ONE

OWL

CHANGING CLASSES

Stratification and Mobility in
Post-industrial Societies

edited by
Gøsta Esping-Andersen

SAGE Studies in International Sociology 45
Sponsored by the International Sociological Association/ISA

SAGE Publications Ltd
6 Bonhill Street
London EC2A 4PU

SAGE Publications Inc
2455 Teller Road
Newbury Park, California 91320

SAGE Publications India Pvt Ltd
32, M-Block Market
Greater Kailash – I
New Delhi 110 048

British Library Cataloguing in Publication data

A catalogue record for this book is available from the
British Library.

ISBN 0 8039 8896 6
ISBN 0 8039 8897 4 pbk

Library of Congress catalog card number 93–84579

Typeset by Photoprint, Torquay, Devon
Printed in Great Britain by The Cromwell Press Ltd,
Broughton Gifford, Melksham, Wiltshire

1001785550

Contents

Notes on Contributors

Zina Assimakopoulou is a doctoral candidate at the European University Institute, Florence.

Hans-Peter Blossfeld is Professor of Sociology at the University of Bremen. He was research scientist at the University of Mannheim, senior research scientist at the Max Planck Institute for Human Development and Education in Berlin and Professor of Sociology at the European University Institute in Florence. His publications deal with educational, family and youth sociology, studies of the labor market, research in demography, stratification and mobility, and methods of longitudinal analysis.

Gøsta Esping-Andersen is Professor of Political and Social Sciences at the European University Institute, Florence. He has published widely in the areas of comparative political economy, welfare states and stratification. His most recent book, *The Three Worlds of Welfare Capitalism*, was published with Polity Press in Europe, and Princeton University Press in the United States (1990).

Jonathan Gershuny was previously Professor and Head of the School of Social Sciences at the University of Bath, and a Fellow of Nuffield College, University of Oxford. He is now Professor of Sociology and Director of the Research Centre on Micro-Social Change at the University of Essex. Among his books are *After Industrial Society* (Macmillan, 1978) and *Social Innovation and the Division of Labour* (Oxford University Press, 1983).

Gianna Giannelli is Researcher in the Department of Economics at the University of Florence. Her research interests include macro and micro labor economics and family economics. She is currently involved in the study of married women's participation in the labor market and its relation with fertility, husbands' employment status and family income in general. The research methods she applies are those of cross-section and longitudinal analysis.

Jerry A. Jacobs is Associate Professor and Chair of the Graduate Program in sociology at the University of Pennsylvania. He has written extensively in the areas of gender and labor markets. His current projects include a study of part-time employment in the United States and a ten-country study of women in public sector employment.

Jon Eivind Kolberg is Professor of Sociology at the University of Bergen, Professor of Social Policy at the University of Tromsø and Research Director at the Luxembourg Employment Study. His research interests include comparative sociology of welfare states, labor markets and social stratification. Among his books are the three edited volumes *The Welfare State as Employer, Between Work and Social Citizenship* and *The Study of Welfare State Regimes* (M.E. Sharpe, 1991). He is now working on a project on patterns of sickness absenteeism and early retirement.

Arne Kolstad is Researcher in the Department of Sociology and Political Science of the University of Trondheim. His main research interest is survey measurement theory and he is currently working on a project on validity and reliability in survey measurement instruments.

Karl Ulrich Mayer is Co-Director of the Max Planck Institute of Human Development and Education, Berlin, and head of its Centre on Education, Work and Societal Development. He is also Adjunct Professor at the Free University, Berlin, and principal investigator of the German Life History Study. His main research interests lie in social stratification and mobility, occupational careers and labor markets, and the sociology of the life-course. Among other works, he is co-author (with N.B. Tuma) of *Event History Analysis in Life Course Research* (1990).

John Myles is Professor of Sociology and Director of the Institute on Aging at Florida State University. Between 1986 and 1988 he was Visiting Fellow at Statistics Canada where he researched issues related to industrial restructuring and its impact on wages and job skills. He has written widely on topics related to labor markets and the welfare state. He is the author of *Old Age in the Welfare State: The Political Economy of Public Pensions* (University Press of Kansas, 1989). He is co-author (with Wallace Clement) of *Relations of Ruling: Class and Gender in Postindustrial Societies* to be published by McGill-Queens University Press in 1994.

Garnett Picot is Manager of the Business and Labour Market Analysis Group in Statistics Canada, part of the Analytical Studies Branch in that organization. He has conducted work in the areas of worker displacement and labor adjustment, the school-to-work transition of college and university graduates, resource planning models, wage polarization and income inequality, and other labor market analysis topics.

Michael Tåhlin is Associate Professor in the Department of Sociology at Stockholm University. His research interests include social stratification, economic sociology and the sociology of work. He is currently engaged in a project on the relationship between individuals' labor market rewards and the structure of the work organizations in which they are employed.

Kees van Kersbergen is Assistant Professor of Political Science at the Free University in Amsterdam.

Ted Wannell is a Senior Analyst in the Analytical Studies Branch of Statistics Canada, and has contributed work on topics such as labor adjustment, micro-simulation planning models, income inequality, and related labor economics topics.

Introduction

Gøsta Esping-Andersen

This is a study of emergent class formation in six advanced societies. Using both longitudinal and cross-sectional labor force data, our chief intention is to examine the validity of the currently reigning views of social stratification in post-industrial society: on one hand, the rosy picture of a meritocratic knowledge-based class order; on the other hand, the gloomy scenario of a swelling service proletariat.

The six-nation comparison which we undertake has a dual motivation. First, the literature has a tendency to assume international convergence; we suspect substantial divergence across nations. Secondly, taking the lead from an earlier work, our theoretical argument is that contemporary social stratification is heavily shaped by institutions, the welfare state in particular.[1] If this is true, cross-national stratification patterns should systematically differ according to the nature of welfare states.

This book should not be read as if it were the final word on post-industrial social stratification. Indeed, serious and systematic research on the phenomenon has hardly even begun. Hence, the work presented in this book could be regarded as a provocation or as an invitation to others to join in. A project which addresses an unfolding, not yet clearly visible, process can hardly ever be precise, let alone definitive. The concepts of class and post-industrialism that permeate this volume remain, therefore, somewhat nebulous. We may be sharply aware that the parameters which defined to us the essence of high industrialism are being irreversibly recast, and we are to some degree capable of identifying the broad contours of an evolving new order. In brief, we live in an era of transition, and cannot pretend to know what will result once the embryonic structural components are cemented and institutionalized. After all, the reigning modern theories of *industrial* society were forged long after the fact. If we are still around twenty or thirty years hence, we might be able to do better than patching the usual 'post-' to our past. I wish to emphasize from the very outset that our use of the terms 'post-industrial' and 'post-fordist' is purely heuristic. We also make liberal use of concepts such as the 'the service proletariat', again a matter of expediency.

Our agenda is both theoretical and empirical. Chapter 1 is an effort to construct a theoretical framework on the basis of which empirical analyses of post-industrial stratification can proceed. The aim is to hypothesize the driving forces behind the process of post-industrialism. Drawing liberally on the earlier insights of Jonathan Gershuny, I locate these in the recast nexus between households and work. In turn, I believe that the ways in which this nexus is recast depends on institutions in general, and on the welfare state in particular. Put somewhat differently, the core idea in this book is that we need an institutional theory of stratification.

The study of social classes often disintegrates into a battle of ideologies. This book is an empirical attempt to explore whether, and to what degree, post-industrial society promotes class closure. Whether classes exist is an open question, not a foregone conclusion. Just as none of the authors in this study is a sworn adherent to post-industrial theory, no one is dedicated to a particular class theory. The kind of open-ended approach we have chosen for this study could be criticized as naked empiricism. True, much of what we have done is to order and re-order the data in the hope of identifying whether or not there emerge the contours of a new class structure. But still, such an accusation would be unfair: unordered data will never reveal anything; our approach is to impose a preliminary theoretical scheme and examine its empirical validity. The second best to having a good and solid theory is to strive towards one. This is the chief purpose of Chapter 1.

Traditional class theory tends to be institution-less, assuming that classes emerge out of unfettered exchange relations, be it in the market or at the 'point of production'. Our study assumes the opposite. If the nexus of households and work is being revolutionized, and if the engines that generate employment function differently, it is because the labor market is now stretched between a set of towering institutions. Mass education, the welfare state and collective bargaining institutions were more or less unknown to Durkheim, Weber and Marx.

The impact of large institutions is difficult to discern in a one-country study. Maybe this is why most stratification theory fails to see them. We have chosen the comparative approach because this is the only means by which their influence can be gauged. Fortunately, the literature is saturated with comparative analyses of welfare states and industrial relations thus providing us with a solid basis for nation-sampling. From the point of view of maximizing institutional variation, and taking into consideration the inevitable constraints of data availability and expertise, our choice fell on a comparison of Germany, Great Britain, the two North American countries, the United States and Canada; and two Scandinavian countries, Norway and Sweden.[2]

The research strategy was chosen by objective constraints. It would have been physically and mentally impossible for anyone to conduct systematic cross-national comparisons alone, even with the aid of a sizable army of research assistants. The data for each nation are complex and assume a particular expertise. For this reason we chose the research-collectivity option. With the aid of two intense workshops (both held at the European University Institute in Florence), a common theoretical and methodological formula, and concurrent back-and-forth communication, we have done our best to conduct and present the research as a unified and coherent whole. Still, no two authors are identical; the contributors use varying analytical techniques, and come to the project with their own unique sociological imaginations. We could not aim for strict comparability.

Chapter 1 serves to present the basic theoretical and conceptual framework for the subsequent empirical analyses. All individual nation-analyses address the same underlying questions and hypotheses, utilizing as far as possible the same concepts and classification system.[3] The actual methodology of the nation-studies will differ; each country's data set stipulates to a large degree what is methodologically appropriate. Thus, the Norwegian study uses merged censuses for 1960, 1970 and 1980; the Swedish analyzes a panel constructed by merging surveys around 1980 and 1988; and the German study also benefits from long panels. In turn, the Canadian and US analyses were constrained by the unavailability of panel data that bridge more than two years. This heterogeneity of data sources, as well as the differences in years covered, obviously diminishes our capacity for sweeping comparative generalizations. The collaborating authors also employ different methodological techniques. Gershuny's study of Britain is, for example, an innovative and unorthodox application of time-budget analysis, while the other nation-studies generally utilize occupational mobility tables coupled with (typically) logistical regression analysis. Again, strict comparability is not possible but we are, nonetheless, convinced that comparative conclusions are warranted as long as we remember that the entire undertaking is meant to be explorative.

The empirical section of the book opens with a comparison of the evolving occupational structure in the six countries (Chapter 2). The aim is to highlight the chief differences in the nations' employment structure so as to provide a framework within which the subsequent case-analyses can more easily be understood and compared. The evidence does confirm that countries cluster. The Scandinavian countries exemplify an extreme case of a gendered, welfare state service-led trajectory; Canada and the United States, in turn, are characterized by their large low-end consumer service labor market. Germany (and, to a degree, Britain) remains comparatively much more industrial and traditional in its employment profile. These differences can be traced to the impact of their respective welfare state and industrial relations institutions, and are important to keep in mind when evaluating the results from the individual case-analyses.

The individual empirical chapters are grouped according to the clusters that emerge in Chapter 2. Since the principal focus of the study is to explore post-industrial class closure, our choice was to center the analyses on the bottom and top of the post-industrial class hierarchies; we are therefore mainly concerned with the potential for a new post-industrial service proletariat, on one hand, and class closure within the professional 'knowledge class', on the other hand. The empirical chapters all present a rich and complex picture of class mobility patterns, some mainly emphasizing the issue of class closure at the bottom; others offering a more general analysis of class mobility. The results that are presented obviously do not condense into a neat and unequivocal finding. Common to all the countries is the degree to which the post-industrial hierarchy is gendered; the female bias is perhaps heaviest at the bottom, but permeates all the way to the top. This does not mean, however, that everywhere a dual gender-distinct class system is evolving.

There is clearly a 'Scandinavian model' insofar as the huge welfare state labor market generates a heavily gendered (female) mobility hierarchy, marked by a large share of unskilled service jobs. The tendency towards class closure is, however, not strong. The Norwegian study, in particular, emphasizes the upward mobility chances for the unskilled service workers; the Swedish, in contrast, suggests that mobility chances of unskilled service workers, while high, are not that different from mobility behavior in the traditional industrial order. This may very well be true, but there emerges nonetheless a strong commonality between Norway and Sweden: the emergence of a distinct, female-biased, career hierarchy in the welfare state.

This stands in sharp contrast to Germany. Here, unskilled service jobs emerge as largely dead-end careers, a closed secondary labor market that is, again, predominantly female. Unlike Scandinavia, these women's mobility chances are few, and low-end service jobs seem to function mainly as a bridge between school and marriage. In Germany, the traditional skill divide that the vocational training system generates is pretty much replicated in the service occupations.

The British study is the one most explicitly concerned with class closure both at the bottom and top of the post-industrial hierarchy. Once again, this study illustrates how female-biased the new service economy is. The analysis hints at an emerging and quite intriguing paradox: while post-industrial society is open at the bottom, that is, not generating a closed proletarian service class, it is closing at the top. Gershuny suggests that education, rather than being the great social leveller, actually blocks mobility into elite positions for all but those with higher educational assets.

It is very tempting to contrast this conclusion with the German findings. Germany's labor market is typically regarded as unusually rigid due to its institutionalization of educational certification for access to good jobs. Yet Blossfeld, Giannelli and Mayer indicate that this kind of rigidity is prominent only at the bottom; at the top, mobility is quite high.

There is, finally, a great degree of commonality in the stratification patterns of Canada and the United States. Both chapters emphasize the openness within the bottom-end post-industrial occupations, but for reasons that diverge from other countries. In North America, unskilled service jobs tend to be very poorly paid, are predominantly filled by youth and immigrants, and function very much as first-entry, or stop-gap, jobs. These jobs do, however, also harbor a large reservoir of uneducated for whom upward mobility may remain very improbable. In both country-analyses a distinct low-end mobility circuit emerges which is unparalleled elsewhere: unskilled sales, clerical and service jobs appear to constitute a common job reservoir for people with low education, and for such people mobility may be very high but generally restricted within this circuit.

The final chapter in this volume (Chapter 9) attempts to pull together the comparative findings of our research. The heterogeneity of data, methods and analytical approach clearly prohibits the elaboration of a list of sweeping conclusions. Instead, this chapter seeks to generalize in the form of concluding hypotheses.

As editor and organizer of this project, I owe a great debt to the individual contributors, who have put an enormous amount of work into each chapter. The project received a great deal of help and encouragement from Karl Ulrich Mayer, Lee Rainwater and Aage Sørensen, all of whom have been essentially quasi-members of the group. I would also like specially to thank one of the anonymous

Sage reviewers. It is exceedingly rare to receive such a thoughtful, detailed and helpful set of comments. Had only he or she been a member of the group from the very start! Personally, I was heavily dependent on the research assistance and collaboration of Zina Assimakopoulou, Kees van Kersbergen and Ursula Jänicken. Unselfishly, they did all the hard work so that I could selfishly devote myself to the easy stuff.

Money is a very encouraging thing and I am very grateful that the Research Council of the European University Institute and the European Commission, Directory General for Social and Labor Market Affairs (DG V), were willing to encourage this study. I hope that the final product will not discourage either from continuing to pursue what is obviously a high-risk investment strategy.

Notes

1   In many ways this research project springs from the conclusions in Esping-Andersen (1990).
2   These represent the three basic welfare regime clusters identified in Esping-Andersen (1990): the United States and Canada are prototypical examples of the liberal model; Norway and Sweden of the social democratic model; and Germany of the conservative model. The United Kingdom was, in my earlier book, somewhat of a hybrid between the social democratic and liberal regime, leaning towards the latter.
3   Our classification scheme is based on three- or four-digit ISCO and ISIC codes and covers six nations. To avoid filling a third of this book with this kind of tedious detail, we refer interested readers instead to Assimakopoulou et al. (1992).

1

Post-industrial Class Structures: An Analytical Framework

Gøsta Esping-Andersen

Much of the discipline of sociology was built around the concept of social class. Today, its privileged analytical position seems less secure, and class analysis may even join the many anachronisms that our immature science has accumulated over the years. As witnessed by the recent, magistral study by Eriksson and Goldthorpe (1992), important studies of social class have certainly not been abandoned entirely. Still, it is symptomatic that Goldthorpe and Marshall (1991) have authored a follow-up paper entitled 'The Promising Future of Class Analysis', which, in large part, defends its relevance against the increasingly vocal skeptics.

However, the skeptics engaged in an active dialogue may be less of a problem than the much larger silent majority for whom the subject has become hopelessly unworthy of mention. The concept of class risks becoming little else than the button we press when it is suitable to invoke the colorful historical imagery of red banners waving on the May Day parades, outraged and sooty mineworkers huddling on the picket-lines, or members of a wild-eyed, revolutionary proletarian mass with patches on their best Sunday suits.

Ideological distaste undoubtedly motivates some to hasten the demise of class theory. But it is probably for its seeming incompatibility with modern social reality that most are partisan as regards its silent death. The notion of a class-ridden society may, today, seem quite moribund. But then so it has numerous times before. In the 1950s, the end-of-ideology thesis argued that the class struggle had been arrested by working-class affluence, only to be followed by the extreme levels of militancy and conflict in the 1960s. Then arose the problem of the new salariat, the ever-growing middle classes, and the professional elites. And now the old cornerstone of class theory, the industrial working class, is in rapid decline. The erosion of our traditional class structure is what many scholars associate with the coming post-industrial society.

Is post-industrial society the culmination of a long and steady process of class structural erosion, or is it the midwife of an entirely new class system? In the voluminous literature on post-industrial society, there is probably no one who argues that inequalities and social stratification will come to an end. On the contrary. But the question is whether the emerging structure of employment, of life-chances and of inequality can be fruitfully understood with our inherited theories of class. The starting point of this book is that any attempt to address this question empirically should lay aside the classical conceptual apparatus of social classes.

Most of the literature that has emerged on the employment effects of post-industrialism shares two common features. One, virtually all such work assumes cross-national convergence, largely because of an exaggerated adherence to technological or growth-based explanations of change. Two, most approaches to 'post-industrial' stratification are couched in the classical conceptual apparatus of class. This means that our understanding of stratification in the 'new' society derives from theories formulated for the purpose of elucidating the era of industrial capitalism. Put differently, such analyses assume a fordist reality in a post-fordist era.[1]

These features constrain both empirical research and theoretical innovation. First, it is not that technology and income growth are unimportant engines of change, only that their impact must be analyzed in terms of how they are institutionally filtered. The point is that similar technological innovations and economic growth take place in institutional settings that diverge. The advanced capitalist societies are regulated by institutions that hardly existed in the era of industrialization: the welfare state, collective bargaining systems, mass education and the modern corporation have emerged as important, if not decisive, institutional filters. Nations vary dramatically with regard to these regulatory institutions, and it is therefore naive to assume convergent trends in employment and stratification.

We should, secondly, question the continued fruitfulness of orthodox class theories. The idea of class in Marxism assumed a naked and unmediated relationship between capital and labor, be it in the labor market or in the workplace. Similarly, the Weberian legacy generally assumes market hegemony as the mainspring of life-chance stratification, although bureaucracy was viewed as an alternative, and, to Dahrendorf (1959), increasingly dominant, means of building social hierarchies. Regardless, orthodox class theory is nested in an institutionally 'naked' world, an Adam Smithian world of unfettered markets.

If, however, institutions not only modify employment relations but also actively shape the direction of change, continued adherence to orthodoxy may seriously block one's capacity to identify qualitatively new axes of social division, hierarchy and social closure. In recent years there has, to be sure, been a flourishing debate on the 'new class', a debate that calls into question the validity of our traditional criteria for class assignment. Thus, in characterizing the distinctiveness of the 'new class', Bell (1976) emphasizes the control of scientific knowledge; Gouldner (1979), the control of culture; Goldthorpe (1982), delegated authority and the exercise of autonomy and discretion; Wright (1985), the control of skill and organizational assets.

While new principles for class analysis have been charted for the professional-managerial cadres, much less attention has been paid to the class structure in general, and to the possible evolution of a new post-industrial proletariat in particular. Is such a class emerging, and, if so, how do we identify it? What are its relations to other classes? What are its specific selection and reproduction mechanisms? And what are the conditions under which it may emerge? The objective of this chapter is, first, to develop a conceptual scheme for the analysis of social stratification in post-industrial society; secondly, to propose a set of hypotheses regarding cross-national divergence with particular address to the size and character of the potential post-industrial proletariat. These shall guide the empirical studies that constitute the core of this book.

Class and Stratification in Post-industrial Society

Post-industrial theory has its pessimistic and optimistic scenarios.[2] In Bell's (1976) pioneering work, post-industrial society is characterized by service employment dominance and the rise of professional-technical cadres, whose privileged social position is a function of their control of scientific knowledge and the means of information. Since meritocracy will emerge as the key criterion for assignment and privilege, Bell envisages a society in which the significance of deep class cleavages will erode. But then his analyses suffer from the lack of attention to the possible rise of a new underclass.

A rather parallel vision is presented in the more rosy literature on 'post-fordism' and flexibility. Here, however, the accent is on the ongoing transformation within manufacturing and its effects on skill upgrading, enhanced worker autonomy and authority, and on the decline of traditional fordist managerial hierarchies (Kern and Schumann, 1984; Piore and Sabel, 1984; Boyer, 1988).

There are essentially two pessimistic versions. One predicts that modern automation and technology will result in a workless society, not far removed from the vision presented in Kurt Vonnegut's *Player Piano*. Gershuny (1978, 1983) argues that rising incomes will not produce a shift in household consumption towards services, but principally engender 'self-servicing' via purchased household commodities. Self-servicing creates demand for household goods that are predominantly material in nature. Thus emerges the paradox that the service society will mainly consume physical goods, and, as a consequence, it will not generate service employment. Moreover, since household capital goods, from video recorders to microwave ovens, are mainly produced in Japan, Taiwan or Korea, self-servicing will hardly promote domestic manufacturing employment in the post-industrial economies.

This kind of jobless growth is one logical outcome of the Baumol (1967) theory of unbalanced growth. His is an application of Engel's Law, but with a new twist: rising incomes will shift demand towards services, and enhanced manufacturing productivity will reduce the need for industrial labor. But, since service sector productivity grows much slower than in manufacturing, the end-result is a cost-disease problem: when wage costs in services follow those in manufacturing, service labor will outprice itself.

In the Baumol model, three outcomes are possible: first, the cost-disease may simply result in mass unemployment; the second possibility is that service jobs can be promoted via government-'subsidized' wages, primarily in the form of welfare state jobs; and the third possibility is that service employment will expand because of low wages that correspond to productivity differentials. The class structural outcome will differ sharply depending on which scenario is dominant, and it should be obvious that each one is institutionally dependent.

The jobless post-industrial scenario can be expected to engender a new kind of insider–outsider cleavage: a closed labor market of insiders enjoying high wages and job security (efficiency wages), and a swelling army of outsiders including youth, long-term unemployed, early retirees and discouraged workers. Jobs themselves may become assets on which the new distributional struggles will center (Van Parijs, 1987). The possibility that such an outsider underclass is evolving has been raised by Auletta (1982), Levy (1988) and Runciman (1990).[3]

The de-industrialization literature presents a second kind of pessimistic scenario. Instead of predicting the growth of an outsider population, the argument here is that industrial decline leads to a powerful downward pressure on wages coupled to mass proletarianization. Hence, the middle declines and the labor market polarizes between the top and the new swelling bottom. Drawing on dual labor market theory, Giddens (1973) also sees the possibility of such polarization with, at the bottom, a new underclass (heavily weighted by women and minorities), trapped into a vicious cycle of underprivilege. A rather similar model is found in the pessimistic variant of the flexibility literature. Piore and Sabel (1984) suggest the possibility of a 'Napoli model' of flexibilization where firms combine their highly qualified internal labor force with a periphery pool of labor reserves. The implication is that post-industrialization *with* wage flexibility (read low wages) generates a new underclass of marginals and stand-by workers in the labor market, what Michon (1981) and Goldthorpe (1990) call 'disponibles.'

The Problem of 'Classes'

Our dominant class theories, be they Marxist or Weberian, identify classes with reference to the axis of ownership, authority or the naked market nexus of industrial capitalism. Along these axes we are presented with a distribution of the *male* workforce; the class membership of women, whether employed or not, is largely defined as an adjunct to the male. Yet one of the revolutionizing characteristics of the post-industrial order is its potential for exploding the traditional class–gender nexus. A lion's share of post-industrial jobs are freed of any natural male bias, many may actually harbor a female bias and, as we shall argue, inherent in the passage towards the service society lies the prospect of a fundamental break with the conventional female life/career-cycle. The constraints on women's capacity to throw themselves into full-fledged career trajectories are sharply reduced. Therefore, seen from both the demand and supply side, it is very possible that the emerging post-industrial labor market will be synonymous with a female labor market (Clement and Myles, 1994). In this section, we shall first address the principles of a post-industrial class conceptualization and, secondly, attempt to integrate the role of women theoretically.

The Construction of a Post-industrial Class Scheme
Marxist theory has been an especially stubborn witness to the transformations of advanced capitalism. A typical example is Ehrenreich and Ehrenreich's (1979) attempt to rescue Marxism by asserting that the new managerial and professional classes, like Renner's service class, were little else than an additional (unproductive) layer in the reproductive logic of capitalist class relations, the key axis still being workers and capitalists.[4] Similarly, it hardly adds much to our understanding of the huge white-collar stratum to force it into the manual proletarian class, as orthodox Marxists still insist on doing (Sobel, 1989).

A much more ambitious and coherent theoretical salvage was attempted in Eric Wright's (1978, 1979) early work. Yet, his solution, to classify the huge number of positions that fall outside the strict class domination axis as semi-autonomous or contradictory locations, was aborted. It is symptomatic that Wright's (1985, 1989) revised class schema, now built around the control and exploitation of assets (ownership, organizational and skills), converges with the Weberian scheme. The labels may differ, but Wright's new class map is only marginally at variance with that of Goldthorpe (1987) or Runciman (1990). Indeed, his 'expert class' is virtually synonymous with Goldthorpe's service class or, for that matter, Gouldner's or Bell's knowledge class.

Those inspired by the Weberian tradition have been more inclined towards theoretical revision. This is to be expected given the much greater flexibility inherent in its standard definition of class: 'classes exist to the extent that groups share a common market condition as the decisive basis for their specific life-chances' (Mayer and Carroll, 1987: 16).[5] In this framework, it is easy to recognize that the burgeoning professional, managerial and executive elites constitute new strata with rather unique life-chances that arise out of a common market condition. Still, the Weberian reformulations also remain unsatisfactory from the point of view of post-industrial society. Their principal shortcoming is a failure to recognize that the 'post-fordist' division of labor may give birth to new axes of stratification.

We propose in the following a tentative 'class scheme' whose principal aim is to distinguish post-industrial from the traditional fordist classes or, if you like, strata. We employ two kinds of criterion that, in our view, are likely to apply differently. The first is essentially a horizontal one: how is a given kind of job inserted in the overall division of labor? The second is dynamic and tries to capture the likelihood of class closure; what we might call life-chance or career regimes.

The New Division of Labor

Most contemporary research follows Gouldner and Goldthorpe and assumes that higher-grade managers, administrators and professionals together form a distinct, elite, class. Gouldner (1979: 19) defends this on the basis of their shared capacity to control knowledge, on the assumption that intellectuals and the intelligentsia are natural allies, and that they are able to appropriate privately larger shares of income produced by the cultures they possess (1979: 20). Goldthorpe (1982), on the other hand, sees the class commonality of his service class in the delegation of trust, which, in turn, results in distinctive conditions of employment in terms of type and level of rewards. He argues explicitly that the difference between managers and professionals is only one of 'situs' position, not class (1982: 170). Furthermore, the role of the state as an employer is unimportant in the Goldthorpe framework, as it is also for Wright's new class map.[6]

If we except the Goldthorpe scheme (and its various applications) and the new Wright scheme, most recent stratification theory has focused only on the above-mentioned 'new class'. In Goldthorpe's larger class scheme, class II brings together both semi-professionals/technicians and lower-level managers; Wright's semi-credentialed group is more or less identical. Also, Goldthorpe's class III encompasses clerical and rank-and-file service workers. To Wright, all service workers are classified together with the 'manual proletariat', which, accordingly, becomes so huge (about 50 percent of the total labor force) that its analytical value is diminished.

Autonomy, human capital assets and the trust relationship are clearly important attributes that unite the 'new class'. But from our point of view there are other attributes which differentiate the scientists-professionals from the managers-administrators. The nature of their human capital and expertise directs them into very divergent kinds of productive (or unproductive) activity. The autonomy of the professional is of a qualitatively different kind than that of the manager, and what they control is not the same. Many professionals, such as engineers, may very well end up as corporate managers, but this will most likely entail a basic change in their working life, social identities, loyalties and functional tasks; hence, it should be regarded as a career, if not class, move. The manager and administrator is a hierarchical creature in the bureaucratic division of control and, as such, assumes authority over others, professionals often included. Outside the state, managers reflect a fordist logic of the division of labor.[7]

In contrast, the professional will usually stand outside the lines of command, possess a great deal of autonomy but probably little authority over subordinates; professionals' approach to work is task-oriented and their authority, legitimacy and collective identity are more likely to derive from the scientific standards of their chosen discipline, and not from bureaucratic office. The professional is, indeed, the antithesis to hierarchy and a fordist system of regulation. In sum, if scientific expertise is emerging as a new and dominant source of power, rewards and status identification that stands in contrast to traditional ones, the managers and professionals may be divided by more than 'situs' differences.[8]

A set of parallel principles can be applied also to the less exalted occupational groups. Thus, semi-professionals and technicians should be differentiated from lower-level management and administration. The former stand in a subordinate relation to the scientists and professionals; the latter similarly to managers; the former execute the more routine professional tasks; the latter execute the more routine managerial prescriptions.

Finally, whereas most class schemes distinguish the broad working classes mainly by skill (credentials in Wright), a parallel 'fordist' divide may also apply to the lower-level wage workers. The division is conceptually clear between manual skilled and crafts workers, on one side, and the unskilled manuals, on the other side. But it seems erroneous to merge skilled and unskilled service workers into these two strata. The former are embedded in the industrial-fordist division of labor and hierarchy, while the latter are mainly employed in inter-personal settings where the labor process is synonymous with a consumption process.[9] For example, a skilled metal worker and a skilled hairdresser would have very little in common be it in terms of autonomy, authority, labor relations or reward system. Similarly, an unskilled factory worker and a fast-food counter worker occupy two distinct worlds of work; the former operates machines in subordination to a managerial hierarchy with a relatively clear productivity–reward nexus; the latter services persons in a setting with blurred hierarchies, usually a fair degree of autonomy and discretion, and only a vague link between productivity and rewards.[10]

Career and Life-chance Regimes

Any kind of class scheme must assume some degree of social closure. Hence, the validity of the class categories presented here depends on the regularities of life-chances and on patterns of class or occupational mobility. To assess the degree of closure, we can think of two criteria of mobility. First, a class is hardly a class at all if it lacks membership stability. Thus, if there is a constant reciprocal flow between managers and professionals, and if their life-chances are similar, the concept of 'situs' would seem appropriate; but if they follow internally ordered, discrete career trajectories with variant life-chance profiles, the concept of class would seem more relevant. Or, in the case of the unskilled service workers, the concept of a new post-industrial proletariat would be wholly inappropriate if virtually no one remains in unskilled service jobs for longer periods. In this case, they are best understood as stop-gap jobs, as an interim within alternative life-cycle trajectories.

Secondly, as emphasized by Mayer and Carroll (1987), the

question is whether job mobility and the life-course are likely to be systematically patterned by class membership. Both Goldthorpe and Payne (1986) and Mayer and Carroll (1987) suggest that the 'post-industrial era' has increased job mobility. But their data also indicate distinct mobility differences. For example, Mayer and Carroll (1987: 25) show that top-level professionals are the least likely to show job changes. Even more dramatically, Oppenheimer (1990) has shown that a large proportion of the low-end service jobs (essentially our unskilled services) constitute youthful stop-gap jobs in a life-cycle career pattern. If this is true, it would be exceedingly difficult to predict future life-chances from incumbency in an unskilled service job. In contrast, there is very little to indicate that the unskilled manual working-class jobs are 'stop-gap'. The utility of making a sharp class distinction between manual and service workers lies in these contrasting 'career-trajectories'. The essence of the 'fordist' manufacturing workers is their highly predictable flat and stable career profile.[11]

As a point of departure, let us briefly re-examine the parameters of the fordist class structure. One of its hallmarks was an extremely high degree of career and life-chance predictability; industrial capitalism produced class closure because the large mass of manual workers shared a very similar life-cycle. The industrial worker and, for that matter, the routine clerical worker would know that significant upward or outward career mobility was unlikely over the life-course. On the other hand, he or she would face a future of good earnings, job and income stability, a package of fringe benefits and welfare state guarantees that allowed, in totem, a satisfactory degree of participation in the prevailing standards of living and consumption of society. The life-chances of a manual worker were such that a single earner sufficed to reproduce the household. Hence, the fordist occupational structure tended to be heavily male, a fact of vital importance for understanding why the post-industrial structure tends to be distinctly feminine.

The question is, does the post-industrial order give rise to a significantly variant set of mobility and life-chance regimes? It is possible that the emerging new job structure turns out to be a replication or perpetuation of our traditional system of stratification. It is also possible that new mechanisms of closure are evolving; that post-industrial society harbors a new class structure based on new social divisions.

In our view, post-industrial society is likely to nurture a novel kind of life-chance structuration in both the service and the industrial occupations. To begin with, there is much to indicate that the fordist system of life-chances is in decay *within* the traditional industrial order; de-industrialization and restructuration is altering the occupational mix, the division of labor and the worker's prospects of sustained high earnings and welfare over the life-cycle. This is what both the 'flexibility' and the 'declining middle' literature suggests.

Secondly, there are many aspects of the service economy which point against the emergence of a stable life-chance and mobility regime at the low end of the occupational structure. As discussed earlier, Baumol's productivity problem seriously inhibits the emergence of a stably employed, well-paid class of service workers in the private sector; services, furthermore, are much less likely to be unionized, and they are much more likely to be organized in small mamma-and-pappa type enterprises. This implies that internal organizational mobility is less likely to occur. Thirdly, career prospects and life-chances in the post-industrial order are certain to be much more dependent on education, human capital resources and, equally important, social skills.[12]

In sum, we posit a divergence in the occupational life-cycle behavior of *traditional* fordist jobs and post-industrial service jobs. It is certainly possible that the traditional industrial economy is undergoing post-industrialization, in the sense of both methods of production and labor force composition. It is also possible that services are undergoing a process of 'fordization', although it is hard to imagine that this could occur on a grand scale.[13] It remains to be seen whether post-industrial society will promote its own class closure, as occurred in the fordist industrial system; is a new class dualism emerging with, at the top, a closed professional elite stratum and, at the bottom, a new servant class, a new post-industrial proletariat, whose chances for mobility are closed?

We cannot assess the degree of class closure on a static, cross-sectional basis. Thus, even if we could identify strong correlations between positions and attributes at any given point in time, as is Wright's approach, we would know nothing about closure. Class formation can only be ascertained through dynamic analysis of mobility patterns across the life-cycle. Our unskilled service class can, once again, serve as an example: *if* it is the case that unskilled manual and service workers constitute one and the same type of people with similar characteristics and life-chances, the case for their separate identity is considerably weakened; especially if we find high rates of mobility and fluidity going *both ways* between the two. The bi-lateral directionality must be stressed since there is a very real possibility that unskilled service jobs serve as a 'dumping ground' for redundant manufacturing workers. In this case, we might consider the low-end service jobs as a functional alternative to early retirement or unemployment. *If*, however, the recruitment and mobility patterns diverge, their separate identity seems warranted. It is evident from this example that we must establish the real class significance of our classes from employment mobility flows.

Class and Gender

The fordist industrial order was built around a very particular sexual division of labor. By the combination of an adequate 'fordist' wage, basic job security and welfare state transfers, families were both able to and encouraged to split their productive efforts between the male's full-time industrial wage employment and the female's full-time dedication to household reproduction. Female labor supply was discouraged not only because of the nature of jobs that high industrialism offered, but also because of inbuilt institutional constraints, ranging from the absence of collective social services to discriminatory tax treatment of two-earner households.

The revolutionary essence of the emerging post-industrial society lies very much in its abolition of this gender logic. First, as the realm of social services expands, the necessity of household self-reproduction declines, thus freeing women from traditional family care obligations.[14] Women's full-time participation and careers depend on the provision of collective social services. Service jobs are not only more flexible and less physically demanding, but they are also frequently 'natural' female career avenues in the sense that they offer paid employment in what are essentially traditional social reproduction tasks. Services for women create jobs for women.

The abolition of the traditional fordist division of labor depends very much on the degree to which the welfare state is service-intensive. If it is committed to social services, it not only frees women from the family, but also generates a vast female labor market. If the welfare state adopts non-discriminatory tax legislation and gives generous provisions for paid absenteeism and sabbaticals, it also grants women the opportunity to pursue uninterrupted work careers.

The consequences for our understanding of post-industrial stratification are, first, that female and male life-cycle profiles will begin to converge; secondly, that the post-industrial job slots are likely to become female slots. As a result, there is the possibility of a gender-divided stratification order with a male-dominated fordist hierarchy, and a female-biased post-industrial hierarchy. In the extreme case, we might envisage two class structural logics, each being gender-specific.

The gender profile of post-industrial societies is particularly sensitive to Baumol's cost-disease problem. Where the welfare state constitutes the main source of service growth, we can expect a greater capacity for women to participate and pursue full-time careers, but the likely consequence is also an extraordinary concentration of the female labor force within the public sector. If, on the other hand, low wages are the main source of service job growth, the capacity of women to enter the labor market may still be substantial (due to the low market price of, say, day-care), and we would be less inclined to expect a strong sectoral concentration of women – although low-paid personal services are likely to show a distinct female bias. The third possibility of jobless growth would predictably result in low female participation and, concomitantly, the continuation of the traditionalist sexual division of labor. In the latter case, we could speak of very incomplete post-industrialization.

A Post-industrial Stratification Scheme

Since the new post-industrial order is still unfolding, its contours and guiding principles remain little more than vaguely distinguishable. We are therefore in no position to elaborate more than a general heuristic device for classifying 'classes.'

Virtually all class theories base their classificatory system on a composite of class attributes. In Marxism, these relate principally to ownership, consciousness and collective action; in the Weberian tradition, they usually include authority, rewards, status and life-chances. For several reasons, our treatment must ignore such attributes. First, it is an empirically open question whether these standard criteria are of equal relevance in the post-industrial order. If the stratification system is in flux, and if we are witnessing the emergence of new bases of class formation (be it knowledge, social skills or alternative resources), it is also likely that accustomed relations between authority, status and rewards will erode.

There are several empirical indications that this kind of flux is, indeed, real. Harrison and Biuestone's (1988) 'declining-middle' thesis suggests that the traditionally stable relationship between job and pay in the American economy has eroded in tandem with de-industrialization, union decline and labor market flexibilization. A similar kind of uncoupling appears to be the case for Canada (Myles et al., 1988). In some European countries, the economic returns on credentials are less and less linear and depend, instead, on such new phenomena as sector (public versus private sector). And, perhaps most important of all, the welfare state has revolutionized labor market behavior. In part, the social wage violates the assumption that classes and life-chances can be identified via 'common market conditions'; as already hinted at, the welfare state introduces the possibility of a welfare state client class. And, in part, the some-times massive expansion in welfare state employment implies not only new occupational groups, but also the emergence of a huge production and reward system isolated from the operation of market forces. The conditions that govern the employment pros-pects in the public sector are only remotely related to productivity and profitability; instead, they have to do with government fiscal capacity and the politics of collective choice.

Traditional class theories were conceived in terms of an under-standing of the state, the economy and the household that reflected the fordist, industrial capitalist order. The classification scheme we shall propose below derives from a set of arguments concerning the distinctive features emerging in these three core institutions and, especially, in their recast interdependency.

The *state* was traditionally understood as a system of domination, social control, legitimation or cohesion in the reproduction of capitalist social relations. Typically, it was viewed as an alien body, essentially divorced from the market, from industrial hierarchy and from the private household. This view hardly corresponds to present-day reality since it is clear that the modern welfare state directly and powerfully determines the welfare and behaviour of the family, the commodity status of labor and the organization of the labor market. Social reproduction can no longer be characterized solely in terms of the relation between families and work; through the expansion of collective social services and transfers, what were once the responsibilities of the household are now provided for by the welfare state. This results in the revolutionary changes we have highlighted regarding women and the economy: the requirements for family self-servicing in terms of social reproduction are dramati-cally reduced, and the possibilities for female/mother employment are vastly increased.

It is, similarly, invalid to assume the existence of autonomous labor market clearing mechanisms. The traditional walls between the welfare state and the labor market have crumbled to the extent that the welfare state provides some of the principal mechanisms by which markets 'clear.'[15] Entry into employment, and subsequent job mobility, is dictated by education and training programs, as to an extent was always the case, but increasingly so also by active labor market measures and direct welfare state employment growth. In Scandinavia, the latter actually accounts for almost the entire *net* employment increase over the past decades. Any theory of labor market clearing must take into account the fact that the welfare state is, in its own right, the employer of up to a third of the entire labor force.

Reciprocally, welfare state institutions dictate the choice of non-entry; either via the provision of a social wage option, or via its tax or service treatment of households. Women with small children are capable of paid employment only if they have access to child-care facilities and enjoy rights to paid absenteeism. In a parallel manner, the welfare state furnishes the basic means for labor market exit. While unemployment insurance has always served this function in a limited way, the real revolution lies in the introduction of early retirement. Thus, the armies of redundant industrial workers may have the option of a social wage rather than being forced to move into bottom-end jobs. In sum, the structure of the welfare state is a key feature in the contemporary process of social stratification: it creates and it abolishes 'empty slots', it helps decide who fills them and how they are to be rewarded, it defines what is to be undertaken within them, and, finally, it shapes the patterns of mobility between them.

Most post-industrial theory argues for the increased importance of education in dictating class outcomes; indeed, the vision of a purely meritocratically based social selection system is what makes this theory appear so optimistic. It is undoubtedly true that a vastly increasing proportion of positions will be defined by educational credentials; upward mobility in the post-industrial job hierarchy will, compared to the fordist, depend much more on credentials. The centrality of education has two major implications. First, the irony of meritocratic assignment is that it introduces a new class filter. Those with few or outdated qualifications will be blocked from competition and upward mobility; education may therefore promote a new class divide. The severity of this filtering will obviously depend on the nature of the educational system. If access to credentials is very broad, and if a system of continued training and retraining exists, the polarizing effect of meritocracy can be lessened. In contrast, a rigid education system is likely to result in class closure. Secondly, since education systems differ substantially among countries, they are likely to strengthen the divergence of class structural trends. As previous research has shown, a rigidly credentialist system, like the German, is much more likely to result in class closure and low occupational or sectoral mobility (Carroll and Mayer, 1986; Blossfeld, 1987a; Mayer and Carroll, 1987; Allmendinger, 1989a,b). In contrast, an active, continuous training system, like the Swedish, should permit a greater degree of career mobility and change.

In addition to formal qualifications, post-industrial society is very likely to put a premium on social skills. These can be purchased, as we know from management sensitivity training centers. But they are more probably socially inherited, and will therefore reinforce two kinds of closures. One, the ghettoization of women in social service occupations and, two, inter-generational closure within the post-industrial elite jobs.

Our assumptions about the *economy* must obviously take into account the insertion of welfare state institutions. They must also be recast because many of the core principles that underpinned industrial capitalism no longer obtain. Industrial production is no longer dominant. This is clear in terms of output and employment shares. More important, perhaps, is its transformation and, especially, the degree to which the logic of standardized mass production and mass consumption, based on the mass worker, is giving way to various forms of flexibilization and de-routinization. The manufacturing system is increasingly built around non-material inputs and specialized technical and professional services, be it through in-house self-servicing or through imports from the business services sector. There is also ample evidence that the traditional industrial hierarchy is undergoing explosive change as taylorist managerialism declines, as technology makes the unskilled worker increasingly redundant, and as flexible work processes demand multi-skilled and more autonomous workers; the boundaries between the worker, the manager and the technician may be eroding.

The entire fordist economy was built around a concept of productivity which is rapidly losing its validity. As Block (1990) suggests, there is a certain neo-physiocratism in our contemporary understanding of the economy since we are really only able to grasp productivity in terms of material outputs; the vast majority of the labor force is, however, engaged in activities that lack an adequate determination of productivity. This obviously affects social stratification since rewards were traditionally pegged to measurable (material) productivity. Today, perhaps the lion's share of economic activity produces leisure or social reproduction for others, much of which may very well take place in the informal economy. It hardly makes sense to regard this as solely a 'tax' on the diminishing productive sector. The shape of our stratification system will depend on the degree to which there evolve 'economies' to service manufacturing, personal leisure or family social reproduction.

It is perhaps in our understanding of the *household* that our assumptions require most revision. The postwar model, around which also the welfare state was built, assumed the male as breadwinner, the female as responsible for social reproduction and the family as the setting for leisure and material mass consumption. Indeed, the postwar promise of full employment was, usually explicitly, limited to adult males; and the postwar welfare state did not – until recently – define its responsibilities as encompassing family social reproduction functions. Intertwined with the trans-formation in welfare states and economy, the nature of the house-hold has been revolutionized. The access to service options in the welfare state (or market), and the access to household technologies, has permitted a drastic reduction of working-time within the most time-consuming fields of household self-reproduction (Gershuny, 1983, 1988). This has, first and foremost, given rise to a wholly new employment sector, typically but not necessarily within the welfare state, catering to such tasks as care of children and the elderly. Since the welfare state increasingly absorbs what are essentially menial household job functions, the marginal stratification effect is an increase in unskilled social service jobs within the welfare state labor market. With the option of outside social servicing, women are in the position to pursue sustained employment and career development. The stratification system is deeply affected as a result. It is likely that the new social servicing jobs will be overwhelmingly filled by the new female labor force, but beyond this effect gender is likely to emerge as a new leading variable in the division of labor. In addition, as the two-earner household unit becomes the norm, it will affect the overall distribution of welfare. The class-biased character of marriage will mean a greater income differentiation between upper- and lower-class household living standards; single-person households are likely to suffer relatively in the income distribution.

Of final importance in the recast household structure is its greater demand for leisure consumption. This is given by smaller family size, by labor-saving household goods and by female employment. Smaller families and female work enhance disposable income, and the introduction of household technologies permits more free time. As Gershuny (1983) emphasizes, the household's greater capacity for leisure may not translate automatically into consumption within the personal services. Since such leisure activities as cinema, restaurants or concerts have their self-servicing option (videos, microwave ovens and stereos), the household faces a price-based choice that will deeply affect the employment prospects within the leisure services. Hence, this employment sector (which is by nature extremely biased towards low-skilled jobs) will be very sensitive to the Baumol cost-disease problem (except where it produces 'pos-itional goods' that are desired because of their limited availability). The marginal price effect of leisure services will depend on the overall income distribution and the wage structure. Where they are affordable to a critical mass of households, the rate of leisure consumption will be high. In turn, this will influence the shape of our stratification system: mass consumption of leisure and fun fuels a large unskilled service proletariat.

Most existing research has focused on either sectoral employment shifts (the rise of jobs in services) or, less commonly, on occupational change. In order to identify the outlines of a new stratificational order, however, we need to combine the two. This we shall undertake in the form of occupation–industry matrices.

The Classification of Industries

It is possible to divide the economy according to two broad logics.[16] In one we find the traditional activities associated with the fordist system of standardized mass production and mass consumption. They encompass mining and manufacturing, distribution (wholesale, retail and transportation) and economic infrastructure (utilities, communication). In the literature, retail sales and transportation are typically classified as services, following the early service-economy theorists (Fisher, 1935; Clark, 1940; Fuchs et al., 1968). But we insist that they should be regarded as functionally integrated activities in the fordist industrial system. Distributive services are, as Browning and Singelmann (1978: 488) point out, the last stage in the processing of goods. Transportation is more ambiguous because it encompasses both goods and people. Yet, in terms of volume its essence lies closer to distribution (Browning and Singelmann, 1978). One can speak of an internal organic interdependency between these sectors in the sense that the logic of mass industrial production necessitates mass distribution linkages, and vice versa.[17]

In the other 'economy', we find the post-industrial services, whose vitality derives from the fundamental changes in societal reproduction discussed above. We distinguish three service industries, each identified by its unique role in reproduction. First, *business services* (or, if you like, producer services) comprise activities that mainly provide intermediate, non-physical inputs into industrial production and distribution (management consultancy, architectural services, software programming and systems design, legal and accounting services, financial services, and the like). Their growth is associated with firms' declining preference for self-servicing and thus increased outside service purchasing, a trend that is fueled by needs for greater flexibility and the growing demand for non-physical, often tailor-made, professionalized-scientific inputs into the production process.

Secondly, the growth of *social services* (health, education and welfare services) reflects household export of the tasks associated with social reproduction; that is, a decline in 'social' self-servicing. This must be understood in terms of a fundamental transformation of the ways in which social reproduction takes place. Social services are increasingly demanded in conjunction with the emerging 'post-industrial' life-cycle, as Block (1990) puts it: the participation of women in the economy, the equalization of career profiles, the reallocation of household time-use, the shrinking size of households and the phenomenal rise in one-person units, and also the changing demographic composition in modern societies. Social services release time for paid employment and for leisure.

Thirdly, *consumer services* are, similarly, an alternative to self-servicing, in this case associated with changing modes of leisure reproduction. On one hand, these changes are connected to the work–social reproduction nexus: when women also work, households are more likely to eat out or send their laundry out (or to self-service via household capital inputs). On the other hand, they are connected to the extension of leisure time and the income capacity to purchase services.

The Classification of Occupations

Detailed occupational titles provide us with a reasonable description of the qualifications, responsibilities and work-tasks of a person. This is, of course, why they lent themselves so well to the construction of status hierarchies in sociological mobility research.

Parallel to our industrial classification, we distinguish a set of occupational classes. In one set, we group those that represent the traditional industrial division of labor; in the second, we group those that are representative of the 'post-industrial' division of labor. For each set, we can then classify occupations according to their place within the hierarchy that is symptomatic of the kind of division of labor that obtains; that is, we distinguish between a fordist industrial hierarchy and a post-industrial hierarchy. The concept of hierarchy used here should be understood as broadly reflecting the degree of authority, responsibility and level of human capital applied.

Our study omits, once again, the primary sector occupations (farmers, etc) and also the military. We thus arrive at the following 'classes':

1   The fordist hierarchy:
   (a)   managers and proprietors (includes executive personnel and the 'petit bourgeoisie');[18]
   (b)   clerical, administrative (non-managerial) and sales

workers engaged in basically routine tasks of control, distribution and administration;
(c)   skilled/crafts manual production workers, including low-level 'technical' workers;
(d)   unskilled and semi-skilled manual production workers, also including transport workers and other manual occupations engaged in manufacture and distribution, such as packers, truck drivers, haulers, and the like.

2   The post-industrial hierarchy:
(a)   professionals and scientists:
(b)   technicians and semi-professionals (school teachers, nurses, social workers, laboratory workers, technical designers, etc.);
(c)   skilled service workers (cooks, hairdressers, policemen, etc.);
(d)   unskilled service workers, or service proletariat (cleaners, waitresses, bartenders, baggage porters, etc.).[19]

It will be noticed that both hierarchies combine a command/authority structure (managers command, clerical workers administer the command and workers execute) and a human capital structure. The command structure is obviously less clear-cut within the post-industrial hierarchy (this is, in fact, a main reason for the distinction between a fordist and post-industrial stratification hierarchy). In many cases, post-industrial occupations will be subject to the authority of managers, and the relationship between professionals and semi-professionals or service workers is not likely to be one of commands as much as one of delegating or sub-dividing tasks. In some cases, of course, we can speak of a 'post-industrial' command structure (surgeons towards nurses; *maître d*'s towards waiters).

The 'outsider' surplus population, consisting of persons unable to enter into employment, is both theoretically and empirically a potentially important 'class' in post-industrial societies. First, the Baumol cost-disease effect (and self-servicing) may block job expansion in the service sector. Secondly, the welfare state may contribute to the creation of an outsider population of early retirees, long-term unemployed or others subsisting on the social wage. Thirdly, public policy or labor market organization may systematically discourage labor supply, as is the case where tax policies penalize women's work, or where efficiency (insider) wages in the labor market create involuntary unemployment (Lindbeck and Snower, 1984). The hierarchical position of the surplus, or outsider, population is difficult to identify precisely because of its outsider status. We have already suggested that it may play the role of a dumping ground for the surplus labor force, just as may also the unskilled service jobs. But it is also likely to be a main alternative to employment in the unskilled service jobs.

Our empirical analyses will build on a cross-classification of these sectoral and occupational groups. Such a matrix is useful because it allows us to trace the post-industrial job-mix in both traditional 'fordist' and in new 'post-industrial' sectors (as well as vice versa, of course). We can therefore examine whether the stratification system of the 'post-industrial' order deviates significantly from the traditional economy.

Conclusion

In this chapter we have emphasized the importance of institutional forces in reshaping our employment structure: the role of the welfare state, education and industrial relations systems. The ways in which these function have powerful repercussions on the transformation of the family, and on the relationship between self-servicing, consumption and paid employment. On one side, all advanced capitalist nations are facing vast institutional transformation. On the other side, cross-national institutional differences are great. Hence, a comparative study like ours promises to uncover both convergent and divergent cross-national post-industrial stratification trajectories.

The basic question that has always guided stratification research has to do with inequality, cleavages and polarization. This is obviously why most have devoted their attention to the industrial working class. As our attention now moves to the post-industrial order, the underlying central question has not changed. It is for this reason that our analytical focus is centered on the 'post-industrial proletariat'. Through an analysis of the relative position and nature of the unskilled service worker stratum and, more importantly, of its life-chances and mobility behavior, we hope to uncover the more general principles that guide contemporary class formation.

Much of the existing literature has studied the emerging class system in terms of structural statics. This may tell us something about the distribution of people across various positions, but is not well suited to an understanding of class *formation*. This is particularly the case with a potentially new service proletariat. Whether people remain service proletarians throughout their entire working lives is a completely different matter than whether the vast majority move on to better positions. In the latter case, we could hardly speak of class formation; our interpretation of the service proletariat would be entirely different. And, in order to draw any conclusions about the principles that operate in class formation, we need to isolate the variables that account for who stays and who moves: in our study, gender and education are the two most important such variables. In sum, our approach must be dynamic, centered on individual life and career trajectories.

The conceptual and analytical scheme presented in this chapter suggests a number of general hypotheses that will guide the subsequent empirical analyses. First, the decline of fordism will lead to stagnation in the relative number of managers, and to a sharp decline among the unskilled manual proletariat. This redundant stratum will, depending on the nature of the welfare state, be absorbed either in welfare state programs or in the unskilled service stratum.

Secondly, the rise of both the professional and semi-professional cadres will depend primarily on the vitality of the business and social services; that is, the degree to which manufacturing and households, respectively, diminish their self-servicing. The service intensity of the welfare state, and its commitment to universal and high-quality collective consumption, are variables that will strongly influence professionalization trends.

Thirdly, the relative size of the service proletariat (the unskilled service workers) is primarily a function of two factors. One, the service proletariat will grow large with a low-wage-based consumer service sector. This will allow individuals and households a price-competitive option to self-servicing their leisure activities.[20] This is most likely to occur where trade unions are weak or entirely absent, but could also occur within informal and hidden economies. Two, the service proletariat will also grow large with the expansion of social services. Since a large share of family reproductive activities are labor-intensive and unskilled, their export into the welfare state (or private market) implies a growth of unskilled service workers. The Baumol cost-disease problem is averted in this case since these jobs are publicly subsidized. Hence, the unskilled *social* service proletariat is unlikely to be low-paid, at least if employed within the welfare state.

Fourthly, the relative size of the outsider surplus population is a function of the combined effect of welfare state policy and the cost-disease problem. The surplus population is most likely to grow large in the jobless growth scenario, that is, under conditions of welfare state resistance to services combined with high labor costs (strong unionism). Its growth is especially encouraged where the welfare state is transfer-biased in its approach to labor market clearing.

Finally, post-industrial societies will, compared to their 'fordist' forebears, exhibit a considerably more positive occupational structure. But since they face a naked trade-off between accepting a large outsider population or, alternatively, a large service proletariat, they may produce two alternative kinds of polarization. In one case, the polarization will be between a small, but highly upgraded, insider structure and a large outsider surplus population. In the other case, a large service proletariat will constitute the pivotal source of polarization.

A genuine analysis of class closure must, however, shift to a dynamic analysis. In particular, we need to establish the mechanisms of life-course occupational mobility. The degree to which the post-industrial class structure is polarizing will, to a large extent, depend on whether a service proletariat is being consolidated; that is, on whether the labor market disadvantages among the service proletariat act cumulatively in a negative manner to suppress upward mobility (Mayer and Carroll, 1987: 18). Our previous discussion suggests several possible scenarios. One, the institutional framework of labor markets may construct de facto mobility barriers that render upward mobility from unskilled service employment improbable. This is likely to happen where (as in Germany) access to skilled positions is strictly linked to educational certification, and much less likely in the more fluid systems of North America where much of a person's training and labor market mobility occurs within the enterprise. It is also less likely to happen in Scandinavia where active labor market policies emphasize continuing adult training and retraining.

Class closure in the sense of a service proletariat may also depend on the welfare state. An expansionary, service-intensive welfare state opens up a huge mobility space which, as a consequence, augments a person's chance of moving up. Moreover, welfare state services and income protection are of vital importance for women's capacity to pursue job careers. We would therefore expect particularly high female upward mobility chances in Scandinavia and, in contrast, much lower ones in Germany.

Recruitment to the service proletariat is likely to come from three main sources, largely depending on the nature of the welfare state. Where the welfare state is very social service-intensive, the service proletariat is likely to be predominantly female. Where, on the other hand, the welfare state is neither service-intensive, nor capable of absorbing mass redundancies from the declining manufacturing sector, the service proletariat is more likely to be a 'dumping ground' for the uneducated, or for laid-off unskilled (largely male) workers. The third possibility is that unskilled service jobs function as first-entry slots, or as stop-gap jobs, for youth and immigrant workers.

The degree of class closure within the service proletariat will depend on its predominant form. If it consists mainly of unskilled welfare state service jobs, its degree of closure will largely depend on the mobility and career-cycle profiles of women workers. Since pay and benefits are likely to be relatively attractive, and since it constitutes an essentially sheltered employment sector, the motivation to move out may be weak. The capacity to do so may be further impaired by the strong probability that workers in these jobs are on part-time.

If, on the other hand, the unskilled service jobs are concentrated in private sector personal consumer services, the nature of recruitment and outward mobility is likely to differ. Since their very existence is mainly due to the presence of a low-wage economy, these jobs are unlikely to be viewed by their incumbents as more than temporary. Whether or not they remain 'stop-gap' jobs will depend very much on overall unemployment levels and the educational profile of the occupants. It is very possible that this kind of service proletariat will be internally divided between a core of permanent proletarians (perhaps circling between unskilled service jobs and unemployment) and mobile transients. In the latter case, we may identify two types: those who are bridging school and careers, and women who are bridging school and marriage/motherhood.

A final note on functional equivalents. Our classification scheme suggests a parallel between the traditional unskilled manual worker and the post-industrial unskilled service worker. As noted, it may even be the case that there is heavy mobility from the former into the latter. However, if there is no reciprocal mobility flow of unskilled service workers into manual jobs, we cannot regard the two strata as equivalents. On the other hand, there may exist alternative kinds of mobility flows and life-chance trajectories that dissolve the uniqueness of an unskilled service proletariat. It is, for example, quite possible that the attributes and mobility flows between unskilled service and (lower-end) sales or clerical jobs are so similar that these should be considered one 'class'. This, however, is also a question of empirical examination.

Notes

1 The concept of fordism, as used by Piore and Sabel (1984) and the French Regulation School (see Boyer, 1988), refers to the epoch of standardized mass production, coupled with mass-consumption, but connotes more broadly the overall macro-arrangement of economic activity and management, including Keynesian demand management to uphold mass consumption and a relatively rigid organization of the production process with its hierarchy of management–

worker relations. In this book, our use of the concept denotes primarily the stratification aspects of fordism, in particular the phenomenon of the standard mass-production worker. This will be discussed in greater detail below.

2 The concept of post-industrial society is often, and rightly, criticized for its implicit assumption of a societal form that supersedes or supplants industrial capitalism (see, in particular, Cohen and Zysman, 1987). In this treatise, I shall use the term in a heuristic way, not as a sworn adherent to the theories that begot the concept.

3 The idea itself is hardly new. Max Adler (1933) identified how long-term mass unemployment provoked a chronic bifurcation of the proletariat with a large section simply unable to enter its ranks. The result was the division of the left parties into the party of the employed, and the party of the unemployed.

4 Note that the Ehrenreichs' thesis comes much closer to the original meaning of the service class intended by Renner than does Goldthorpe's. Karl Renner (1953 emphasized that the service class was unproductive, but functionally necessary to uphold capitalist society. This certainly does not form part of Goldthorpe's definition.

5 Note, however, that the precise (English) text in Weber is somewhat more restrictive since it emphasizes (1) that people must have in common a specific causal component of their life-chances, insofar as (2) this component is represented exclusively by economic interests, and (3) is represented under the conditions of the commodity or labor markets. This, to Weber, (1978: 927), is class *situation*. The addendum regarding markets may, in fact, turn out to be decisive for our understanding of post-industrial classes, not only because a large share of the labor force is in state employment (without being necessarily equivalent to the traditional hierarchical structure), but also because of the often closed, monopolistic class character of many professions.

6 Wright's argument (1989: 345) is that state employment hardly alters class relationships since state activities are subordinate to the essence of capitalist society.

7 We may very well wish to qualify this point as post-fordist management principles find their way into the modern corporation, and as management training becomes scientized and professionalized.

8 There are two criteria often used to argue for a common classification of managers and professionals. One is Gouldner's stress on ideological similarity, a criterion that seems weak in light of the new conservatism and 'Yuppie' wave of the 1980s. The other, especially emphasized by Goldthorpe, is that they share similar privileges in the economic reward structure. It can be questioned whether, in fact, professionals and managers are embedded in similar reward structures. Parkin (1968) makes a distinction similar to ours on ideological grounds. To Parkin, there is a clear division between business-related occupations and the scientific professions. In the end, however, these are criteria requiring empirical verifications, and should not be assumed a priori.

9 Surprisingly, on the basis of the assets criterion, the Wright approach ends up defining the proletariat as a residual. See, in particular, Wright and Martin (1987: 9).

10 In fact, the marked differences in autonomy and authority between manual and service proletarians are evident from the data provided by Ahrne and Wright (1983: 229). Surprisingly, this is ignored in their analyses.
    We may very well be overplaying the difference between unskilled manual

and service workers. Flexible specialization and job upgrading in manufacturing may reduce the fordist character of the factory worker, while taylorist efforts in services (such as we find in McDonald's) may 'fordize' the service worker. It should be understood that the fordist–post-industrial divide which we impose on the labor market is to be seen in ideal-typical terms.

11 Probably the dominant outward mobility channel for unskilled manual workers has been early retirement. See, for example, Aaron and Burtless (1984) or Esping-Andersen (1990).

12 Reconsider the McDonald's fast-food counter workers. Their jobs may be highly taylorized, but they nonetheless have to possess social skills that, in a factory, are quite irrelevant: an engaging smile, courtesy, youthful enthusiasm. For career promotion into, say, McDonald's management, these kinds of social skills are very likely to be determinant.

13 McDonald's and Burger King outlets represent probably the most advanced type of taylorism and mass standardization in the consumer services. But since customers seek personal services precisely because they are personal and cater to individual demands and tastes, the potential for massive fordization should be modest indeed.

14 We should not forget the ways in which the fordist system itself has helped propel the gender revolution. Mass production and mass consumption has made household production goods, such as dishwashers, dryers, microwave ovens, etc., affordable. As a result, the amount of necessary household working time has been sharply reduced (Gershuny, 1983, 1988).

15 For a detailed treatment of this point, see Esping-Andersen (1990: Chapters 6 and 7).

16 Our study will disregard the primary sector entirely.

17 The industrial classification system proposed here follows, with some minor modifications, the influential contribution of Singelmann (1974) and Browning and Singelmann (1978). The main differences are that we exclude communications from producer services, and exclude postal services and government from social services. For an overview of the Browning and Singelmann scheme, see Browning and Singelmann (1978: 487).

18 It would be more appropriate to divide this group into higher-level managers with larger proprietors, and lower-level managers with small proprietors, as does Goldthorpe. On the basis of even detailed census data (three to four-digit ISCO codes) this is difficult since we are provided with virtually no information on size and, in many cases, the managerial group is not well differentiated. In the analyses that follow we will accordingly have to accept a less than satisfactory managerial classification.

19 The operational definition of the unskilled service proletariat follows the criterion that an unskilled service job is one that any one of us could do with no prior qualifications. Hence, it corresponds to a proletarian situation in Wright's sense in which there is a complete lack of any asset (skills, capital or organization) with which to undertake exploitation.

20 To this we should add the huge employment effect of tourism, which, in non-competitive situations, may give rise to a large service proletariat that is not necessarily low-paid. Thus, Monte Carlo, Rome or Venice are hardly low-wage economies.

2

Trends in Contemporary Class Structuration: A Six-nation Comparison

Gøsta Esping-Andersen, Zina Assimakopoulou and Kees van Kersbergen

As a first step towards an understanding of the evolving 'post-industrial' employment order, this chapter examines almost three decades of industrial and occupational change. We do this by the way of comparative statics, presenting a snapshot of the employment structure around 1960 and, again, in the 1980s.

From the accumulated evidence of previous research, we should anticipate a favorable trend. Virtually all research rejects Braverman's de-skilling and mass proletarianization thesis while pointing, instead, to a pervasive momentum of skill upgrading and professionalization (Kern and Schumann, 1984; Goldthorpe, 1987; Mayer and Carroll, 1987; Block, 1990; Erikson and Goldthorpe, 1992).

The overall trend may very well be favorable, but there remain a number of unresolved and disputed issues. First, the white-collar mass within clerical and sales jobs is often identified as a source of proletarianization. This mass is not only large and, of course, heavily female, but it is also one in which technology and work rationalization is likely to promote at least selective or partial downgrading of jobs (Crompton and Jones, 1984; Hartman, 1986; Applebaum and Albin, 1988). Applebaum and Albin (1988) show a growing white-collar polarization in terms of rewards and working conditions between jobs in the information services, on the one hand, and in the more labor-intensive, low-technology tertiary services, on the other hand.

Secondly, there is the possibility of polarization as posited by the 'declining-middle' thesis (Harrison and Bluestone, 1988). The traditionally well-paid, middle-layer jobs within industry disappear, creating a huge pool of cheap labor available for bottom-end service jobs. This polarization scenario may have empirical support from earnings data over the past decade, but may not be valid if our focus is on jobs rather than pay. Virtually no studies have shown a disproportionate growth in the unskilled ranks, and most conclude that unskilled manual workers are declining much faster than their better-skilled comrades (Kern and Schumann, 1984; Kutscher, 1988).

Thirdly, there is also the potential for polarization in the 'insider–outsider' scenario; in this case, in terms of access to jobs. This kind of dualism is, of course, much more likely to evolve under conditions of jobless growth, and is only marginally pertinent to economies, such as the American, which are capable of massive and sustained employment growth. As was suggested in Chapter 1, we may very well be facing a trade-off between the two evils of insider–outsider cleavages or a large bottom-end service proletariat.

Fortunately, class structural outcomes are not historically pre-ordained, but are conditional upon the institutions that pattern job growth. Within any country, institutional change may recast the functioning of labor market supply and demand. In the United States, for example, education and affirmative action have changed the kinds of jobs offered (more teachers, for example) and the labor supply mix (more women and educated workers). The influence of cross-national institutional differences on stratification has only recently become subject to systematic research (Mayer and Carroll, 1987; Allmendinger, 1989a,b; Featherman et al., 1989; Mayer et al., 1989).

Institutional Determinants of Employment Change

As argued in Chapter 1, the welfare state, the industrial relations system and education emerge as key institutional filters for employment structuration. These are the main forces that dictate the family–work nexus.[1] If the welfare state is service-intensive, it will bias service employment trends; if it provides a high social wage guarantee, the scope for a low-wage-based service economy is sharply reduced; if the welfare state is committed to full employment and active labor market policies, both female and overall participation rates are likely to increase. Inversely, if the welfare state actively reduces labor supply and is biased against social service provision, the result is almost certainly low female participation and a large outsider population of welfare state clients.

Similarly, employment trends are affected by the nature of industrial relations. Where, as in Germany and Scandinavia, trade unions are strong, centralized and bargain nationally, the employment outcome will be very different than in North America (and to an extent Britain), where unions tend to be weak, fragmented and localized. For example, Streeck (1987) shows that skill upgrading and flexible specialization are much more likely to occur where unions are powerful and capable of negotiating mutually acceptable terms with the employers. Also, the growth of low-wage service jobs is unlikely where trade unionism is comprehensive, centralized and committed to wage equalization. In contrast, American-style industrial relations reinforce labor market dualisms and segmentation; and since trade unionism penetrates only marginally into the services, the growth of a cheap labor force is made possible. The result is likely to be more low-productivity jobs at low pay.

The differences in union coverage within the service sector (combined social and personal services) are notable. At one extreme we find very strong unionization in Norway and Sweden (68 and 87 percent, respectively); at the other extreme, unionization in the United States is very weak (19 percent). The German rate is also quite low (28 percent), but this is unlikely to produce a large, unorganized, low-wage sector since union contracts typically cover most employees. Canada and Britain lie in the middle with 53 and 52 percent, respectively (OECD, 1991: 110).

The structure of labor supply and demand, as well as job mobility patterns, is, finally, conditioned by the education system. The German system is unique in the degree to which employer hiring decisions and job attainment are tied to vocational training and educational certification (König and Müller, 1986). Occupational change after first job is therefore less prevalent, and the unqualified labor force smaller and more marginal. Hence, unskilled service jobs are more likely to be filled by persons marginal to the labor force (immigrants and women), and mobility out of unskilled employment is likely to be especially restricted. Few other nations present such a rigid and pervasive job-matching process, and most rely more on on-the-job training and 'organizational' mobility, as in the United States, or on active labor market training programs, as in Scandinavia.

The educational system should be especially important for mobility into the post-industrial knowledge-based jobs. On the one hand, this may imply a future of diminished occupational mobility to the extent that access to the elite jobs depends less on internal career-lines, and more on initial educational attainment. On the other hand, welfare states may circumvent such mobility rigidities with sponsored adult training programs.

In this chapter we examine trends in post-industrial stratification within our six advanced nations: Canada, Germany, Norway,

Sweden, the United Kingdom and the United States. These nations were selected for comparison precisely because of the huge differences in their key institutional structures. At one extreme, the United States and Canada (and to a lesser degree, the UK) have relatively residualistic welfare states, characterized by only a modest social wage guarantee, and by their passive approach to full employment policy. They are also welfare states with a comparatively low *public* commitment to collective social services, although their use of generous tax-expenditures helps subsidize social service expansion in the private sector. Canada and the United States (with Britain) are also quite similar with regard to labor market training, both exhibiting a residualism that is parallel to their welfare state commitments.

At the other extreme, both Norway and Sweden feature welfare state and industrial relations institutions that are explicitly designed to influence the employment structure. The social wage guarantee is extraordinarily high, thus reducing the individual's compulsion to accept unattractive jobs; both welfare states feature a strong commitment to collective services, thus directing employment towards welfare state service jobs; both are internationally the epitome of a full employment guarantee. In both cases, we find extraordinarily comprehensive and centralized trade union systems which, for decades, have pursued solidaristic wage bargaining policies aimed at minimizing earnings differentials.

Germany represents a third regime. Its welfare state is both generous and quite comprehensive; yet social rights are strictly tied to one's employment record. Also, the German welfare state retains a strong commitment to preserve the traditional caring functions within the family. This results in a bias against collective social services (except for health care), and an implicit discouragement of female participation. It is, on the other hand, a heavily transfer-biased welfare state, especially in its approach to labor market intervention. Germany has been a leader in the use of early retirement schemes for purposes of reducing labor supply and aiding industrial reorganization. The German tax system discourages female labor force participation, while this is much less the case in the other countries. Germany's system of labor market education is, as noted, unique in its emphasis on skill certification via apprenticeship. In terms of industrial relations, the German falls closer to the Scandinavian model in terms of centralization, but with a markedly lower level of trade union density.

With these institutional differences in mind, we would anticipate a rough three-way divergence in terms of employment change: a Nordic, a North American and a German model. For institutional reasons, Britain can be expected to lean towards the North American model. The residual nature of their welfare states and their decentralized industrial relations framework should facilitate the growth of a large low-wage service proletariat. The absence of a comprehensive employment training system may produce a substantial labor force lacking in skills. It follows that a sizable proportion of the active population is likely to be blocked from upward occupational mobility.

In contrast, this is less probable in either of the North European countries. The social service bias of Sweden and Norway will have two concomitant implications: first, it will facilitate high levels of female participation; second, it will fuel the growth of a large (probably female-dominated) unskilled social service stratum which owes its employment to the welfare state, not – as its North American counterpart – to low wages; demand for social services is fiscally subsidized and thus relatively price inelastic. With access to the active labor market training programs, the Nordic social service proletariat is granted a high probability of outward and upward job mobility.

The institutional framework of Germany can be expected to result in two basic features: first, due to unionism, credentialism and its welfare state bias, employment growth within either of the two service proletarian groups will be only marginal.[2] This implies both less overall employment and less female labor force entry. At the same time, it implies less job polarization and almost certainly a less proletarian service economy; the skill mix within services, like industry, should be higher. Secondly, due to modest job expansion and its transfer bias, the German system may produce an unusually large 'outsider', or labor market surplus, population chiefly embracing women, early retirees and the long-term unemployed.

The Analytical Approach

We will describe the principal trends in employment structure by monitoring overall change between 1960 and the latest possible date in the 1980s.[3]

The choice of 1960 as our starting point is partly motivated by practical considerations. For most countries, it is virtually impossible to construct genuinely comparable occupation and industry data for pre-1960 censuses.[4] But for a study of post-industrial stratification the period around 1960 also offers a logical starting point since it represents a 'high point' in the postwar era of fordist industrial mass production. As Singelmann (1978) has shown, the industrial sector reached its maximum relative size in all advanced countries around this period. The same holds for the size of the manual working class (Kalleberg and Berg, 1987: 79). It was not until after 1960 that non-distributive services gained their real growth momentum. The two to three decades that our study covers can, accordingly, be regarded as an era of unfolding post-industrial employment, whether by this we mean the emerging dominance of services, the declining significance of industrial employment or the rise of professional and related occupations.

Our examination will proceed as follows. We shall, first, examine *sectoral* shifts in employment with particular emphasis on changes in the size of the consumer, social and business services. Secondly, we analyze *occupational* shifts separately in order to characterize evolving hierarchies. Here, we will focus especially on the new service proletariat and the outsider population. We will then, thirdly, examine the *interaction* of sectors and occupations. This serves to specify class differentiation within the new service economy, and to identify the job composition effect of differential sectoral growth. The fourth part of our investigation focuses directly on emerging patterns of polarization.

Sectoral Employment Shifts

The sectoral data presented in Tables 2.1 and 2.2 portray the widely recognized shift towards services. Their share of total employment more or less doubled over the period. But there is considerable international divergence in both the scope and composition of change.

Table 2.1   *The sectoral distribution of employment, 1960* (percent)

	Germany	Norway	Sweden	Canada	USA	UK[a]
Primary	14.2	20.5	14.1	12.2	7.4	2.6
Industry	48.5	33.3	42.2	31.7	35.3	44.3
Distribution	18.7	26.0	20.2	26.0	23.1	21.1
Traditional economy	**81.4**	**79.8**	**76.5**	**69.9**	**65.8**	**68.0**
Government	**4.9**	**4.0**	**2.9**	**6.4**	**5.1**	**5.6**
Consumer services	5.8	6.9	8.2	9.0	11.4	8.9
Social services	4.5	6.4	9.3	9.2	11.2	11.2
Business services	3.4	1.9	2.9	5.5	6.8	6.4
Service economy	**13.7**	**15.2**	**20.4**	**23.7**	**29.4**	**26.5**

[a] 1971

Table 2.2   *The sectoral distribution of employment, 1980s*
(percent)

	Germany 1985	Norway 1985	Sweden 1985	Canada 1981	USA 1988	UK 1981
Primary	4.9	7.6	6.5	5.4	3.1	2.2
Industry	39.7	26.6	28.5	27.2	25.4	37.1
Distribution	20.7	23.8	19.2	24.6	22.7	22.2
Traditional economy	**65.3**	**58.0**	**54.2**	**57.2**	**51.2**	**61.5**
Government	**7.8**	**6.5**	**6.8**	**7.7**	**4.8**	**9.6**
Consumer services	6.4	5.6	5.4	8.7	11.9	9.2
Social services	12.0	22.8	26.4	15.0	20.9	11.5
Business services	7.8	7.2	7.3	11.6	11.2	8.3
Service economy	**26.2**	**35.6**	**39.1**	**35.3**	**44.0**	**29.0**

The share of services in 1960 varied a great deal, from a low of 14 percent in Germany to a high of 29 percent in the United States. Starting from a much higher initial base, it is only to be expected that the service share would grow more slowly (about 50 percent) in the United States and Canada. In evaluating the very modest British growth we must remember that our data begin in 1971. But initial base certainly does not dictate subsequent growth rates. Norway started at a higher point than Germany, yet its growth rate is 134 percent, compared to Germany's 91 percent. The Swedish rate was slightly higher at 92 percent.

Measuring growth in terms of shares does not take into account national variations in overall employment expansion. We should therefore also compare absolute levels of employment growth. In this case, the rank-order of the countries changes substantially. Total absolute service employment grew by 90 percent in Germany, 256 percent in Norway, 58 percent in Sweden, 150 percent in Canada and 113 percent in the United States (1960–80). At any rate, the degree of post-industrialization in sectoral terms differs widely, with the United States and Sweden as the undisputable vanguards. Germany (as Britain) not only follows far behind the others; its level of post-industrialization in 1985 is indeed lower than for the United States in 1960!

In terms of service sector composition, the countries converge in the sense that the social and business services are the most dynamic, except in Britain. But there are also sharp differences: Sweden and Norway are extreme cases of a social service-led transformation. With Germany, these are also countries with a small (and even declining) consumer service sector. The United States and Canada have both a social service sector that is larger than the German and

British, and there is an obvious Anglo-Saxon bias towards a large consumer services sector.

Occupational Employment Shifts

Judging from Tables 2.3 and 2.4, the degree of occupational transformation is somewhat less dramatic than was the case for sectoral shifts. In 1960, the rural classes remained large in several nations, Norway especially. Since the 1960s, both the rural classes and the manual industrial workers have declined sharply. In this sense, our epoch unites the ultimate demise of the 'pre-industrial' classes with the accelerated erosion of the industrial working class.

There is a certain degree of cross-national convergence in the profile of occupational change. Within our fordist hierarchy, the clerical sales occupations continue to grow, albeit modestly, thus helping to offset the general decline among the manual workers. Within our post-industrial hierarchy, the share of professionals and semi-professionals has almost doubled everywhere.

Still, the post-industrial hierarchy emerging in each country is quite distinct. The German, as we expected, is not only much smaller than elsewhere, but also much more skilled. Its unskilled service proletarians have declined sharply, so that their share is less than half of that elsewhere (but then the German manual working class has declined less than elsewhere).[5]

Britain's profile is surprisingly similar to the German, being still

Table 2.3   *The occupational distribution of employment, 1960 (percent)*

	Germany	Norway	Sweden	Canada	USA	UK[a]
Primary occupations	14.3	20.4	13.6	12.3	6.5	2.9
Managers	3.3	2.8	4.7	1.8	7.8	8.8
Clerical	14.9	10.0	9.2	19.0	16.1	17.2
Sales	7.8	8.1	6.9	5.6	7.2	6.2
Skilled manual	25.3	11.2	18.6	14.2	13.2	15.1
Unskilled manual	16.1	26.3	21.6	20.8	21.6	25.7
'Fordist occupations'	**67.4**	**58.4**	**61.0**	**61.4**	**65.9**	**73.0**
Professional	2.9	3.4	2.7	5.4	5.4	4.6
Semi-professional	4.9	5.2	8.9	5.1	6.2	7.0
Skilled service	1.7	3.7	4.3	6.2	4.2	3.1
Unskilled service	8.7	7.9	9.5	9.6	11.9	9.5
Post-industrial occupations	**18.2**	**20.2**	**25.4**	**26.3**	**27.7**	**24.2**

[a] 1971

Table 2.4   *The occupational distribution of employment, 1980s (percent)*

	Germany 1985	Norway 1985	Sweden 1980	Canada 1981	USA 1988	UK 1981
Primary occupations	**5.2**	**7.5**	**4.4**	**5.6**	**3.1**	**2.5**
Managers	4.5	8.7	4.0	5.0	9.1	8.7
Clerical	21.1	13.1	11.7	19.3	16.1	15.6
Sales	8.5	8.4	6.9	9.9	12.2	6.5
Skilled manual	17.3	9.5	15.2	11.7	8.7	12.3
Unskilled manual	16.5	15.9	12.4	16.2	14.4	24.5
'Fordist occupations'	**67.9**	**55.6**	**50.2**	**62.1**	**60.5**	**67.6**
Professional	6.6	5.0	7.3	7.2	8.8	6.5
Semi-professional	10.7	12.7	14.6	8.9	9.3	9.1
Skilled service	5.0	7.3	4.4	7.0	6.6	3.8
Unskilled service	4.5	11.5	16.9	9.3	11.7	10.5
Post-industrial occupations	**26.8**	**36.5**	**43.2**	**32.4**	**36.4**	**29.9**

very industrial. But, unlike in Germany, there is a heavy unskilled worker bias in both the fordist and post-industrial hierarchy. Comparatively speaking, Britain appears very proletarian.

The Nordic, and especially Swedish, trajectory is biased towards the semi-professionals, on the one hand, and the unskilled service strata, on the other hand. This, as we shall see, is almost entirely attributable to the welfare state effect.

Finally, the United States and Canada show a fairly common pattern, characterized above all by a much more even distribution along the post-industrial hierarchy. The stagnant share of the American unskilled service proletariat suggests that the 'declining-middle' thesis may not apply to jobs. Indeed, the American post-industrial hierarchy seems much less polarized than the Swedish. In Sweden, the ratio of professionals to service proletarians in the 1980s is 0.43, compared to 0.75 in the United States.

The industry occupation profiles that emerge give substantial credence to our institution-based stratification hypotheses. There is a clear Nordic welfare-state-led employment trend, highly advanced in a post-industrial sense, albeit in a rather one-dimensional direction; Germany (with Britain) stands out clearly as a post-industrial laggard; and Northern America, also very post-industrial, shows a continued emphasis on private market, consumer service jobs. On one point, namely managerialism, the United States is extreme. Still, in the 1980s, it had almost twice as large a managerial class as did Canada. As argued elsewhere, this is partly a function of the United States' unusual reliance on managers in the manufacturing sector and partly associated with the huge consumer service economy which is so heavily characterized by small outlets.[6]

The Labor Market Outsiders

If our thesis is correct, service sector stagnation is the alternative to a large service proletariat. However, with concomitant de-industrialization and lack of service growth, we should expect the emergence of a labor market surplus population. Employment stagnation will obviously have different dis-employment effects, depending on demographic pressures. Germany, for example, has experienced stagnation in both jobs and people. Yet, what matters is the size of younger cohorts, the rates of net immigration, and trends in female labor force supply. If there are strong pressures for labor market entry for any of the latter three reasons, the insider–outsider cleavage should be especially noticeable.

In distributional terms, the surplus population will depend on either the social wage or spouse's earnings. In either case, this kind of distributive dependency may actually reinforce the insider–outsider cleavage. To finance the outsider populations, be they housewives or welfare state clients, direct and indirect labor costs will rise, thus further discouraging the emergence of service jobs, in the consumer services especially. The effect may also be to block welfare state job expansion since the fiscal burden of maintaining a large transfer-dependent population will preclude social service investments.

It is clearly very difficult to estimate the size of the outsider population. We lack comprehensive information on the degree to which, for example, housewives and early retirees would prefer to work. The problem extends also to youth in education. There is little doubt that the education system in many countries serves as a parking lot for unemployable youth cohorts.

In this overview, we estimate the relative size of the outsider population by proxies. Table 2.5 presents a surrogate index of the degree of 'outsiderness', based on four variables: (1) the employment gap, which measures the difference in overall participation from the Swedish rates (being the highest); (2) the percentage of long-term unemployed (one year or more); (3) the percentage of long-term (same as above) unemployed among youth (aged 16 to 24); (4) and the percentage of workers who are involuntarily in part-time jobs.

Table 2.5 supports the hypothesis that outsiders pay the price for a small service proletariat. The German score on our outsider index is systematically higher than in the other countries, while the

Table 2.5   *Indices of the 'outsider' population, 1980s*

	Germany	Norway	Sweden	Canada	USA	UK
Employment gap[a]	15.9	3.5	0.0	9.2	4.9	5.0
Long-term unemployed in labor force[b]	2.7	0.2	0.2	0.8	0.6	2.3
Youth long-term unemployed in labor force[c]	2.8	0.2	0.1	0.8	0.7	4.3
Involuntary part-time in labor force[d]	1.1	n.d	3.1	5.2	3.7	2.8
Summary outsider index	22.5	3.9	3.4	16.0	9.9	14.4

[a] Percentage labor force participation below Swedish level.
[b] Persons, aged 16–64, unemployed for more than one year as percent of the labor force (average 1986–8).
[c] Percentage long-term unemployment (one year +) in labor force cohort, aged 16–24 (average 1986–8).
[d] Persons on involuntary part-time schedules as a percent of total labor force.

Sources: OECD, 1984, 1985, 1987, 1990a,b

German service proletariat is 6 percentage points below the average. Of course, the size of an, at least latent, outsider population tells us very little about the cleavage structure. First, we do not know what proportion within the 'participation-deficit' group would prefer to work *if* conditions were favorable (i.e. attractive jobs and child care were available, or households did not face a negative tax effect). Secondly, it is difficult to speak of a cleavage when one side of the divide is extraordinarily heterogeneous and fragmented.

Women in the Post-Industrial Labor Market

The post-industrial job structure is likely to be very feminine, for reasons of both supply and demand. To illustrate this point, let us reconsider the historical dynamics of change. Until the 1950s (more or less), women's participation in industrial jobs was quite high, typically concentrated in such sectors as textiles, leather and the food industries. Women's return to the home in the postwar era coincided with two decisive events: one, these were among the first industries to 'de-industrialize' and rationalize, thus shedding large numbers of female workers; two, the 'familialization' of women workers was made possible by the institutionalization of fordism, including job security, high pay and life-cycle family-income guarantees. Fordism thus permitted families to live decently on the male breadwinner's earnings.

The vast expansion in the post-industrial service jobs since the 1960s occurred therefore in a unique context of (near-) full employment among males and a huge latent labor reservoir of women. The largely male-dominated industries, such as autos or steel, experienced their first major waves of 'de-industrialization' during the 1970s and 1980s. Early retirement and unemployment programs, however, helped channel this excess male labor supply out of the market. Accordingly, the male labor supply for the expanding post-industrial jobs would be more marginal.

Nonetheless, for the post-industrial job structure to become heavily feminine, it must furnish women with the means for participation. Hence, a social services-biased expansion will be more likely to produce a post-industrial labor market that is gendered across the entire occupational hierarchy. In contrast, where social services are under-developed, women's insertion in the service economy is likely to be of a more marginal nature; in this case, we would expect women to be more concentrated in easy-entry service (or sales) jobs on a temporary basis.

From Table 2.6 we see that post-industrial job growth is, indeed, quite female-biased. Except for Germany, women account for the lion's share of total post-industrial employment growth since 1960. Women are everywhere over-represented in the three post-industrial service sectors, accounting for two-thirds of all in Scandinavia.[7] And within the service economy, it is especially the *social services* that have experienced a female-led expansion. In this case, Sweden is extreme with 70 percent of total net female employment growth concentrated in the welfare state.[8]

The female bias is also pronounced when we turn to the post-industrial occupations. Women tend to be extremely over-represented in the unskilled service jobs, but are also surprisingly well represented in the more elite occupations. The feminine bias would appear even stronger if we had adjusted for the lower rates of female labor force participation. In terms of both sectors and occupations, the Scandinavian countries are exceptionally gender-biased. This is what one would expect given the welfare state dominance and its effect on both female labor force supply and demand. Vice versa, Germany's unusually low degree of feminization can be attributed to the welfare state's discouragement of female employment.

The bottom half of Table 2.6 depicts women's performance in the post-industrial hierarchy. Women are extraordinarily over-represented in the bottom-end unskilled service jobs, particularly in Scandinavia, and the over-time trend seems to reinforce this bias in all countries except the United States. Britain is an extreme case of

Table 2.6   *Women and post-industrial employment, 1960–1980s (percent)*

	Germany	Norway	Sweden	Canada	USA	UK
Women's share of post-industrial service sector (1980s)	52.9	67.7	68.6	60.6	61.6	58.6
Women's share of growth 1960–80s	45.0	71.3	73.6	63.1	64.0[a]	62.5[b]
Women's share of post-industrial occupations (1980s)	44.6	60.1	59.0	48.0	49.7	54.0
Women's share of growth 1960–80s	51.4	67.4	67.1	55.5	46.5[a]	61.7[b]
Women's share of unskilled service jobs (1980s)	65.9	78.7	83.0	62.2	59.0	75.3
Women's share of growth/decline 1960–80s	−29.8[c]	81.2	87.9	74.5	51.3[a]	101.8[b]
Women's share of professional and semi-professional jobs (1980s)	38.8	43.3	46.1	47.1	50.9	42.1
Women's share of growth (1960–80s)	42.7	51.5	55.3	53.2	52.9	50.8

[a] 1960–80
[b] 1971–81
[c] Women account for 29.8 percent of total decline in unskilled service jobs in Germany.

a female-concentrated proletarianization, but it is also interesting to note that the large net decline that has occurred in Germany has been disproportionally among men. At the other end of the spectrum, women have generally benefited within the post-industrial elite jobs. Had we adjusted for their lower rates of participation, women's growth would have been stronger than men's in the professional and semi-professional (including technical) cadres.

Structural change has certainly not been gender-neutral, and we might very well see the emergence of a strong gender dualism. As the service economy becomes a predominantly female labor market, the post-industrial occupational hierarchy becomes a female hierarchy. Yet there are significant national variations in this tendency. The trend is least evident in Germany, and most powerfully so in Scandinavia. Comparatively speaking the female hier-archy is very unbalanced in Britain, and most balanced in the United States.

The unskilled service workers may become a proletarian *class* if there exists powerful social closure. This we shall be able to ascertain through mobility analyses in the subsequent chapters. But if, indeed, this turns out to be the case, such a class would obviously be a feminine one. Unskilled service jobs are, above all, character-ized by virtue of being easy first-entry jobs for unskilled persons. This may be one reason why their female bias is so strong. For exactly the same reasons, we would also expect them to be over-represented by immigrants and under-privileged minorities. This is in fact the case. In Sweden, the foreigner share in the unskilled service jobs is about 9 percent (which is more than twice the overall proportion of foreign workers); in Germany, their share is 12 percent (compared to an overall proportion of 7.6 percent).

For the United States, we saw a low and declining female over-representation in the unskilled service jobs. Does the same obtain for minority workers? Both yes and no. In 1960, Blacks accounted for more than 27 percent of all unskilled service jobs, but by 1988 their share had declined to 15.4 percent. This is no doubt related to the demise of the domestic servant. Hispanics, on the other hand, have more or less filled the gap, growing from a 2 percent share to 12.1 percent of the unskilled service jobs. If we were to add Black and Hispanic *males* (16.3 percent) to the total female share, constructing so to speak a combined minority share, the United States would look more like the other countries with a combined 'minority' share of 75.3 percent.

The Service Proletariat

Generally speaking, post-industrial society seems to produce much less proletarianization than did its industrial predecessor. While the unskilled manual working class has declined sharply over the past decades, the size of the service proletariat has been quite stable in the Anglo-Saxon nations, and has declined sharply in Germany. Unskilled service jobs have, on the other hand, been a major source of job growth in the Nordic countries. Judging from the compara-tive trend, it appears that the unskilled service workers' share may stabilize around a maximum of 10–15 percent of the labor force; this compares to roughly 20–5 percent unskilled industrial workers in 1960.[9]

It may be argued that our unskilled service class vastly under-estimates the total share of effectively proletarian *non-industrial* jobs, since a large proportion of clerical and sales jobs are genuinely unskilled (Crompton and Jones, 1984; Hunt and Hunt, 1985).[10] This proportion can be estimated for the United States on the basis of Hunt and Hunt's (1985) data. Excluding the jobs already classified in our service proletariat (messengers and mail carriers being the two largest groups), the unqualified share of clerical occupations was, in 1982, roughly 8 percent (1.5 million). This is equivalent to approximately 1.5 percent of the total labor force.[11] In other words, our data may underestimate the total non-industrial proletariat, but certainly not vastly so. Moreover, there is little evidence to suggest that the trend is towards a disproportionate growth within the ranks of the low-skilled clerical jobs. Kutscher's (1988) projections on the basis of BLS data indicate that administrative support occupations will grow by only 10 percent between 1986 and 2000, which is much lower than the projected growth for most professional, semi-professional and managerial jobs.

There is also a large proportion of sales jobs that could rightly be held to fit the unskilled worker defintion, although here we lack any concrete information on the internal differentiation among sales personnel. In most of our countries, the sales job share of employment is about 6–8 percent; the United States is an extreme with 12 percent. So, even if as much as half of sales jobs were to be considered genuinly unqualified, the total service proletariat would not have to be considered huge anywhere.[12]

If we turn our focus directly to the unskilled service worker class, its traditionally heavy female and minority concentration does *not* appear to be in decline. If by minority we mean women and racial-ethnic minority populations, the evidence is clear that their share has increased. In our interpretation of these trends, we should bear in mind the fact that the growth of the female and 'minority' labor force has been disproportionally large. If we take the growth trend into account, the female and minority bias in the recruitment to service proletarian jobs would clearly remain, but would appear somewhat less extreme.

It is to be expected that the *sectoral* bias of the service proletarian jobs will also influence their gender and minority composition. Concretely, the extreme level of female over-representation in Norway and Sweden is almost certainly related to the fact that female-dominated jobs are concentrated within the social services.[13] Table 2.7 indicates that, in the past, service proletarian jobs were largely (about half of the total) associated with the consumer service industries. This sectoral bias declined significantly by the 1980s. The data suggest that the service proletarian share is mainly a function of the social and consumer services. It declines

Table 2.7   *The sectoral distribution of unskilled workers,*
1960–1980s (percent)

	Germany	Norway	Sweden	Canada	USA	UKª
Industry						
1960	17.0	5.3	10.4	10.4	8.4	10.2
1980s	9.7	8.8	4.1	3.5	3.8	8.3
Distribution						
1960	34.1	18.7	12.6	14.1	14.1	12.9
1980s	16.6	16.9	8.5	11.6	7.7	13.0
Government						
1960	5.7	3.3	2.0	5.1	1.5	7.1
1980s	13.4	10.1	7.2	5.4	9.2	20.4
Consumer services						
1960	33.7	54.6	40.5	46.9	52.9	30.8
1980s	25.8	18.5	13.3	41.7	40.6	30.3
Social services						
1960	6.8	16.5	30.5	20.0	18.8	34.2
1980s	25.8	41.0	61.3	29.9	28.7	24.3
Business services						
1960	2.4	1.6	3.5	2.9	3.1	4.6
1980s	8.2	4.2	4.4	7.7	9.7	3.5
Other						
1960	0.3	0.0	0.5	0.6	1.2	0.2
1980s	0.5	0.5	1.2	0.2	0.3	0.2
Total	100.0	100.0	100.0	100.0	100.0	100.0

ª 1971

when the consumer industries decline, but rises with the growth of social services.

This supports the hypothesis (discussed in Chapter 1) that the export of traditional family self-servicing activities fuels a disproportionate growth of unskilled service jobs. Hence, where, as in Scandinavia, the welfare state has taken over many traditional family care functions, the result is the mushrooming of unqualified (female) service jobs. Where, as in Germany, the consumer services decline and household care functions are not exported, the result is a decline in the service proletariat. In contrast to these two polar cases, Canada and the United States exhibit a much more balanced growth within the service economy. This may also explain their much *less* imbalanced service proletarian distribution.[14] The survival and growth of unskilled service jobs is, except for the social services, likely to depend on wage differentials. In a previous (time-series) study, we have shown that consumer service jobs are the only major group in which employment trends are related to wage costs (Giannelli and Esping-Andersen, 1991). This is also what we find in a cross-sectional national comparison. In the 1980s, in both

Sweden and Germany, earnings in these jobs average 89–90 percent of a skilled manual worker, whereas in the United States they average only 63 percent.

Post-industrial Polarization?

If it is true that the service proletariat, or its outsider equivalent, stabilizes at a relatively modest maximum, this alone suggests that post-industrial societies will generate cleavages that are numerically less substantial than their industrial forebears. Polarization, however, depends on the overall employment configuration.

In the literature there seems to be no agreed upon definition of polarization. The 'declining-middle' thesis predicts a swelling bottom *and* top at the expense of the middle layer skilled manual and non-manual occupations. The empirical studies have almost exclusively examined earnings, while our emphasis is on jobs. The validity of the 'declining-middle' thesis would obviously be strengthened if job shifts correlate with earnings shifts.

A second approach to polarization follows the logic inherent in the de-skilling debate. The thesis here is that jobs will be downgraded (except at the top, of course), be it for reasons of managerial taylorism or technological skill displacement. Most research in this tradition has focused on the labor process and the actual tasks performed by workers. Hence, it suggests that occupational titles may be misleading. Virtually all recent research casts serious doubt on the de-skilling thesis, including its erstwhile priests (Kern and Schumann, 1984). But it is nonetheless possible that a process of downgrading is unfolding in the sense that the long-term trend systematically generates more job growth in the lower than in the higher echelons of the occupational structure; that is, employers shift from hiring professionals to semi-professionals, from semi-professionals to skilled service workers, and so on down the line. The net effect of such a trend is perhaps not so much polarization as generalized occupational downgrading.

A third, and clearly superior, approach to polarization takes into account a more comprehensive set of positional attributes that, when combined, define cumulative privilege or under-privilege (Giddens, 1973; Mayer and Carroll, 1987). Polarization would then exist where a significantly large labor market group is systematically excluded from access to upward mobility. Aside from the extraordinarily comprehensive indicator approach in the Scandinavian 'Level of Living' studies, clearly education, earnings and mobility probabilities constitute key variables with which to gauge the presence of systematic and cumulative under-privilege. Analyses of this will be undertaken in the subsequent chapters.

In this section, we shall examine polarization with three different measures. First, we examine the changing ratio of top–bottom jobs within the fordist and post-industrial occupational 'hierarchies' taken separately. In the fordist hierarchy we take the ratio of unskilled manual workers over managers; in the post-industrial hierarchy, unskilled service workers over professionals (excluding semi-professionals). Secondly, we examine the 'declining-middle' thesis by taking the percentage share of the middle within each of the two hierarchies. Clerical-administrative occupations constitute our middle in the fordist hierarchy, semi-professionals, technicians and skilled service workers the middle in the post-industrial hierarchy. Thirdly, we examine 'downgrading' by comparing over-time growth rates across the occupational hierarchy.

Beginning with the bottom–top ratios in our two hierarchies, Table 2.8 indicates a clearly declining degree of polarization. The decline is obviously more dramatic within the fordist hierarchy due to the substantial unskilled worker decline. Britain is an exception to this trend, while Norway and Canada are extreme cases of industrial de-proletarianization, most likely due to their once dominant, and now marginal, mining and raw-material processing industries (like iron, wood and paper pulp). Also the post-industrial hierarchy is becoming less bottom-heavy, again as we would expect. Germany is an extreme case with only 0.68 service proletarians for every professional in the 1980s! Except for Norway, it is also evident that the post-industrial sector is far less 'polarized' than its fordist equivalent.

Turning to the 'middle', Table 2.9 depicts a more mixed picture

Table 2.8 *Occupational polarization in the fordist and post-industrial hierarchies: the ratio of bottom–top occupations, 1960–1980s*

	Germany	Norway	Sweden	Canada	USA	UK
Fordist hierachy[a]						
1960	4.87	9.51	4.58	11.65	2.77	2.93[c]
1980s	3.64	1.83	3.08	3.32	1.58	2.81
Post-industrial hierarchy[b]						
1960	2.95	2.32	3.54	1.78	2.20	2.09[c]
1980s	0.68	2.30	2.30	1.49	1.33	1.62

[a] Fordist hierarchy: unskilled manuals/managers
[b] Post-industrial hierarchy: unskilled service workers/professionals
[c] 1971

Table 2.9   *The percentage share of the middle within the*
fordist and post-industrial occupational hierarchies, 1960–1980s

	Germany	Norway	Sweden	Canada	USA	UK
Fordist hierachy[a]						
1960	59.6	35.8	45.6	54.1	44.5	44.2[c]
1980s	56.6	40.6	53.6	49.9	41.0	41.3
Post-industrial hierarchy[b]						
1960	36.3	44.2	52.0	43.0	37.5	41.7[c]
1980s	58.6	54.8	46.6	49.1	43.7	43.1

[a] Fordist hierarchy: clerical and skilled workers
[b] Post-industrial hierarchy: semi-professionals, technicians and skilled service workers
[c] 1971

from the point of view of polarization. The fordist hierarchy is becoming more middle-heavy only in the Scandinavian countries. There is a declining middle trend within the rest. But, turning to the post-industrial hierarchy, the trend is very favorable. Sweden's very strong accent on unskilled service jobs means, however, a significant decline in the post-industrial middle. Again, our data confirm the thesis that a small post-industrial labor market assures a more favorable occupational mix, while a large one tends to promote greater polarization. Generally speaking, however, the data from both Table 2.8 and 2.9 give a consistent impression that the post-industrial employment trend is positive.

Unfortunately, the occupational earnings structure can be studied only for Germany, Sweden and the United States. The pervasive low-wage effect on job trends within the American consumer service sector stands out clearly. In 1980, the average hourly earnings of workers within eating establishments were only 44 percent of average manufacturing wages in the United States, compared to 65 percent in Germany and 80 percent in Sweden.[15]

Table 2.10 presents earnings differentials between our occupational groups with average skilled manual worker equal to 100. As is well known, the Swedish wage structure is very compressed, as our data also show (with the exception of the very highly paid managers).[16] The German wage structure is similarly quite compressed, but with an extraordinarily high earnings premium for the elite occupations, managers and professionals. In both cases, we see once again the famous Baumol cost-disease effect of high relative pay among the unskilled service workers. The American earnings distribution is almost the exact opposite of the German. Instead of an extraordinarily privileged top, the United States is characterized by its extremely under-privileged bottom. The unskilled service

Table 2.10   *Occupational earnings differentials in Sweden and the United States (skilled manual workers = 100)*

	Germany 1985	Sweden 1988	USA 1960	USA 1988
Managers	185	156	143	130
Clerical	105	108	74	81
Sales	106	97	96	94
Unskilled manuals	98	91	79	81
Professionals	210	134	138	146
Semi-professionals	116	111	97	108
Skilled service	88	98	79	86
Unskilled service	89	89	50	63

The data are not strictly comparable. The Swedish are based on hourly earnings, the US on annual earnings and the German on monthly earnings. For Sweden, the data refer to pooled labor force samples, 1986–9. For a detailed explanation, see Chapter 4 below. For the United States, the 1988 (March) CPS file used here reports earnings for 1987. For Germany, the data are derived from the 1985 Mikro-census. The earnings data refer only to full-time employed.

workers are clearly a very badly paid workforce.[17] For most of the other occupations, the American differentials are not dramatically different from the Swedish or German. Indeed, the position of American sales workers is surprisingly favorable. The United States has become internationally notorious for its over-paid executives. This seems, however, to be contradicted by our data. The reason is almost certainly that our managerial group is so heterogeneous, comprising a large share of 'petty-managers' whose relatively modest earnings outweigh the effect of the overpaid executive.

For the United States we can compare the 1960 and 1988 earnings distribution. From this perspective, there does not appear to be much support for the 'declining-middle' thesis since exactly the opposite has happened: in every case, the middle-layer occupations have improved relatively while the top levels have lost.[18]

In summary, there is evidence that suggests polarization within the post-industrial occupational hierarchy, but only to a limited extent, and only with regard to the unskilled service class. In the United States, this class is associated with extremely low earnings, but then its minority over-representation is not extreme. In Sweden, it is a virtual female ghetto, but since it is largely concentrated in the welfare state, earnings are not low. The real test of polarization will, however, have to await the mobility analyses conducted in the subsequent chapters.

Turning, finally, to the occupational downgrading trends in Table 2.11, we are struck by the wide national differences. But the overall trends hardly point to an impending polarization. In both the fordist

Table 2.11   *Occupational upgrading and downgrading:*
percentage relative change within occupational groups,
1960–1980s

	Germany	Norway	Sweden	Canada	USA	UK[a]
Managers	36.4	29.9	−14.9	177.8	16.7	−1.1
Clerical/sales	30.3	11.4	15.5	59.3	21.5	−5.6
Skilled manuals	−31.6	−34.9	18.3	−17.6	−34.1	−18.5
Unskilled manuals	2.5	−53.5	−42.6	−22.1	−33.3	−4.7
Professional	127.6	19.0	170.4	33.3	63.0	41.3
Semi-professional	120.0	95.4	87.6	74.5	50.0	30.0
Skilled service	194.1	58.7	2.3	12.9	57.1	22.6
Unskilled service	−48.3	17.3	77.9	−3.1	−1.7	10.5

[a] 1971–81

and post-industrial hierarchy, higher-grade occupational groups are undisputably growing faster than their lower-grade equivalents. Similarly, the bottom-end jobs decline more rapidly than those at the higher rungs of the ladder. There are only two exceptions to this rule. One is the much steeper decline of skilled than non-skilled manuals in Britain and Germany. This seems to contradict the analyses of Kern and Schumann (1984) and Streeck (1987), both of which argue that the German model of industrial restructuration has generated a noticeable degree of skill upgrading. The explanation may lie in the huge influx of foreign guestworkers after 1960, but the contradiction may also be more apparent than real. The skill and task upgrading that these studies note may not be reflected in official occupational titles. Sweden provides the other exception with its accentuated unskilled bias in the post-industrial workforce.

Conclusions

The analyses in this chapter are based on cross-sectional employment data, and therefore provide only a snapshot of the major trends. Since we cannot trace the movement of persons between positions, we cannot make any conclusions about class formation in the strict sense of the word: we can say nothing about openness or closure. Hence, the real answer to whether post-industrial labor markets are more or less polarized must be found in the career trajectory analyses presented in the subsequent chapters. At this point, therefore, our task is to identify the aggregate trends associated with processes of class structuration.

The scenarios that emerge from our data suggest a mix of convergence and divergence. First, we are hardly surprised to find that services are becoming the major source of employment in both relative and absolute terms. It is also evident that the social and business services are much more dynamic than the consumer services. Yet, beneath this common development we find three distinct trajectories: the Nordic welfare state-led social service economy; the German slow-growth model, biased against the social and consumer services; and the North American trajectory with its more evenly distributed growth on the backdrop of a very large, but now stagnant, consumer services industry. Britain's uniqueness lies in the way in which it straddles the German and North American models: it is slow to post-industrialize, but it boasts an American-sized consumer service sector.

Secondly, although the overall pace of occupational change has been slower, it too combines convergence and divergence. The fordist hierarchy has everywhere experienced a marked decline of the traditional manual working class; to a degree this has been offset by a modest rise in clerical and sales occupations. Fordism is, so to speak, becoming post-industrialized. The rise of professionals is also a general trend. Still, the post-industrial hierarchy diverges considerably. It is top-heavy in Germany, while relatively bottom-heavy in Scandinavia (the social service proletariat) and in North America (the consumer service proletariat).

Two conclusions emerge from these trends. One, it is fairly evident that diminished household self-servicing translates into service proletarian growth; either in the private consumer services if it is cost-competitive, meaning low wages; or in the welfare state if there is political will or fiscal scope. Two, it seems plausible that the post-industrial future will face a trade-off between a large service proletariat and a large outsider population. Of course, this kind of trade-off may be considerably relaxed depending on demographic trends. Also, its class structural consequences depend greatly on the reward structure, on the population composition, and on the mobility opportunities and life-chances available to the service proletariat and the outsider population, respectively.

Despite the divergent shape of the post-industrial hierarchy, there is very little evidence to suggest strong polarization. Everywhere, the trend favors the higher-grade occupations such that the shape of the post-industrial occupational hierarchy is biased towards the top and the middle, rather than the bottom. Women and minorities remain very concentrated within the inferior post-industrial jobs, but then the top-end of the system is very open to minorities and especially female, entry. Hence, it is possible that the post-industrial structure may be more sexually democratic in its mode of recruitment.

However, it is also very possible that women's greater access to elite positions occurs within a highly gender-segregated order. The post-industrial structure that permits female career achievement is, in itself, threatening to become a predominantly female hierarchy, especially in its Scandinavian welfare statist version. If this is so, we may very well face a second kind of trade-off: the democratization of women's career opportunities may depend on structural segregation; women may be better able to pursue careers, but only within female job hierarchies. The strong performance of women in the much less segregated American occupational hierarchy suggests, however, that this need not be so.

From our survey of aggregate trends emerge a number of questions of major importance for any understanding of our class structural future. First, it is very possible that the rising salience of education for access to the new elite post-industrial 'knowledge class', while held to be a leap towards meritocracy, may instead promote class closure. If proper educational credentials become the passport to the top, upward mobility through internal promotions and ladder-climbing will diminish. Hence, class formation becomes a function of the system of educational opportunity. If access to higher education is class-selective, we should expect increasing closure within *both* the post-industrial elite professions *and* the bottom-end service class. This emerges as a very real possibility in the subsequent country chapters.

A second important issue has to do with the character of the post-industrial bottom jobs. These are potentially the seed-bed for a new proletariat, but from a life-chance perspective the question is whether they are primarily way-stations, or whether they become long-term parking lots. That is, *if* tenure within these positions is typically brief *and* followed by upward career mobility, their relative size and composition is of minor importance. If, on the other hand, job tenure is long and mobility typically restricted, chances are that post-industrial society will produce class cleavages parallel to its industrial forebears. This is especially the case since unskilled service jobs are unlikely to offer significant opportunities for on-the-job skilling.

The evolving system of social stratification will depend very much on the mobility prospects of the low-end service workers. They are in jobs which require essentially no skills whatsoever. This implies that 'downward' mobility is possible only in the sense that persons may slide into the outsider population, be it into unemployment or into housewife status. Indeed, the extreme degree of female over-representation in the unskilled service jobs may simply mirror the choice of many women to utilize them as a bridge between school and marriage. Horizontal mobility offers one alternative, implying moves into other essentially unskilled jobs, such as lower-grade sales, clerical or manual positions. It is exceedingly possible that the unskilled service workers find themselves rotating between unqualified jobs within a secondary unskilled labor market. Upward mobility from unskilled service jobs may occur in a variety of ways. But, except in the case of becoming owner or manager, upward mobility will depend on educational credentials. The evolution of a distinct post-industrial proletariat will therefore depend very much on the distribution of skills and qualifications.[19]

The remainder of this book is dedicated to finding answers to these questions.

Notes

1 This is not to say that these are the only important institutions affecting employment trends. A truly comprehensive study might wish to examine also the impact of the monetary system or nations' integration in the global economy. This is obviously beyond the scope of this study, and, anyhow, with the current levels of global integration, it is doubtful whether any nation can deviate markedly from others in its monetary and fiscal policies. Our focus on these three institutions is motivated by their obvious *direct* impact on the functioning of labor markets.

2 This hypothesis should be modified to the extent that there are large immigrant populations willing to take low-end and low-paid jobs, to a large degree outside the formal economy.

3 As our data base, we have predominantly used population census files, occasionally supplemented with labor force surveys. For *Canada*, we use the 1961 and 1981 Census. For *Germany*, we use the 1961 Census and the 1985 Mikro-census (weighted to mirror the actual population distribution). For *Norway*, we use the 1960 and 1980 Census, and the 1985 Addition to the Labor Force Survey (the sample, as in Germany, has been weighted). For *Sweden*, we use the 1960 and 1985 Census. We will, on occasion, also refer to data for '1987'. These are in reality merged survey files for 1986–9. Because of the modest sample size (N = 1,755), and thus a fairly high error probability within many cells, we hesitate to make direct comparisons with the census-based data. For *Britain*, our data base is a 10 percent sample based on the 1971 and 1981 Census. Lack of comparability makes it impossible to go back to 1960. Finally, for the *United States*, we use the 1960 and 1980 Census and the 1988 (March) Current Population Survey (weighted). The 1988 data for the United States should be fully comparable with the Census files.

4 The comparison of industrial and especially occupational categories across nations and time is notoriously difficult since census and survey classification procedures differ. In this study we have sought to achieve as much direct comparability as possible by reclassifying the raw three- or four-digit level data for each country/year on the basis of an adapted version of the 1968 ISCO system. In most cases, we believe we have achieved a high level of comparability. However, it should be noted that some uncertainty remains, in particular with regard to the managerial occupations (in the US data, especially, the 'managers, not else classified' group is very large). For a detailed technical overview of our reclassification procedures, see Assimakopoulou et al. (1992).

5   Again, this is consistent with the results from cohort studies. Blossfeld and Becker (1989) show an actual decline in first entry for each successively younger cohort of −6 percent in the private sector and −9 percent in the public sector.

6   In our data we are unable to distinguish, say, a McDonald's franchise manager from an industrial plant manager.

7   The other side of the coin is an overwhelming male dominance in the traditional industrial fordist sector. Excluding sales and distributive services, the male share is almost identical in all six countries with a high in Canada of 79.6 percent, and a low in the US of 72 percent.

8   The welfare state effect is marked even in Germany. Blossfeld and Becker (1989) show that the welfare state effect on first job entry increases dramatically for each new cohort. The public sector absorbed 13 percent of the 1929–31 cohort, and a full 24 percent of the 1949–51 cohort. However, they also show that the effect is substantially larger for males than for women (27 percent compared to 21 percent).

9   For the United States, we have historical data that are fairly comparable to the classification system used for 1960 and the 1980s. Our estimates suggest that the share of unskilled manual workers was 25 percent in 1920 and 26 percent in 1940; the share of the service proletariat, in turn, was about 5 percent in both 1920 and 1940 (computed from US Congress, 1978: 140–5). This indicates that the major decline among the unskilled manuals occurred *after* 1960, while the major growth among the unskilled service workers occurred between 1940 and 1960. For Norway and Sweden, it is probably fairly safe to assume that the size of their (welfare state-based) service proletariat will stabilize. By the mid-1980s the provision of social services had more or less reached saturation point, and fiscal overload will anyhow preclude a new wave of public sector job expansion.

10 To a degree, our unskilled service worker classification has taken this into account since we have included a number of menial administrative service jobs (such as messenger boys and fast-food counter personnel) within our service proletariat. Yet many completely unskilled 'junk-jobs' undoubtedly remain within the clerical/sales class (copy machine operators, telephone receptionists, to give a couple of examples).

11 We have classified as proletarian the following clerical jobs: phone ad takers, receptionists, phone operators (reception), shipping packers, coin machine operators, switchboard personnel, xeroxers and keypunchers.

12 Here we may note that the lion's share of sales and clerical jobs in Germany presume vocational training. Hence, it is impossible to believe that Germany's service proletariat would swell had we included unskilled clerical and sales workers.

13 They are, of course, also to a large extent part-time jobs, a phenomenon that is difficult to analyze via the Census data sets we have available. We know that the part-time share for women in the social services is especially high in both Sweden and Norway (accounting for 30–5 percent of all women workers in this sector). On the other hand, part-time employment among women, at least in Sweden, has declined steadily during the 1980s (OECD, 1987: 29–30). This decline suggests that women's labor force participation is moving in the direction of full-time career status.

14 It is difficult to explain the large proportion of unskilled service workers in government administration in Britain. It may be due to undetectable classifi-

cation procedures whereby, for example, parts of the health service are classified as 'government administration' rather than as social services. It may also be that British government administrators surround themselves with an unusually large army of cleaning and serving personnel.

15 Computed from *Statistisches Jahrbuch* for Germany, *Arbetsmarknads Aarsbok* for Sweden, and *Employment and Earnings* for the United States. Other, less comparable data show that the average earnings of unskilled service workers in Germany equal about 80 percent of average manual industrial workers (OECD, 1987: Chart 3.3).

16 There are two reasons why the Swedish managerial earnings are so relatively high. The American managerial group comprises a much larger share of low-level managers than does the Swedish, hence the comparative difference. Secondly, these are pre-tax data, and Swedish managers are probably paid high gross salaries to offset their extremely high marginal tax rate.

17 Comparing the average earnings of unskilled service workers across these nations is somewhat misleading due to their very different sector mix. In fact, if we examine only the unskilled service workers within the *consumer* services, both Germany and Sweden begin to approximate the United States. In Germany, (full-time) unskilled consumer service workers earn 76 percent of the average earnings of the skilled manual worker; in Sweden, 85.7 percent (males only).

18 Ours is not necessarily a rejection of the Harrison and Bluestone (1988) study. First, our time-span is much longer than theirs; secondly, our data are much more aggregated; and, thirdly, the considerable earnings improvement evident for the unskilled service workers may, in large part, be attributed to the decline among domestic servants.

19 Education systems are, generally speaking, premised on the concept of national citizenship. If the unskilled service jobs tend to be disproportionally filled with unskilled immigrants, we would therefore expect less mobility and, hence, a fossilization of a distinct service proletariat. This, in fact, could very much be the case in the United States where, as we saw, immigrant Hispanics are replacing Blacks as the dominant minority within the unskilled service jobs.

3

The Post-industrial Stratificational Order: The Norwegian Experience

Jon Eivind Kolberg and Arne Kolstad

This chapter addresses two set of questions: (1) does the post-industrialization of modern society involve the emergence of a new proletariat in the service sector of the economy; and (2) what is the welfare state impact on social stratification via its retirement and employment functions? The chapter will make four main points.

First, the categories of stratification used in this volume make sense in terms of the standard level of living indicators (authority, earnings, fringe benefits, health risks, job autonomy, hours worked, educational attainment) commonly assumed to be correlated with social position. The unskilled service workers are characterized by subordination, low wages and fringe benefits, low autonomy, low job variation, high health risk exposure and low educational credentials. They resemble the unskilled blue-collar workers, but tend to score even lower.

Secondly, the fluidity of individual trajectories is substantial. In particular, this is the case with respect to the unskilled service workers who are at the heart of this investigation. Hence, these workers can hardly be called a new service proletariat, because unskilled service work tends to be temporary in terms of people's careers. In fact, there is a considerable amount of upward mobility from the ranks of the unskilled service workers.

Thirdly, the upward mobility chances for unskilled service workers depend upon the type of service industries one works in. Thus, social services (which are 90–95 percent public in Norway) definitely provide the best chances of mobility into managerial, professional and semi-professional positions. Here, too, the gender bias as regards promotion has almost evaporated.

Fourthly, at the aggregate level, the net effect on social stratification seems to be a complex combination: the welfare state reduces the numerical strength of the proletariat, fordist and post-industrial, via early retirement. It promotes the growth of the middle class via the rise of professional, semi-professional and skilled service jobs, thus diminishing the relative importance of the manual proletariat. The combined result is to tilt the stratificational order towards the middle class.

Points of Departure

This chapter follows the analytical framework set out in Chapters 1 and 2 in this volume. Our ambition is primarily to explore the Norwegian case empirically. However, the empirical program for this study has wide-ranging theoretical implications. The chapter is based on the following assumptions.

First, class theory would gain considerably by establishing much stronger links to social mobility research. Our understanding of social stratification cannot be based on separate snapshots in time; it should rest on data on the actual life-chances of individuals, implying a panel approach.

Secondly, the observation that the number of unskilled service workers is rising rapidly does not necessarily mean that a new class structure is in the making. In our view, it is meaningful to speak about the emergence of a new (service) proletariat only if the increasing number of unskilled service workers are, and will be, trapped in low-end, low-paid jobs in the core of the new service economy. Thus, the significance of the numerical expansion of unskilled service workers for the stratificational order of modern society depends on the extent to which people are permanently locked into unskilled service jobs, or are unable to leave such low-standard jobs for something better.

Thirdly, the empirical study of the present chapter encompasses the influences of gender and education. This is because sex segregation appears to be a major characteristic of the emerging stratificational order. In fact, the gender biased nature of modern social stratification constitutes a critical theoretical challenge for modern sociological class analysis. However, the ambition here is not to try to integrate class analysis and feminist concerns, but mainly to demonstrate empirically that the post-industrial social order is strikingly feminized, as opposed to the old fordist social order. There should be no need to persuade anybody about the importance of educational credentials. A strong tradition in theories of post-industrial society maintains that meritocracy will be the foundation of social stratification in future society. In this study, we want to specify the relative importance of education in leaving unskilled service jobs.

Fourthly, one important point of departure for this chapter is that the sociology of the welfare state and modern class analysis should increasingly be companion areas of sociological inquiry, to the benefit of both. Thus, this chapter is based on the assumption that the emerging system of social stratification in modern society is filtered through major institutions, such as the welfare state. Of course, this filter (i.e. the welfare state) must be regarded as a variable, in the sense that the impact of the welfare state on social stratification varies over time, and in space.

Finally, from among a variety of possible designs, this study will concentrate on unskilled service workers, and investigate their degree of mobility within the system of social stratification. The chapter will also indicate the range and direction of mobility out of what some scholars call the new service proletariat. In conclusion, the unskilled service workers (in the post-industrial segment) will be compared to the unskilled manual workers (in the so-called fordist segment).

The Context

In Chapter 2 we saw that Norway's development of a post-industrial employment structure started late, but then accelerated in the last two decades. By the 1980s, the Norwegian employment profile begins to resemble the Swedish. However, there are differences that deserve to be mentioned. In contrast to Sweden, the Norwegian 'fordist' hierarchy is, at the bottom, unusually biased towards unskilled jobs while, at the top, almost American in its managerial dominance. In turn, the Norwegian 'post-industrial' structure is much less dominated by the semi-professionals than in Sweden.

As in Sweden, the Norwegian road to post-industrialism is heavily welfare state-driven. As shown in earlier research, in this respect Norway is a Scandinavian laggard, but rapidly catching up (Hagen, 1991). Similarly, welfare state employment in Norway is heavily female-biased. Due to the one-sidedness of the industrial structure, and to the territorial dispersion of welfare state services, women working in dying industries could readily find new work in the expanding social services. Thus, to take but one example, a stunning 45 percent of the women who worked in the textile industry in 1970 were employed in the welfare state ten years later. In addition, the degree of welfare state employment expansion was so strong that a considerable share of new jobs were filled by recruits from outside the labor market. And because the rate of female labor market participation was lower than in the other Scandinavian countries, the household represented a significant labour reservoir.

In many respects, Norway conforms to the general idea of a

'Scandinavian' model. Yet in some respects it displays a set of unique characteristics that stem from the peculiar timing of the expansion of the Norwegian economy in general, and that of the welfare state in particular.

The Correlates of Social Stratification

The generally heuristic approach to the concept of post-industrial 'classes' taken in this volume calls for a method of empirical validation. Do the categories of stratification make sense in terms of the standard level of living indicators (authority, earnings, fringe benefits, health risks, job autonomy, hours worked, educational attainment) commonly assumed to be correlated with social position? The discussion of this issue is organized around our key class, namely the unskilled service workers, in comparison to other groups in terms of the overall profile of class correlates. We employ survey data from the mid-1980s.[1]

The unskilled service workers are characterized by subordination, low wages and fringe benefits, low autonomy, low job variation, high health risk exposure[2] and low educational credentials. They resemble the unskilled blue-collar workers, but tend to score even lower. This profile emerges even more clearly when we examine their status in terms of the cumulation of attributes, adding together the scores on authority, autonomy, health risk and wages.[3] In cumulative terms, we find that 14 percent of the unskilled service workers are situated at the 'bad' end of the distribution. This percentage is significantly higher than for any other occupational group (with the exception of primary sector occupations). It is of vital importance to keep in mind that the gender differences are substantial (in the expected direction) within a majority of the occupational groups, and to such a degree that they outweigh the differences between the stratificational categories.

In summary, even if class differences in Norway are relatively small, there emerges a consistent differentiation between the occupational classes, coupled with strong gender-based distributional cleavages. As we shall find, there is considerable overlap between gender and occupation in Norway.

Stability and Change among Unskilled Workers

The study of the impact of industrial transformation on job trajectories requires panel data. Our analyses are based on a 10 percent sample of the Norwegian censuses of 1960, 1970 and 1980. Of course, it is very unfortunate that our analyses are restricted to the period 1960–80. The inability to cover the recent past (1980–92) is due to the fact that Norway's censuses do not yet provide panels for the 1980–90 period.

In addition to our basic stratificational categories, we have also included five categories at the boundary of the labor market: housewives[4], pensioners[5], students[6], immigrants[7] and individuals who died between two points in time. This permits us to analyze concomitantly both mobility between jobs and mobility in and out of the labor market. Our aim is to examine over-time transitions across gender, age and education so as to identify the interactions between the labor market, the welfare state and the household.

The dynamics of social mobility cannot be adequately captured via bivariate transition tables. We expect the mobility rates to vary over time and between different industries; the influence of education should also vary. Our ambition is to determine if differences between occupational groups, and changes between periods, reflect substantial differences in the sex and age composition of occupational positions, rather than mere differences between industries. And we want to know how education influences career trajectories.

Our approach is based on a multivariate logit analysis of transition probabilities. We anticipate finding gender-specific differences in the mobility patterns among the unskilled service workers, but not necessarily to the same degree and in the same direction in all industries, and during both decades. Men and women are treated in separate models to take these interaction phenomena into account.[8]

Our experience is that raw logit coefficients are difficult to interpret and therefore often poorly understood. Probabilities, and change in probabilities, expressed in percentages, are commonly used and easily calculated for so-called model cases with specific values on the variables included in the models. These probabilities will vary for persons of different age and educational levels. We solve this problem by letting the model cases be persons of mean age and average education (for women and men, respectively, at the beginning of the decade in question). The variation of age and education around these means allows us to specify under what circumstances, and how much, age and education matter.

The industry-specific membership of the unskilled manual and unskilled service workers constitutes the starting point of our model cases. The panel data make it possible to trace the probabilities of either stability or mobility. Shifts can be of several kinds: horizontal, short-range and long-range upward mobility, as well as mobility out of the labor market (i.e. to either pensioner or housewife status).

The analysis is restricted to persons between 16 and 64 at both ends of the time periods considered, so as to concentrate on persons who are possible candidates for transitions to other occupations. The overall transition rates cannot easily be deduced from the logit models. Consequently, we shall first examine the simpler bivariate distributions (Appendix Tables A3.1 and A3.2).

Rates of Stability
It turns out that the unskilled service workers are particularly mobile: only one-third of the unskilled service (and sales) workers remain in the same position over a ten-year period, compared to more than 50 percent of the unskilled manual workers. Stability is greatest at the top of the occupational structure; still, approximately 40 percent of managers, professionals and technicians/semi-professionals have moved in the course of a ten-year period.

The multivariate logit analyses, shown in Table 3.1, are restricted to the unskilled service and unskilled manual workers. Low-status men tend to be more stable than women, but this difference is clearly diminishing. During the twenty-year period we study, men have become less stable, and women more so.

Age reduces the probability of mobility. For unskilled service jobs, the effect of ten years of age is to raise the stability rate by 10–15 percent for both men and women. The age effect is generally higher for men. More education, on the other hand, reduces the degree of stability, especially among women.

In contrast to the service proletariat, the traditional unskilled industrial male workers are highly stable, while the female workers are slightly less stable than their sisters in the unskilled services.

In order to gain a clearer picture of how mobility trends affect social stratification, we must turn to an analysis of their occupational composition.

Occupational Mobility from Proletarian Positions
We shall distinguish between two kinds of upward mobility. Long-range upward mobility implies a movement from either unskilled service or unskilled manual work into managerial, professional or technical- and semi-professional work. We shall call these MPT occupations. The transition from unskilled service work into skilled service or clerical work, or from unskilled manual jobs into skilled manual occupations, skilled service jobs or clerical work, will be labeled short-range upward mobility.[9] Movements between unskilled categories or into sales jobs are defined as horizontal mobility.

From Appendix Tables A3.1 and A3.2 we see that between 1960

Table 3.1 *Probabilities of retention in the service proletariat
and in unskilled manual worker positions in manufacturing,
Norway, 1960–70 and 1970–80 (percent)*

	1960–70		1970–80	
	Men	Women	Men	Women
Service proletariat				
Average age, years	33.2	32.6	32.5	35.2
Average education, years	7.5	7.4	8.8	8.3
Number of observations	1694	4741	2102	7042
Consumer service:				
Model case	34.2**	26.1	34.8*	33.1*
Education 1+ year	−0.8	−2.4*	−3.4**	−6.8**
Age 10+ years	16.9**	13.4**	14.8**	9.8**
Retail service:				
Model case	19.9**	34.6	11.4**	37.6
Education 1+ year	0.6	−2.8*	−1.4**	−7.3**
Age 10+ years	13.4**	14.9**	7.8**	10.1**
Social service:				
Model case	60.1**	29.0	49.9**	37.2
Education 1+ year	0.8	−2.6*	−3.8**	−7.3**
Age 10+ years	15.1**	14.1**	14.9**	10.1**
Business service:				
Model case	54.0	20.3	27.4	34.9
Education 1+ year	0.9	−2.0*	−2.9**	−7.0**
Age 10+ years	16.2**	11.7**	13.7**	9.9**
Unskilled manual workers in manufacturing				
Average age, years	35.9	33.0	34.6	33.5
Average education, years	7.3	7.3	8.4	8.2
Number of observations	21177	3102	22551	3827
Model case	64.8**	27.9	61.1**	26.3
Education 1+ year	−7.3**	−2.2	−6.1**	−2.6**
Age 10+ years	2.3**	10.9**	2.1**	8.0**

Notes for Tables 3.1–3.4:
* Significant with alpha-level 0.05; ** Significant with alpha-level 0.01.
For the model case, this is understood as significantly different from persons in other industries or outside the labor force at the beginning of the decade.
– Too few observed transitions to calculate rates (in Table 3.2).
The reference group includes persons going to all positions inside or outside the labor market other than the industries included in the table. Individuals who died between 1960 and 1970, or between 1970 and 1980 are excluded. Also excluded are individuals in military occupations and persons whose occupational category is missing or not ascertained.
The probabilities are expressed as percentages, separately for men or women.

Source for all tables in this chapter: Own calculations based on a data set from the Census Data Bank of the Norwegian Social Data Archives, University of Bergen; for documentation, see Holm, 1988.

and 1970 16 percent of those who began as unskilled service workers in 1960 experienced upward mobility; in the subsequent decade, this increased to no less than 28 percent. In comparison, the probability of upward mobility among the unskilled manual workers, at 21–2 percent, remained stable.

A similar trend is evident in terms of long-range mobility among the unskilled service workers, rising from 4 percent in the first decade to 10 percent between 1970 and 1980. In Table 3.2 we see that the only case of notable long-range mobility between 1960 and 1970 were men in consumer services. This would indicate a

Table 3.2 *Probabilities of transition from the service proletariat and from unskilled manual worker positions in manufacturing into MPT-occupations (long range mobility), Norway, 1960–70 and 1970–80 (percent)*

	1960–70		1970–80	
	Men	Women	Men	Women
Service proletariat				
Average age, years	33.2	32.6	32.5	35.2
Average education, years	7.5	7.4	8.8	8.3
Number of observations	1694	4667	2102	7042
Consumer service:				
Model case	17.6**	1.6*	12.7**	5.2*
Education 1+ year	4.5**	1.5**	7.9**	3.6**
Age 10+ years	−1.2	−0.3*	−6.3**	−1.5**
Retail service:				
Model case	2.6	–	6.6	4.7
Education 1+ year	−0.2**	–	4.6**	3.3**
Age 10+ years	0.8	–	−3.4**	−1.3**
Social service:				
Model case	2.7	3.1	12.1**	10.0**
Education 1 + year	0.9**	2.7**	7.6**	6.4**
Age 10+ years	−0.2	−0.5*	−6.0**	−2.7**
Business service:				
Model case	4.5	–	10.7	2.4
Education 1+ year	1.4**	–	6.9**	1.8**
Age 10+ years	−0.3	–	−5.4**	−0.7**
Unskilled manual workers in manufacturing				
Average age, years	35.9	33.0	34.6	33.5
Average education, years	7.3	7.3	8.4	8.2
Number of observations	21177	3102	22551	3827
Model case	5.6	2.2*	6.2**	4.1**
Education 1+ year	3.7**	0.5	4.4**	3.0**
Age 10+ years	−1.7**	0.5*	−2.4**	−1.0**

relatively modest impact of education. Yet, however small, its effect is highly significant. One additional year of education explains most of the small movement that can be observed among women.

With one exception (men working in the consumer service industry), the rate of upward occupational mobility increased in the second decade. The most important finding, for our purposes, are the remarkable industry-specific differences. The social services are special in at least three important respects. First, this is where significant upward mobility is most common. Secondly, this sector stands out as offering almost identical upward mobility chances across gender. Thirdly, women's return to education is consistently the highest in the social services.

The effects of education and age are larger in the second decade (as we should expect when aggregate mobility rates increase). The effect of age is higher for men than for women. In the second decade, men ten years older than average have a 3.4–6.3 percent lower probability of reaching MPT positions, whereas the effect for women is 0.7–2.7 percent. This difference cannot be fully explained by differences in the general mobility level.

The change in the effects of age and education over time means that unskilled service workers have improved their chances of upward mobility, especially if they have above average education, and, in the case of men, if they are relatively young.

How do the occupational careers of the unskilled service workers compare with the traditional, fordist working class? In Table 3.2 we see that the chances of long-range upward mobility have been constant over time in the case of male unskilled manual workers. In the period from 1960 to 1970 their probability of reaching MPT status (5.6 percent) was slightly higher than the corresponding rate for men in the social and business service industries, but much lower (by 12 percent) than for men in the consumer services. From 1970 to 1980, the probability of considerable upward mobility among the unskilled manuals was only around 50 percent of that of their fellow unskilled service workers. For women, the rate of long-range upward mobility increased from 2 percent during the first decade to 4 percent during the second. Given these low aggregate rates, the modest effects of education imply that education has been an important determinant for long-range upward mobility from the fordist segment of the proletariat as well.

The patterns of short-range mobility, shown in Table 3.3, are quite parallel. Compared to MPT mobility, short-range moves are more typical among women than men. In the decade from 1970 to 1980, our model women in the social and business services have short-range mobility chances amounting to 18 percent and 21

Table 3.3 *Probabilities of transition from the service proletariat and from unskilled manual worker positions in manufacturing into skilled service or clerical occupations (short range mobility), Norway, 1960–70 and 1970–80 (percent)*

	1960–70		1970–80	
	Men	Women	Men	Women
Service proletariat				
Average age, years	33.2	32.6	32.5	35.2
Average education, years	7.5	7.4	8.8	8.3
Number of observations	1694	4741	2102	7042
Consumer service:				
Model case	9.4	8.8	10.1**	14.5
Education 1+ year	1.0*	1.8**	0.3	1.5**
Age 10+ years	−2.9**	0.3	−1.8**	−3.6**
Retail service:				
Model case	4.1*	5.0	11.2*	10.5
Education 1+ year	0.5*	1.1**	0.3	1.2**
Age 10+ years	−1.3**	0.2	−2.0**	−2.7**
Social service:				
Model case	8.8	12.7**	5.6**	17.8**
Education 1+ year	1.0*	2.4**	0.2	1.8**
Age 10+ years	−2.7**	0.5*	−1.0**	−4.3**
Business service:				
Model case	6.3	11.3	7.3**	20.7
Education 1+ year	0.7*	2.2**	0.2	2.0**
Age 10+ years	−2.0**	0.4	−1.3**	−4.8**
Unskilled manual workers in manufacturing				
Average age, years	35.9	33.0	34.6	33.5
Average education, years	7.3	7.3	8.4	8.2
Number of observations	21177	3102	22551	3827
Model case	15.4**	7.2	11.4**	12.7
Education 1+ year	0.6	1.2	0.3	3.3**
Age 10+ years	−3.3**	−0.2	−2.5**	−2.2**

percent, respectively; this is three times that of their male colleagues. For both sexes, age and education have only a marginal influence on short-range mobility throughout the two decades.

In the unskilled manual strata, males were twice as likely as women to engage in short-range mobility during the first decade, but this gap was subsequently reversed. The effect of education was significant only for women from 1970–1980, being the strongest among all the sub-groups we have analyzed.

We have defined horizontal mobility as movements between unskilled or sales jobs. In Table 3.4, we see that the transition from

Table 3.4   *Probabilities of transition from the service proletariat and from unskilled manual worker positions in manufacturing into sales or other unskilled occupations (horizontal mobility), Norway, 1960–70 and 1970–80 (percent)*

	1960–70		1970–80	
	Men	Women	Men	Women
Service proletariat				
Average age, years	33.2	32.6	32.5	35.2
Average education, years	7.5	7.4	8.8	8.3
Number of observations	1694	4741	2102	7042
Consumer service:				
Model case	20.6	5.8**	16.9	8.8*
Education 1+ year	−4.1**	−1.4**	−5.1**	−1.8**
Age 10+ years	−8.2**	−1.2**	−4.9**	−1.9**
Retail service:				
Model case	37.9**	11.0	22.3	14.9
Education 1+ year	−6.1**	−2.6**	−6.5**	−2.9**
Age 10+ years	−12.9**	−2.1**	−6.2**	−3.0**
Social service:				
Model case	6.7**	4.1**	9.8	3.9**
Education 1+ year	−1.5**	−1.0**	−3.2**	−0.8**
Age 10+ years	−2.9**	−0.8**	−3.0**	−0.9**
Business service:				
Model case	22.2	8.1	22.9*	11.3
Education 1+ year	−4.3**	−1.9**	−6.6**	−2.3**
Age 10+ years	−8.7**	−1.6**	−6.4**	−2.4**
Unskilled manual workers in manufacturing				
Average age, years	35.9	33.0	34.6	33.5
Average education, years	7.3	7.3	8.4	8.2
Number of observations	21177	3102	22551	3827
Model case	3.7**	11.9	4.7**	19.3
Education 1+ year	0.6**	0.2	0.5**	−3.0**
Age 10+ years	−0.5**	0.2	−0.6**	−2.4**

unskilled service to unskilled manual work is mainly a male phenomenon. The social services are, once again, exceptional; this time because of the exceptionally low propensity for horizontal mobility within both sexes.

Education and age are both negatively related to the horizontal mobility from unskilled service to blue-collar jobs.

Transitions from the blue-collar proletariat to the service proletariat, on the other hand, are more usual among women. This reflects the persistent numerical dominance of women in the unskilled service occupations, and the general male dominance in unskilled manual jobs. In line with our earlier observation that service jobs in general, and welfare state jobs in particular, constitute a mobility target for workers in dying industries, women's probability of moving from unskilled blue-collar to unskilled service and sales increases noticeably in the second decade.

To sum up, long-range mobility is more frequent among men than women, but the gap is closing. Education plays an important role for this kind of mobility within both our unskilled strata. Short-range mobility, in contrast, is less associated with education and tends to be predominantly female. Horizontal movements, finally, are very gender patterned. Men tend to move from the services into industry, while women tend to move in the opposite direction. With the expansion of the service sector, mobility from industry to the service proletariat is growing, especially among women. To complete the mobility picture for the unskilled workers we must now turn to an analysis of the flows out of the labor market.

Employment Exits among the Unskilled
Again, we will focus upon working age individuals in 1970 and 1980, respectively, and specify to what extent they leave the labor market before they reach the age of 65. The two main roads of exit comprise early retirement and exit into the household. As shown in Appendix Tables A3.1 and A3.2, the combined exit probabilities vary considerably by occupation.

Surprisingly, women are consistently more likely than men to take early retirement. The logit probabilities (not shown here) range from zero to 5.5 percent, and increase in the second decade (for details see Kolberg and Kolstad, 1991: 10, Table 9). In the second period, our model case women in the consumer and business services were the most likely to take early retirement; the lowest probabilities were found among men in the social services.

Age has, obviously, a large and significant effect on the probability of retirement, while the effect of education is marginal except for women in the last period, where each year of education reduces the probability of early retirement by 2–3 percent. A comparison with blue-collar workers in manufacturing brings out the same pattern: women's early retirement is more prevalent, and has been rising faster, and the effects of age and education are about the same as for the service proletariat (see Kolberg and Kolstad, 1991).

It turns out that exit from the labor market to the household for women of average age and education does not vary significantly across industries (except for women in business service industries). High rates of female mobility from unskilled service jobs to the household would indicate that these jobs constitute natural 'stop-gap' positions between school and family formation. While this was fairly true for the 1960s, it is no longer the case. The rate of exit to the household has declined dramatically among unskilled female service workers, from about 30 to 11 percent (see Kolberg and Kolstrad, 1991: 11, Table 10). Age, but not education, has an important effect on female exits into the household. For unskilled women, the probability of moving into housewife status is halved if they are ten years older than average.

The Recruitment into Unskilled Positions
Our analysis of employment recruitment is based on those who in 1970 and 1980, respectively, occupy proletarian positions. We will here trace their locations in the stratificational order ten years earlier. Table 3.5 makes it clear that the recruitment behavior of men and women differs dramatically.

The most typical 'origin' of female unskilled service workers is previous housewife status. Half of all women who worked in unskilled service jobs in 1980 were housewives ten years earlier. In contrast, unskilled male service workers arrived most commonly from manual occupations, in particular from unskilled manual jobs. Put differently, the expanding social service-dominated unskilled service jobs tend to absorb two specific groups especially: women from the household and men from industry. There is accordingly a strong link between the traditional (blue-collar) working class and the service proletariat.

The recruitment to unskilled manual jobs is, first, affected by the high degree of male stability. Secondly, there is a noticeable degree of male mobility between skilled and unskilled manual work, including a significant amount of downward mobility. Thirdly, there is a considerable (and declining) influx from the primary sector. For women, the recruitment patterns resemble those of the service proletariat. Of women working in blue-collar jobs in 1980, about 40 percent had been housewives in 1970.

International Comparison

Drawing broader international comparisons is made difficult by the variability of country data sets in this volume. First, the time-frame of the individual nation analyses differs considerably. For example, the Norwegian data span the census years 1960, 1970 and 1980,

Table 3.5 *Recruitment to proletarian positions by gender, age (16–64 years) and stratificational position ten years earlier, Norway, 1960–70 and 1970–80 (percent)*

	Men 1970 Unskilled service	Men 1980 Unskilled service	Women 1970 Unskilled service	Women 1980 Unskilled service	Men 1970 Unskilled manual	Men 1980 Unskilled manual	Women 1970 Unskilled manual	Women 1980 Unskilled manual	Men 1970 Total	Men 1980 Total	Women 1970 Total	Women 1980 Total
Managers	2.1	2.5	0.2	0.3	1.1	1.7	0.1	0.2	4.7	6.2	0.5	0.7
Professional	1.1	0.9	0.0	0.1	0.9	0.5	0.0	0.1	3.8	4.6	0.3	0.6
Technical-scientific professional	1.4	1.6	0.6	0.5	0.4	1.1	0.5	0.6	4.1	6.5	2.2	5.7
Skilled service	4.6	2.9	1.7	2.4	1.2	1.3	0.5	1.1	3.0	3.2	1.4	3.8
Unskilled service	34.2	31.4	19.4	24.3	1.6	1.6	5.0	8.3	2.2	2.7	6.0	9.0
Clerical	3.9	2.3	1.1	3.1	0.9	1.1	1.2	2.0	6.0	5.7	7.0	12.3
Sales	1.9	3.1	1.5	3.8	1.3	2.1	1.5	4.5	3.4	4.4	3.8	6.7
Skilled manual	8.8	11.8	0.4	0.5	9.9	12.5	2.6	2.3	13.4	15.2	0.6	0.6
Unskilled manual	22.3	28.0	3.8	4.9	60.5	65.2	26.6	31.6	28.1	29.5	3.9	4.9
Primary sector	10.0	4.9	0.4	4.0	15.9	5.5	0.3	2.7	20.1	9.8	0.5	4.6
Not yet immigrated	5.7	5.3	3.9	1.0	3.8	1.9	3.8	1.9	3.9	2.1	4.0	1.5
Housewives	0.2	0.1	64.6	50.4	0.0	0.6	56.0	39.0	0.0	0.4	64.1	39.3
Pensioners	0.4	0.9	1.0	2.1	0.2	0.4	0.8	2.7	0.5	2.1	1.1	3.4
Students	3.3	4.2	1.2	2.6	2.3	4.3	0.9	3.0	6.8	7.5	4.6	6.9
N	22,130	24,310	75,590	115,140	235,910	222,280	34,790	33,950	807,810	871,770	822,640	884,720

Individuals who died between 1960 and 1970, or between 1970 and 1980 are excluded. Also excluded are individuals in military occupations and persons whose occupational category is missing or not ascertained.

while Jacobs' American mobility data cover a one-year interval between 1971–2 and 1987–8 (see Chapter 8).

Secondly, there is some variation in how the individual country-analyses have applied the common classificatory framework. Thus, some studies (like the Swedish one – Chapter 4) have introduced special occupational sub-divisions, and the various case-analyses have been compelled to operate with different kinds of collapsed categories. Both the different time-spans and the different application of stratificational categories should serve as warnings against jumping too fast to firm conclusions.

Yet, as with Norway, the country chapters of this volume (with the one exception of Chapter 5, on Germany) uniformly indicate very high rates of mobility out of unskilled service jobs. Moreover, these mobility rates are increasing over time. This suggests that it is unlikely that unskilled service jobs will crystallize into a genuine new service proletariat. In this respect, Norway follows the common trend.

However, closer inspection reveals two important differences. First of all, the Norwegian study highlights the existence of significant industry-specific differences regarding the probability of leaving unskilled service jobs for higher destinations in the social structure. Thus, in Norway, the social service sector gives the best opportunities, since the chance of upward mobility from the bottom-level social service jobs is both higher overall, and hardly differs according to gender. The US study shows exactly opposite industry-specific patterns of upward mobility. There, the rate of mobility out of unskilled service occupations is highest for retail sales workers, followed by the consumer and business services; mobility rates in the social services and public administration are shown to be substantially lower. Also, in the United States, mobility out of unskilled service jobs increases in retail sales and consumer services, but declines in the social services and public administration. The social services clearly play different roles in the mobility systems of these countries. It is tempting to explain the mobility differences in terms of where the momentum of expansion is centered. Norway's welfare state-led post-industrialization has opened a huge mobility space within the social services that furnishes not only a large reservoir of easy first-entry unskilled jobs, but also a vast number of new jobs along the entire hierarchy. In the United States, as is well known, public sector employment has stagnated.

This interpretation receives added credibility when confronted with the Swedish study, although a direct comparison is made difficult since it lacks detailed disaggregated industry data. Still, like in Norway, the mobility prospects of Swedish unskilled workers are better in service industries than in the traditional ones. Mobility out of unskilled jobs in Sweden has increased over time, so that the younger cohorts show the highest rates of mobility.

In Norway, there has been a substantial increase in upward mobility from the service proletariat while, at the same time, the career chances of the blue-collar workers have stagnated. This contrasts with Tåhlin's argument that occupational sector in Sweden (the distinction between fordist and post-industrial jobs) is of no significance in determining upward class mobility (see Chapter 4 below). These contrasts may, of course, be due to differences in job classification or to the different time-spans that have been analyzed. Still, the differences may very well be real, due to the possibility that class structuration is more firmly consolidated in Swedish than in Norwegian society. Norway is, from the point of view of employment transformation, a 'catch-up country'. The transition towards a service economy came later than in Sweden, and accelerated in the later (1970–80) period of our study. In other words, the comparatively high degree of dynamism we have found in Norway may be attributed to a 'period effect'. If so, chances are that the powerful institutional parallels which exist between Norway and Sweden will result in greater future convergence in the two countries' employment and mobility structure. More truly comparative research is clearly called for.

The Impact of the Welfare State on Social Stratification – Empirical Results

There are at least three good reasons for examining the effect of the welfare state upon the evolving pattern of social stratification. One is the abundance of theoretical positions with uncertain empirical validity. A second is the lack of concrete information on critical empirical distributions. The third reason is that the process of post-industrialization in Norway has been strongly patterned by the welfare state. On one hand, social service employment rose from 7 percent of the working population (below 65 years of age) in 1960 to 20 percent in 1980. On the other hand, early retirement grew in the same period. Between 1960 and 1970, 4 percent of those who were below 65 years of age had taken early retirement, rising to 7 percent between 1970 and 1980.

How do we examine the impact of the welfare state on the pattern of social stratification? There are different options. One would be to specify the stratificational effects of the welfare state by calculating the difference between the actual distributions on one hand, and the pattern of social stratification that would have existed without welfare state employment, and without the existence of early retirement.

Using this kind of approach would force us to conclude that the impact of the welfare state is profound. Without the welfare state, the share of technicians and semi-professionals would have been 6 percent lower than (or half of) its actual share in 1980; the shares of skilled service workers would have been reduced by 33 percent; the service proletariat by slightly less than 20 percent; and the professional category by approximately 10 percent. The absence of the welfare state would, on the other hand, have augmented the size of the fordist economy: both management and the blue-collar workers would have been some 20 percent larger in a situation without early retirement and without social sector employment.

This kind of simulation exercise is, of course, unrealistic in the sense that it is difficult to imagine the complete absence of a welfare state in a modern democratic society. Another, and less unrealistic, approach would be to estimate the consequences of a situation where early retirement is not graded by class, and where the social

Table 3.6   *The impact of the welfare state on social stratification: the distribution of early retirement across stratificational categories, Norway, 1960–70 and 1970–80 (percent)*

	I 1960 All actives	II 1960–70 Retire-ment	III 1960–70 II−I	I 1970 All actives	II 1970–80 Retire-ment	III 1970–80 II−I
Managers	4.6	2.5	−2.1	7.2	3.4	−3.8
Professionals	3.6	3.3	−0.3	4.3	1.7	−2.6
Technical-scientific professionals	5.6	2.4	−3.1	8.0	2.8	−5.2
Skilled service	3.9	4.3	0.5	4.6	4.7	0.1
Unskilled service	7.2	13.8	6.6	8.7	15.4	6.7
Clerical	11.2	5.1	−6.1	10.8	7.3	−3.5
Sales	6.2	4.3	−1.9	7.1	7.1	0.0
Skilled manual	12.1	9.3	−2.8	10.6	9.5	−1.1
Unskilled manual	27.9	32.4	4.5	24.1	32.9	8.8
Primary sector	17.7	22.5	4.8	14.7	15.2	0.5
N	976,240	48,280		1,124,570	76,240	

The figures refer to persons who were less than 65 years of age in 1960, 1970 and 1980, respectively.
Rounding affects some totals.

Table 3.7 The impact of the welfare state on social stratification: the distribution of social service employment across stratification categories, Norway, 1960–70 and 1970–80 (percent)

	I 1960 Total	II 1960 Social service	III 1960 II–I	I 1970 Total	II 1970 Social service	III 1970 II–I	I 1980 Total	II 1980 Social service	III 1980 II–I
Managers	4.6	3.1	-1.5	7.2	2.8	-4.4	7.2	2.9	-4.3
Professionals	3.6	20.7	17.1	4.3	29.8	25.5	4.4	28.7	24.3
Technical-scientific professionals	5.6	59.5	54.0	8.0	82.4	74.3	11.8	69.8	58.0
Skilled service	3.9	12.3	8.4	4.6	54.1	49.5	6.8	54.6	47.8
Unskilled service	7.2	17.6	10.4	8.7	34.1	25.4	11.3	40.8	29.5
Clerical	11.2	4.1	-7.1	10.8	10.1	-0.7	13.6	12.8	-0.9
Sales	6.2	0.0	-6.2	7.1	0.6	-6.5	8.5	0.5	-8.0
Skilled manual	12.1	0.5	-11.7	10.6	1.0	-9.5	8.3	1.1	-7.2
Unskilled manual	27.9	0.2	-27.8	24.1	0.5	-23.5	21.0	0.8	-20.2
Primary sector	17.7	0.1	-17.6	14.7	0.4	-14.3	7.2	1.4	-5.8
N	976,240	63,730		1,124,570	168,180		1,715,920	345,400	

The figures refer to persons who were less than 65 years of age in 1960, 1970 and 1980, respectively.

services grow only at the average rate. A third approach would be to apply, for example, the values for the United States to Norway and then calculate the consequences in terms of social stratification. None of these possibilities has been pursued here. Instead, we have chosen the straightforward, and perhaps less sophisticaed, approach by simply comparing the distributions of total and social service employment across the stratificational categories we have chosen, and observing the differences.

Returning to the results of Appendix Tables A3.1 and A3.2, we would have to conclude that the welfare state's early retirement programs tend to be class-biased. They are, however, hardly biased towards the traditional industrial older male blue-collar workers. Indeed, early retirement is more frequent among unskilled service workers, and it tends to affect women more than men (see also Kolberg, 1991). The structure of early exit among women changed, if not dramatically, during the twenty-year period we have studied; the importance of the pension system increased and the significance of the household declined. Hence, the common thesis about the impact of the welfare state on the stratificational order via early retirement has to be reformulated. The Norwegian welfare state does affect the stratificational order by reducing the numerical strength of the entire proletariat, both 'fordist' and post-industrial, male and female. In this broader sense, the class-specific character of early retirement seems to have increased over time. (See Table 3.6.)

Turning to the welfare state's impact on the employment structure, we have already seen in Chapter 2 how welfare state employment trends in Norway (and Sweden) have been biased towards professional, semi-professional and skilled service occupations. This is demonstrated here in Table 3.7.

On the one hand, then, the welfare state is an important vehicle in the formation of the modern middle classes. On the other hand, it also contributes significantly to the growth of bottom-end unskilled service jobs. This net effect on social stratification is a complex combination. It reduces the numerical strength of the proletariat, fordist and post-industrial, via early retirement. It promotes the growth of the middle class via the rise of professional, semi-professional and skilled service jobs, thus diminishing the relative importance of the manual proletariat. The combined result is to tilt the stratificational order towards the middle class. But the welfare state also helps expand the service proletariat. Of the two mechanisms – early retirement and social service employment – the latter is by far the most influential, but they clearly reinforce each other.

Appendix

Table A3.1 Inflow-outflow patterns of the Norwegian stratificational structure, 1960–70 (persons who were above 15 years of age in 1960 and less than 65 years of age in 1970 in percent)

1960	Managers	Professionals	Technical-scientific professionals	Skilled service	Unskilled service	Clerical	Sales	Skilled manual	Unskilled manual	Primary sector	House-wives	Pensioners	Students	Total (N)
Managers	60.2	2.3	4.5	1.7	1.5	7.1	7.1	3.8	6.3	1.1	1.8	2.9	0.0	42,120
Professionals	6.0	58.0	5.1	1.0	0.8	3.8	1.0	9.6	6.3	2.2	1.1	5.0	0.2	32,250
Technical-scientific professionals	9.8	8.1	59.3	2.7	1.5	3.1	1.7	1.7	2.2	1.1	6.1	2.3	0.4	51,630
Skilled service	4.1	0.6	2.3	52.2	6.4	3.9	2.0	1.7	8.6	1.7	9.8	5.9	0.2	35,580
Unskilled service	1.9	0.2	2.0	6.6	33.9	3.1	2.5	1.8	8.3	3.7	25.6	10.1	0.2	65,710
Clerical	11.4	1.8	2.4	1.4	1.7	51.5	4.4	1.1	2.5	0.9	18.3	2.4	0.2	104,560
Sales	14.3	0.6	2.0	1.3	2.7	8.1	34.3	1.5	6.3	1.8	23.5	3.6	0.1	58,190
Skilled manual	4.3	0.7	4.1	1.1	2.0	1.6	2.2	55.3	21.5	1.4	1.7	4.0	0.2	112,610
Unskilled manual	3.3	1.2	2.3	1.5	3.0	2.0	2.6	10.9	58.9	2.8	5.4	6.1	0.1	258,000
Primary sector	1.3	1.0	1.0	1.4	1.5	1.0	0.9	4.7	22.8	56.8	0.7	6.6	0.2	165,330
Not yet immigrated	3.9	4.5	2.5	3.7	6.7	7.2	4.5	7.0	16.1	5.8	23.7	8.2	1.0	63,500
Housewives	0.6	0.2	0.3	2.1	9.3	5.1	5.8	0.4	3.7	9.4	54.5	6.9	0.2	525,140
Pensioners	0.9	0.2	0.1	2.5	6.2	2.5	2.8	1.1	5.1	2.2	5.1	70.2	0.1	13,220
Students	4.9	13.5	25.5	3.0	1.7	13.6	4.4	5.2	6.3	3.1	13.8	0.9	4.1	92,090
Total	5.0	3.0	3.6	3.2	6.0	7.5	4.9	7.3	16.7	10.2	24.0	6.2	0.4	1,619,930
N	81,250	48,380	98,440	51,260	97,720	121,050	79,630	118,790	270,700	165,350	388,610	99,790	6,960	1,619,930

Individuals who died between 1960 and 1970 excluded. Also excluded are individuals in military occupations and persons whose occupational category is missing or not ascertained.

Table A3.2 Inflow–outflow patterns of the Norwegian stratificational structure, 1970–80 (persons who were above 15 years of age in 1970 and less than 65 years of age in 1980 in percent)

1970	Managers	Pro-fessionals	Technical-scientific pro-fessionals	Skilled service	Unskilled service	Clerical	Sales	Skilled manual	Unskilled manual	Primary sector	House-wives	Pensioners	Students	Total (N)
Managers	58.5	3.3	3.4	1.2	1.5	6.7	8.5	3.1	6.6	0.9	1.8	4.4	0.2	58,930
Professionals	11.7	63.6	7.3	0.5	0.7	3.1	1.3	2.2	2.8	1.8	1.9	2.9	0.3	43,900
Technical-scientific professionals	9.6	7.1	63.4	1.6	0.9	2.9	2.1	1.4	2.5	0.8	4.8	2.0	0.6	105,990
Skilled service	3.4	2.2	9.3	48.9	5.7	4.6	2.2	1.4	5.6	1.5	8.6	6.0	0.5	59,900
Unskilled service	2.3	1.1	6.6	8.6	36.3	7.7	4.1	1.7	6.5	1.1	11.6	12.0	0.5	97,950
Clerical	12.8	2.7	4.3	1.7	2.7	52.0	4.6	0.9	2.0	0.8	11.0	3.6	0.7	153,760
Sales	13.5	1.0	3.9	3.0	5.5	9.6	35.2	2.3	6.5	1.0	12.2	5.8	0.4	93,500
Skilled manual	4.9	2.1	5.2	1.5	2.6	1.5	2.4	45.4	21.5	1.8	5.6	5.4	0.3	133,270
Unskilled manual	4.1	1.6	3.4	2.6	4.3	2.5	3.2	7.6	54.2	3.2	4.3	8.7	0.3	287,480
Primary sector	1.4	1.6	2.7	1.7	4.9	1.6	1.2	2.3	11.1	54.7	6.9	9.7	0.3	119,170
Not yet immigrated	5.8	7.3	14.9	4.6	9.8	7.4	3.0	6.3	19.1	1.2	15.6	3.3	1.7	25,390
Housewives	1.3	0.3	5.4	5.2	18.4	11.8	8.8	0.7	4.6	2.4	29.2	11.4	0.6	315,760
Pensioners	0.4	0.2	1.6	1.9	6.0	2.6	1.8	1.1	4.3	1.5	3.5	74.8	0.4	43,710
Students	5.8	10.9	26.2	5.6	3.3	13.2	4.1	5.4	8.8	2.4	9.7	1.8	2.7	121,100
Total	7.2	4.2	10.1	5.0	8.4	10.5	6.1	6.4	15.4	5.7	11.4	8.9	0.6	1,659,810
N	119,210	70,010	168,110	82,430	139,450	174,850	101,070	106,100	256,230	94,750	189,510	147,830	10,260	1,659,810

Individuals who died between 1970 and 1980 excluded. Also excluded are individuals in military occupations and persons whose occupational category is missing or not ascertained.

Notes

The data sets for the empirical parts of this chapter were provided by the Norwegian Social Science Data Archives (NSD), University of Bergen. The authors alone are responsible for the analyses and interpretations.

1 The data in this section are based on own calculations of the Addition to the Labor Force Survey 1985, and of the Level of Living Survey 1987. For operationalization and results, see Kolberg and Kolstad (1991). For documentation of these surveys, see Håvorsen (1987) and Kiberg (1989).

2 This health risk indicator captures the ergonomic dimension. For results and operationalization, see Kolberg and Kolstad (1991: 5, Table 4).

3 The variables were first dichotomized and then added. For specification of operationalizations and for results, see Kolberg and Kolstad (1991: 9, Table 8).

4 A housewife is defined here as a married person who is not economically active, and whose main source of income is another person's earnings or pension.

5 A pensioner is defined as a person whose main source of income is a pension and who is economically non-active.

6 Note that a student here is somebody who does not combine studies with paid work.

7 These are individuals who are present in the Census at t2 but not at t1, and who are born abroad.

8 Note that no other interactions are found throughout any of the following analyses, a fact that helps us to keep the models reasonably simple.

9 The definition of short-range mobility is not symmetric for the two unskilled occupational groups. This is to make concepts clearer. As the skilled manual worker group is heterogeneous, it is not clear whether this position should always be regarded as higher than unskilled service. The same might be said for the unskilled manual versus skilled manual categories, but we expect that the main tendency for such a transition is promotion from the person's starting position.

4

Class Inequality and Post-industrial Employment in Sweden

Michael Tåhlin

Most accounts of the 'post-industrial' transition emphasize the shift from manufacture towards services as the major source of employment. In purely descriptive terms, this is uncontroversial. But, as Kumar (1978: 199f.) has pointed out, such statistical trends are often presented as if this transformation carries some self-evident and far-reaching implications for the societies concerned. Only rarely do we get to know something more specific about what these consequences actually are.

Labor market inequalities have traditionally been structured mainly by class and sex. Compared to managerial positions, working-class jobs have been less rewarded, and provided quite limited opportunities for upward mobility. Within any given class, women's rewards have been smaller than men's, and their mobility prospects have been bleaker. Does post-industrial society change these traditional axes of inequality?

As discussed in Chapter 1, there are optimistic and pessimistic post-industrial employment theories. According to the liberal 'logic of industrialism' thesis (Parsons, 1960; Treiman, 1970; Kerr et al., 1973), average job rewards will rise in terms of both wages and non-pecuniary factors, especially skills, while overall inequality will diminish, and opportunities for job mobility will increase. Reward attainment will increasingly be governed by univeralism and achievement, and less by ascription. Service sector jobs are, in this perspective, the vanguard in the process of change. Sectoral divisions between occupations or industries may even become more important than class as the basis for stratification (Bell, 1976).

Sharing roughly similar assumptions, a second, more pessimistic, perspective draws essentially opposite conclusions with regard to skills and mobility. At the bottom, the mass of unskilled service jobs are difficult to automate away and, at the top, the increasing importance of formal credentials, such as education, means class closure in the recruitment to higher positions. The chances for promotion through work experience will accordingly decline (Collins, 1979; Parkin, 1979; Goldthorpe, 1985).

Finally, retaining the analytical primacy of class, the Marxist perspective denies the relevance of the service sector as a separate, and qualitatively different, structure. Hence, any changes that occur in the level and distribution of job rewards, including mobility opportunities, should be understood within the framework of capitalist domination or exploitation. Changes are expected to be mostly negative, favoring de-skilling, low wages and slim chances of advancement for the majority, combined with an increasingly privileged and closed top (Braverman, 1974; Kumar, 1978; Wright and Singelmann, 1982; Bluestone and Harrison, 1986).

To apply these hypotheses to Sweden requires that we first recognize its peculiar traits. In terms of income distribution between the social classes, Sweden is unusually egalitarian, both before and after taxes and transfers (Smeeding et al., 1990), and inequalities have declined during the recent decades, at least until the 1980s (Vogel et al., 1988; Gustafsson and Uusitalo, 1990). The welfare state is probably more developed than anywhere else, with comprehensive social policies in areas such as education, employment security, health care and pensions (Esping-Andersen, 1990; Olsson, 1990). Hence, the working class is probably relatively less disadvantaged with regard to general living conditions than in most other countries.

Still, the implications of these characteristics for the salience of class as an axis of stratification are not self-evident. In the case of work-life mobility, the high security of employment (if not of a particular job) and the comparatively small class inequalities might have a positive as well as a negative effect on the rate of class transitions during working life. On the one hand, since the material risks associated with changing jobs are small, and the distance between classes narrow, class mobility should be more common than elsewhere. According to this view, egalitarian policies promote more dynamic and efficient labor markets because workers are empowered with strong resources and high aspirations. The alternative, neoclassical view insists that these kinds of egalitarian policies will distort labor market incentives and signals, engendering suboptimally low rates of mobility. This issue is difficult to settle conclusively, but voluntary job mobility does not seem to be less common in Sweden than, for instance, in the United States (Åberg, 1984). Indeed, Swedish labor market policies are to a large extent designed to facilitate job mobility in response to industrial restructuration.

International comparisons of work-life *class* mobility (as distinct from mere job mobility) are quite rare. Most studies have compared class mobility between rather than within generations, and here the evidence shows that Sweden has a relatively high rate of social fluidity, although the differences between nations are not large (Erikson and Goldthorpe, 1992). It has been suggested that Sweden's relatively high rate of intergenerational mobility is especially due to the low degree of income inequality, and to the egalitarian educational system (Erikson, 1990). Still, we should not assume that intergenerational and work-life mobility patterns can be explained similarly. Low class inequalities in material living conditions may be more important for the rate of class shifts between generations than for the rate of class transitions during working life. Some mechanisms may even operate in opposite directions for the two kinds of mobility. For example, if educational attainment and work-life mobility are two complementary alternatives in the allocation of individuals to higher class positions, then a decrease in class inequality in education might have a positive effect on inter-generational mobility, but a negative effect on work-life mobility.

In Chapter 1 it was suggested that there are counteracting forces in Sweden with regard to the mobility opportunities of unskilled service workers. On the one hand, the active labor market policies might enhance outward mobility from unskilled work. On the other hand, the welfare state's dominance in the category of unskilled service work might imply relatively high levels of job rewards, and thus act as a disincentive to leaving. A similar logic may very well apply to manual workers; they, too, can benefit from training programs, and, as we shall see, their relative reward level does not differ much from that of working-class jobs in the service sector. In fact, it is reasonable to expect comparatively little variation in job rewards and mobility opportunities across employment sectors in Sweden.

In sum, we should not expect the Swedish rate of work-life class mobility to be either consistently lower or higher than elsewhere. Matters are more clear-cut with regard to the relative importance of class compared to the impact of sectoral distinctions in the determination of job rewards. In the case of wages, Sweden's centralized system of wage bargaining has, until very recently, meant that wage rates were influenced mainly by the characteristics of jobs, and not of firms or sector (Hibbs, 1990). Indeed, a prominent motive behind this policy was to accelerate the process of industrial restructuring and squeeze out the low-profit firms. In any event, a major consequence of the system has been to equalize wages within, rather than between, classes. Accordingly, class should be more salient than sectoral divisions in determining rewards in the Swedish labor market.

Data, Definitions and Analytical Strategy

To address the above hypotheses, I use data on earnings, working conditions and work-life mobility among Swedish employees during the period 1979 to 1989 (for mobility, we are able to extend the period further back). As we saw in Chapter 2, in this period the service sector became the largest source of employment in Sweden, in terms of both occupations and industries. The data were collected in the ULF surveys on living conditions, conducted by Statistics Sweden (for further information, see Vogel et al., 1988). In most of our analyses, we shall combine samples of employees aged between 18 and 65 from the surveys carried out from 1979 to 1981 and 1986 to 1989, respectively.[1]

Our time-frame is of course quite short for an analysis of change. Nevertheless, if the arguments of theories of post-industrial society have any force in the Swedish case, the impact of sectoral divisions on the pattern of social stratification should be clearly evident in our data, which cover such a recent period as the 1980s. Should we find only small sectoral effects, we may at least conclude that the importance of cleavages by sector has not grown very much; and should we find large effects, we would assume that the importance of sectoral cleavages has grown over the past decades, although the latter cannot be conclusively shown. Retrospective information on occupational histories permits us to examine longer-term trends in work-life mobility by comparing patterns of class transitions between different birth cohorts (see the final, empirical section below).

We shall employ a sectoral classification system based on three separate dimensions. Following the scheme outlined in Chapter 1, we, first, distinguish between traditional and service occupations; the former include managers, clerical and sales employees, and manual workers. Service occupations comprise the professionals, semi-professionals (including technicians) and service workers.[2] Secondly, we examine six different industrial sectors, excluding the primary sector. These will be grouped into a broad traditional sector (manufacturing and distribution, including sales) and a broad service sector (government, consumer, social and business services). Thirdly, for Sweden it is vital to distinguish between the private and the public sector. The public sector has grown markedly in size, occupying over 40 percent of all employees at the beginning of the 1990s. Hence, post-industrial development in Sweden is characterized not only by a strong growth of services, but also by a rapid expansion of public employment (Esping-Andersen, 1990, and this volume).

The importance of the three kinds of sectoral divisions will be assessed in two ways. First, we will examine their explanatory power in contrast to other determinants, mainly class, in accounting for the variation in job rewards. Secondly, we shall determine the extent to which sectoral divisions explain rates of mobility between classes. Class is thus a crucial concept in the analyses; it is seen as a hierarchically structured dimension cutting across the occupational sector cleavage. Each class includes both traditional and service occupations. The occupational categorization we use reflects not only different domains of work, such as manufacturing and service, but also different levels of authority, autonomy and skill. On the basis of these criteria, we collapse the occupational schema of ten categories into four classes.[3] Class I contains the top-level groups in the traditional and service sector, respectively; that is, managers and professionals. Class II consists of white-collar employees below the top of the hierarchy in both sectors – clerical employees, skilled sales occupations and semi-professionals (including technicians). Skilled workers, both manual and service, make up class III, while class IV contains all unskilled workers (manual, service and sales). Employees in primary occupations are not included in the class schema, and will not be considered in the analyses below.

In what follows, I will first briefly examine the distribution of basic job characteristics, including average wages, among the different occupational groups. I then explore in more detail the determinants of wage dispersion. Finally, work-life occupational and class mobility is analyzed.

Job Characteristics in Different Occupational Categories

Class has an obvious impact on both physical and mental working conditions. Our objective in this section is, first, to examine whether the distribution of job characteristics by occupation is due to factors beyond traditional class differences; and, secondly, to identify whether this distribution has changed, either in a positive or negative direction. In other words, are there any signs of a distinctively 'post-industrial' profile in terms of working conditions within jobs?

The distribution (and change) of physical and mental job characteristics in the different occupational groups is shown in Table 4.1. Working-class jobs are of course more physically demanding than white-collar jobs.[4] Less obvious is the similarity in the physical character of jobs across the dividing line between traditional and service occupations. The unskilled occupations score virtually the same, while the skilled service workers enjoy somewhat lighter physical demands than skilled manual workers. A regression analysis (not shown in the table) confirms this.[5] Class is strongly and significantly related to the physical character of work, while neither occupational sector, industrial sector, the private/public divide nor sex plays any important role. An interaction effect between class and occupation accounts for the lighter physical character of the skilled service jobs.

The difference in mental stimulation on the job is substantial between all the four different classes, with managers and professionals at one end, and unskilled manual and service workers at the other.[6] Excluding managers and professionals, opportunities to learn new things in work appear to be slightly better in the service occupations than in the traditional sector, although class remains the dominant explanatory variable. There is practically no difference between services and traditional industries, nor between the public and private sector. However, the post-industrial vision of skill upgrading is given some support by the over-time increase in the possibility of learning new things on the job.

The same general pattern of class differences obtains in the case of autonomy at work.[7] Manual workers have the least autonomy, while managers and professionals have the largest. Here we find a 'post-industrial' effect since the scope for individual decision-making is larger in service occupations than elsewhere. Hence, in the service sector the average autonomy is greater, and there is also an interaction effect such that the degree of class inequality is lower than among traditional occupations. There is no significant difference between service and traditional industries, while jobs in the private sector appear to be slightly more autonomous than in the public sector.

The degree of occupational wage inequality is low by international standards, but remains nonetheless clearly structured by class.[8] Managers and professionals have the highest wages, and unskilled workers the lowest. The differences are fairly stable over time, except for the negative development for class I (managers and professionals). Interestingly, the traditional and the service occupations exhibit quite similar patterns of wage dispersion. (We will explore this issue more closely in the next section.)

In summary, variations in the quality of work remain principally

Table 4.1 *Job characteristics in different occupational groups among employees (age 18-65) in Sweden, 1979-89*

	Physical demands		Stimulating work		Autonomy		Wage per hour	
	1979–81	1986–9	1979–81	1986–9	1979–81	1986–9	1979–81	1986–9
(1) Managers	0.3	0.3	0.81	0.89	4.8	4.9	100	91
(2) Clerical	0.7	0.8	0.55	0.63	3.4	3.7	67	66
(3) Skilled sales	0.4	0.6	0.67	0.89	4.6	4.7	83	75
(4) Unskilled sales	1.5	1.7	0.37	0.41	2.7	2.7	58	55
(5) Skilled manual	2.2	2.3	0.57	0.64	2.7	3.0	64	65
(6) Unskilled manual	2.3	2.5	0.35	0.36	2.3	2.6	63	64
(7) Professionals	0.2	0.3	0.88	0.90	4.7	4.7	100	91
(8) Semi-professionals	0.8	0.8	0.78	0.78	4.1	4.1	78	74
(9) Skilled service	1.5	1.7	0.68	0.73	2.9	3.2	69	66
(10) Unskilled service	2.2	2.2	0.38	0.41	3.0	3.0	61	58
All occupations	1.5	1.5	0.56	0.63	3.3	3.5	70	68
N	3,347	10,640	3,352	6,547	3,325	6,489	9,118	11,250

For variable definitions, see notes 4, 6, 7 and 8 at the end of this chapter.

determined by class, and it is only with regard to job autonomy that we find a service occupation effect. Hence, in terms of typical job attributes, the post-industrial stratification order in Sweden differs only marginally from the traditional class society.

Determinants of Wage Dispersion

We will now more closely examine the interplay of class and employment sector, along with education, age (as a measure of experience) and sex in the determination of wages. According to the optimistic post-industrial perspective, the sectoral variables should influence wage inequalities, and since service jobs are held to be superior, one would have to expect that average wages should be higher in the service sector than in traditional employment. Further, since inequality should be relatively more influenced by achievement than ascription in the service occupations and industries, one would expect the pattern of wage determination to differ between the sectors in this regard. We shall use education and experience (age) as indicators of achievement, while sex is the only clearly ascribed characteristic. The results of regression analyses with wage level as dependent variable are shown in Table 4.2.

The first column of the table shows the regression estimates for the entire labor market.[9] Class, sex and age have strong effects on the size of the wage. Class I, II and III all differ significantly from the reference category of class IV (unskilled workers), and in the order implied by their class numbers. Men are consistently better paid than women, by a differential roughly corresponding to the difference between class II and unskilled workers.[10] Wage levels are positively related to age, most clearly so during the early phases of working life. In contrast to the recent trend in North America, there are no signs of a steepening age wage gradient. Sweden's overall egalitarian wage distribution implies also that young employees are relatively well-paid.

Occupational sector (traditional versus service) has a moderate, albeit significant, effect, such that service employment pays more by an amount slightly exceeding the difference between skilled and unskilled workers. This means that the simple schema of four classes accounts quite well for the occupational dispersion of wages, almost as well as the more extended occupational schema with ten categories. Disaggregating the industrial sectors, we find that business services and manufacturing pay the highest wages, while employers in consumer services pay the lowest. The service industrial sector is thus markedly heterogeneous with regard to wages, and on average its employees actually earn less than employees in

Table 4.2 *Regression analyses of wage (in wage per hour) predicted by class, industrial sector, occupational sector, private/public sector, sex, age and education among employees (age 18–65) in Sweden 1986–9*

		All	Industrial sector		Occupational sector	
			Traditional	Service	Traditional	Service
Class	I	.294	.295	.302	.320	.304
	II	.127	.130	.130	.115	.152
	III	.046	.017	.087	.016	.085
Industrial sector	Manufacturing	(-.012)	.021		-.035	(.008)
	Distribution	-.025			-.055	(.010)
	Government	-.048		-.034	-.100	(-.012)
	Consumer services	-.124		-.125	-.123	-.110
	Social services	-.077		-.064	-.107	-.062
Occupational sector	Traditional	-.060	-.054	-.057		
	Private	(-.000)	-.029	.028	(.000)	(-.004)
Private/public sector	Private	.142	.163	.119	.157	.122
Sex	Men	-.206	-.182	-.226	-.191	-.211
Age	18–24	-.129	-.098	-.160	-.092	-.163
	25–9	-.055	-.030	-.078	-.034	-.075
	30–9	(-.010)	(.001)	-.021	(-.001)	-.020
	40–9					
Education	University	.068	.066	.074	.069	.065
	Secondary	.027	.020	.027	.014	.034
R^2 (adj.)		.360	.337	.387	.297	.409
N		11,175	5,483	5,692	5,610	5,565

Unstandardized regression coefficients and proportions explained variance. Non-significant estimates at the 95 percent level appear within parentheses.

The reference categories are the following: for class, class IV; for industrial sector, business services (except in column 2, where it is distribution); for occupational sector, service occupations; for private/public sector, the public sector; for sex, women; for age, 50–65; and for education, only compulsory schooling.

traditional industries. Finally, it does not seem to matter at all whether one works in the private or public sector.

To sum up, the traditional pattern of wage determination has hardly changed; class remains the major explanatory factor, while sectoral divisions matter much less. It might of course be that the effects of other determinants are mediated by sector. If such interaction effects are present, it could still make a real difference for the employee whether he or she works in a post-industrial sector or in a more traditional one. In the second and third columns of Table 4.2, we therefore examine wage inequality separately for employees in traditional and service industries and occupations.

In general, the sector differences are small. They can basically be summarized as three interaction effects. First, in the service sector, skilled workers earn markedly higher wages than unskilled workers; this pay differential is quite small in the traditional sector. Secondly, the wage gap between the sexes is larger in traditional than in service industries and occupations. Thirdly, wages differ more by age in the service sector than in traditional industries and occupations. Apart from these rather small effects, the wages are determined in the same manner in both sectors.[11]

This pattern of similarities between sectors in reward determination weakens the post-industrial hypotheses. Of the apparent deviations from the pattern, the lower degree of sex inequality in the service industries and occupations is, however, in line with the optimistic post-industrial scenario. The larger wage differences between skilled and unskilled workers and between age categories in the service sector are more difficult to interpret. If they reflect greater returns to human capital, they fit into the vision of meritocracy inherent in much post-industrial reasoning. If not, they add to the already strong case against the view that a fundamentally new type of stratification order is emerging.

As a conclusion to this section, it might safely be said that whatever the advent of a post-industrial society in Sweden might mean, the process of wage determination has not changed much. In this sense, industrial and post-industrial society appear to be intimately rather than distantly related.

Work-life Mobility during the 1980s

Class, then, remains the single most important dynamic determinant of job rewards in Sweden. In comparison to sex and age, it is dynamic in the sense that individuals can (in principle, at least) change their conditions by moving between classes at any speed and in any direction. Hence, mobility chances are of key importance in the stratification order. In this section, we analyze work-life mobility with panel data from the two previously used time-points, 1979–81 and 1986–9.[12]

Table 4.3 presents a summary of outflows from, and inflows to, our ten occupational groups by sex. For each occupation, it shows the proportion of individuals who remain stable over the eight-year period, as well as the two most common destinations and origins for those who leave or enter the occupational category.

Six out of ten male employees belong to the same occupational group on both occasions. Professionals are the most stable, while managers and sales personnel are the most mobile. The extreme (but rare) case is the group of unskilled sales workers, with almost no stable male incumbents at all. Mobility is generally more common among traditional than service occupations, an exception being the slightly greater stability among unskilled manual workers as compared to the unskilled service workers. There is a fair amount of sectoral exchange within the male working class, that is, between manual workers and unskilled sales workers on the one hand, and service workers on the other. Those who leave manual jobs tend to move to lower-grade white-collar service occupations, which is also the most common destination among those who leave the bottom-end service jobs. Further, of the men who exit from unskilled service work, a large proportion end up in unskilled manual jobs. It is also noteworthy that the majority of male entrants into service worker jobs are former manual workers, but they are few in absolute numbers since the low-end service jobs are so heavily dominated by women.

Two out of three female employees have remained in the same occupational category, which is slightly more than among men. The exit rate is lowest among semi-professionals, and highest among managers, sales employees and skilled manual workers. As in the case of men's mobility, there is a good deal of exchange between occupational sectors. Unskilled service jobs are, by far, the most common destination for women who leave traditional manual jobs. Similarly, the chief source of female recruitment to manual work is previous unskilled service workers. A different pattern obtains, however, when mobility is examined from the viewpoint of the service workers. Semi-professional jobs is the dominant destination for women who leave working-class service jobs, either skilled or unskilled. Likewise, the most common recruitment source among female skilled service workers is previous semi-professionals. Inflow into unskilled service work is generally low, and the most common origin is from unskilled sales work.

To assess whether post-industrial society engenders a new kind of

Table 4.3 *Occupational mobility between 1979–81 and 1986–9 among employees (age 18–65) in Sweden.*

	Outflow (men)			Outflow (women)			Inflow (men)			Inflow (women)		
	Stable	Dest. 1	Dest. 2	Stable	Dest. 1	Dest. 2	Stable	Orig. 1	Orig. 2	Stable	Orig. 1	Orig. 2
(1) Managers	.48	7(.18)	2(.17)	.46	2(.24)	7(.15)	.29	7(.16)	8(.16)	.23	2(.48)	8(.11)
(2) Clerical	.52	1(.12)	7(.11)	.72	1(.08)	8(.06)	.46	1(.13)	6(.08)	.81	10(.06)	4(.04)
(3) Skilled sales	.37	1(.30)	8(.14)	.27	8(.25)	2(.15)	.42	4(.15)	8(.12)	.27	2(.37)	4(.22)
(4) Unskilled sales	.07	3(.28)	1(.19)	.53	10(.16)	2(.12)	.27	5(.39)	1(.19)	.70	10(.17)	5(.03)
(5) Skilled manual	.57	6(.21)	3(.13)	.38	10(.27)	6(.20)	.79	6(.13)	8(.04)	.49	6(.16)	10(.15)
(6) Unskilled manual	.65	5(.14)	3(.06)	.60	10(.13)	5(.08)	.61	5(.30)	10(.02)	.66	10(.15)	5(.13)
(7) Professionals	.69	8(.13)	1(.13)	.74	8(.17)	2(.04)	.61	8(.16)	1(.08)	.55	2(.17)	8(.15)
(8) Semi-professionals	.66	7(.11)	1(.08)	.81	7(.06)	10(.04)	.55	5(.20)	7(.07)	.66	10(.13)	9(.06)
(9) Skilled service	.61	8(.12)	2(.08)	.55	8(.20)	10(.17)	.56	6(.18)	5(.07)	.49	10(.30)	8(.09)
(10) Unskilled service	.58	8(.11)	6(.09)	.66	8(.12)	9(.09)	.59	5(.16)	6(.11)	.77	9(.05)	4(.04)
All	.59			.67			.59			.67		

Proportions stable incumbents, the two most common destinations for those who exit each occupational category, and the two most common origins among those who enter. N = 4,341.
Outflow proportions are shares of all employees in each of the ten occupational categories at the first time-point (1979–81) who either belong to the same category (see the 'Stable' columns) or have moved to some other category (see the figures within parentheses after each destination) between the first time-point and the second (1986–9). Conversely, the inflow proportions are shares of all employees in each of the ten occupational categories at the second time-point who either belonged to the same category at the first time-point ('Stable') or have moved from some other category between the time-points (see the figures within parentheses after each origin).

proletariat, the occupational mobility patterns of unskilled workers are central. We will examine this issue more closely below, but some trends are already evident in Table 4.3. First, the degree of stability is about the same for both unskilled manual and service workers. For men, who dominate the manual group, the stability is slightly higher in the manual category, while the reverse pattern obtains among women, who dominate the service group. Unskilled jobs do not appear to be of a 'stop-gap' nature. Rather, both unskilled manual and unskilled service jobs are close to the average level of job stability. This brings Sweden closer to the German than to the North American pattern. The small difference in retention rates between unskilled manual and unskilled service jobs is, however, also a characteristic of the Canadian labour market. Sweden and Canada differ with regard to the general level of stability of working-class jobs, which appears to be higher in Sweden.

Secondly, mobility opportunities seem to be slightly better for unskilled service than for unskilled manual workers. The most common destination among women as well as men who leave the service jobs is lower-level white-collar occupations. In contrast, those who exit from unskilled manual jobs mainly move to other working-class jobs; for men skilled manual work, and for women unskilled service jobs.

Thirdly, the inflow patterns of unskilled manual and service jobs are roughly similar. For men, the most important source of recruitment to both categories is skilled manual workers. Among women, service workers are the most common recruitment category both for unskilled manual and unskilled service workers. In addition to similar overall mobility rates, there is therefore substantial exchange between unskilled service and unskilled manual occupations. This is what was also found for Germany, but in Sweden the opportunities for career mobility among unskilled workers seem greater.

Hence, when we consider men and women separately, there are greater similarities than differences in the mobility patterns of unskilled manual and service workers. This conclusion is supported by two additional results, not shown in Table 4.3. First, the unskilled manual workers and the unskilled service workers are recruited among individuals previously outside the labour force to a roughly equal extent. Among men, this proportion is about one in ten, and among women about one in five, with only minor differences between the manual and service categories. Secondly, the median age of these entrants is 22 and 25 years among male unskilled manual and service workers, respectively, while the corresponding ages among women are 33 and 34 years. For the men, this is about the same age as new entrants into other occupational categories. For the women, however, the entrants into unskilled manual or service jobs are clearly older than other recent joiners of the labor force. Apparently, women who have been away from the labor market for an extended period are not able to compete successfully with younger women (or with men) for the more rewarding jobs. As in several other countries, unskilled jobs are a typical entry position for women with long labor force interruptions, and at least in Sweden this is true for traditional and service jobs alike.

We now turn to a more detailed investigation of the determinants of work-life mobility. As spelled out above, the ten occupational categories are merged into four different classes. Five types of class shifts will be considered: (1) any move from one of the four classes to another; (2) upward moves, defined as implied by the classes' numbers; (3) downward moves, defined in the same manner; (4) moves out of class IV; and (5) moves into class IV. In addition, we will examine the determinants of exit from the labor force into early retirement and long-term unemployment. The method of analysis is logit models (see, Aldrich and Nelson, 1984), which are well-suited for explaining variation in dichotomous dependent variables, especially when the distribution of the outcome variable is skewed.

Central to our analyses is the impact of employment sector. Even if conditions among employees do not vary much by sector at any given time-point, opportunities for mobility between different classes could vary by sector. In the optimistic post-industrial scenario, the rate of mobility, especially upward, should be higher in the services than in the traditional sector. In order to examine this proposition, we use the three sectoral divisions as independent variables in predicting class mobility, along with sex, age and education. In addition, class position at the outset is used as an explanatory variable in all instances, except when a single origin class is the object of analysis. It is reasonable to assume that mobility depends not only on the individual's resources, but also on the characteristics of the starting position. In particular, the propensity to move should depend on the reward level of the initial job (Tuma, 1976; Sørensen and Tuma, 1981). As we have shown, job rewards are mainly determined by class, so the latter may be used as a control variable to tap the reward dimension in our analyses.[13] Results for all the different kinds of mobility under consideration are given in Table 4.4.

About one-third of all individuals have changed class during the

Table 4.4 *Logit models of class transitions between 1979–81 and 1986–9 predicted by occupational sector, industrial sector, private/public employment, sex, age and education among employees (age 18–65) in Sweden.*

	Any move	Upward move	Downward move	Out from class IV (trad. sec.)	Out from class IV (serv. sec.)	Into class IV (trad. sec.)	Into class IV (serv. sec.)	Out from labor force
Occupational sector	(-.065)	(-.158)	(-.008)			-.643	(.070)	(.239)
Industrial sector	(.095)	.441	-.382	.882	(.484)	-.681	(.163)	(-.351)
Private/public sector	-.329	-.309	(-.244)	(-.479)	(-.368)	-.857	(.214)	-.742
Sex	-.187	-.432	.274	(-.276)	(-.079)	-.533	1.593	(.302)
Age								
18–24	.784	.461	1.069	.719	1.282	.597	1.003	-3.268
25–29	.514	.400	.565	.730	.943	.736	(.175)	-2.997
30–9	.457	.443	.419	(.256)	.903	.570	(.232)	-3.062
40–9	(.183)	(.104)	(.305)	(-.230)	(.250)	(.442)	(.434)	-1.690
Education								
University	(.204)	1.282	-1.328	1.464	1.536	-1.776	-.987	-.904
Secondary	.260	.767	-.684	1.073	.661	-.581	-.506	(-.331)
Class								
I	-.387	-1.465	-1.754			-2.461	-2.563	(-.616)
II	-.346	-.904	-1.172			-1.915	-1.161	-.800
III	.358					(-.613)	(.089)	(-.083)
Mobility rate	.307	.217	.168	.325	.299	.066	.044	.042
χ²	205.09	298.40	226.16	74.15	70.27	375.94	164.33	411.57
N	4,341	3,863	2,946	695	700	3,646	3,641	5,082

Logistic regression coefficients and χ² values for the models are given. Non-significant estimates at the 95 percent level appear within parentheses.
The service occupational sector, the service industrial sector, the public sector and women have value 1 while their counterparts have value 0. For age the reference category is 50–65 years, for education thge reference category is only compulsory schooling, and for class the reference category is either class I (column 3) or class IV (columns 1, 2, 6, 7 and 8).

period under consideration. This substantial degree of mobility is not significantly related to either occupational or industrial sector. Hence, the rate of class transitions is roughly the same regardless of whether one initially belongs to the service sector or not. The public/private division, however, makes a notable difference since public employees are much less prone to change. If public employment is considered as post-industrial, which makes sense at least in the Swedish context, then the relatively low mobility rate among public employees would appear to speak against the expectations of optimistic theories of post-industrial society.

Age is the most important determinant of overall class transitions. Young employees are much more likely than older ones to move between classes; it is well-known that occupational careers tend to stabilize with age. Additionally, the overall rate of class shifts is affected by class, sex and education. Class moves are least common in the white-collar categories, especially among managers and professionals. Although to some extent due to a ceiling effect, that is, that only downward moves are possible, this result is in line with the notion of a particularly strong holding power in the top class (Goldthorpe, 1982, 1987). The highest general propensity to change class is found among the skilled workers. A large proportion of this mobility is downward, into the category of unskilled working-class jobs. Women's rate of class mobility is lower than men's, mainly because they have fewer chances of upward mobility. Finally, mobility is positively influenced by education: class shifts are comparatively common among individuals with more than compulsory schooling.

The majority of class shifts are upward, the determinants of which are analyzed in the second column of Table 4.4. (Individuals starting from the top class are excluded here, since they have no possibility of making an upward move.) As in the case of overall class transitions, there is no effect of occupational sector on upward class mobility, indicating once more that the simple class schema is sufficient without a sectoral elaboration. But the other two sectoral distinctions do have a significant influence on upward class mobility: as the optimistic post-industrial theorists would predict, there is greater career mobility in the service industries than in manufacturing and distribution. By contrast, upward mobility is less prevalent in the public than in the private sector.

Education, sex, age and class of departure all have significant effects on upward mobility. As expected, having an education above the compulsory level enhances one's career prospects, especially so for schooling at the university level. Women make career moves to a considerably lesser extent than men. The size of this differential implies that the relatively low propensity to change class among women is entirely due to the inequality in career prospects between the sexes. Again, we see that upward shifts are most common among the young. The influence of class is also in the expected direction; that is, the higher the class of departure, the lower the rate of upward mobility. This would appear to be due to two main factors: first, other things being equal, the probability of being under-rewarded relative to one's capabilities is greater at the lower end of the class structure (Tuma, 1985); secondly, there is simply more room to move upward the lower one's initial position in the structure.

There has been less (17 percent) downward than upward class mobility. The determinants of downward shifts are examined in the third column of Table 4.4. (In this case, individuals in class IV at the beginning of the period are excluded, since their probability of a downward move is zero.) The cleavage between traditional and service industries is the only significant sector variable, implying that downward moves are less common in the services. The influence of the public/private divide and of occupational sector is negligible. Hence, downward class mobility is also invariant across the traditional and 'post-industrial' occupations.

Downward mobility is explained by basically the same variables as upward moves: education, sex, class of departure and age. Hence, just as education is a lever for moving upward, so it protects against downward mobility. Again, women are disadvantaged since they are more likely than men to experience demotion. Further, downward moves are more common the higher the position one starts from, which may again be explained by differential probabilities of mismatches between resources and rewards, and by variations in the sheer number of positions below the one initially held. Finally, downward moves are much more common among the young.

Leaving class IV should be considered separately, since the position as unskilled worker is the most disadvantaged of all. Reward levels are low, but this may be of less importance if individuals' stay in these positions is transitory. The traditional and service occupational sectors are examined separately, which means that the pattern of outflow from the category of unskilled service workers may be compared with the corresponding pattern among unskilled manual workers (see the fourth and fifth columns of Table 4.4).

Regardless of sector, slightly less than one-third of the unskilled workers advance into some other class within the time-span under consideration. This means that unskilled service workers and unskilled manual workers have roughly identical chances of upward mobility. And, with minor exceptions, their mobility is explained by more or less the same factors. For unskilled manuals, the service industries offer better mobility opportunities, but this is not the case for the unskilled service workers. In either case, there is no effect of gender, nor of public/private sector. Schooling has a similar and positive impact on mobility for both manual and service workers, while age has the customary negative effect – young individuals are more likely than older ones to leave unskilled work. The age effect is stronger among the unskilled service workers.

The recruitment into unskilled jobs is examined in the sixth and seventh columns of Table 4.4. Once again, we examine the two occupational categories separately. In this case, a number of interaction effects emerge. Unskilled manual workers are recruited chiefly from traditional occupations, traditional industries and the private sector. They are also predominantly men. Individuals entering unskilled service work, on the other hand, come equally from traditional and service occupations and industries, and from the public and private sectors; women are highly over-represented among the entrants. The class recruitment, however, is rather similar between the two categories of unskilled workers: newcomers arrive chiefly from within the working class. Age and education also have similar effects in the expected direction. In the unskilled service jobs, the youngest age group (below age 25) is dominant, while all age categories below age 40 are more likely than others to move into unskilled manual work. As for education, schooling has a somewhat stronger negative impact on the rate of entry into class IV in the traditional sector as compared to service occupations.

It is also important to consider the process of exit from the labor force, especially when the destination is early retirement or long-term unemployment. Such exits are typically a sign of unusually bad conditions, often involving severe health problems (Hedström 1987). Not surprisingly, age is the chief determinant of this kind of drop-out mobility (see the final column of Table 4.4), but there are several other factors of importance. Class and education are both significant, implying that, quite as expected, white-collar employees and highly educated individuals are unlikely to drop out from the labor force. Of greater interest are the sectoral effects. The occupational and industrial divisions are both non-significant. Thus, the early retirees and the long-term unemployed are recruited from the service and the traditional sectors of the economy to a roughly equal extent. Neither sector appears to have a disproportionately large number of employees with potentially severe labor market problems. There is, however, a considerable difference between the private and public sector in this regard, implying that private sector jobs are more impairing than others.

To sum up, the amount of class mobility is substantial, but this mobility is only marginally related to the division between 'post-industrial' and traditional occupations. The major exception lies in the recruitment patterns to unskilled jobs: unskilled manual workers are recruited chiefly from the traditional jobs, while unskilled service workers are recruited evenly from all the different sectors of the labor market. This implies (as we would expect) a net mobility from the traditional to the service sector.

The divisions between traditional and service industries, and between the private and public sectors, matter more. The effects of industrial sector are in the direction expected in the optimistic post-industrial perspective; that is, upward class shifts are more, and downward moves less, common in the service sector. On the other hand, career mobility and class transitions in general are less common in the public than in the private sector.

These caveats aside, the impact of our sectoral divisions is very small in comparison to the more traditional factors like age and education. The lack of a powerful 'post-industrial' effect on mobility patterns may, of course, be due to the brief time-span that our data cover. We therefore turn now to an analysis of longer-term mobility during the life-course.

Work-life Mobility in a Long-term Perspective

Some restrictions apply to the information we have available from the longer work histories, based on the sample interviewed in 1981. It includes only individuals aged 25 and above, and excludes occupations of less than two years' duration (several jobs may be included in each occupational episode). The mobility thus registered is therefore more limited than what would have been the case if entire job histories were collected. In fact, 40 percent of the sample we will use, individuals born between 1920 and 1956, have only held one occupation. On the other hand, it might be argued that the most important part of work-life mobility takes place between positions held for some significant duration of time, even if a limit of two years appears unnecessarily strict.

Further, apart from occupational codes (including class) and time (entry and exit years), nothing is known about the positions. It is therefore not possible to examine the impact of industrial sector or the distinction between private and public employment on the rate of mobility. The sectoral influence is assessed simply by using the division between traditional and service occupations. Other independent variables are sex, age, education and number of previously held occupations.[14] In order to make the analysis more comparable to the results in the previous section, the occupation held at age 18 (if any) is used as the starting point of each respondent's career, which is then followed until the time of the interview (1981).[15] Trends are established by comparing mobility rates between different birth cohorts. The method we use is known as the Cox proportional hazards model (Allison, 1984; Tuma and Hannan, 1984; Blossfeld et al., 1989). The dependent variable is the length of time until some specified event (such as a class shift) occurs. Effects of the independent variables (or covariates) are expressed as differences between the transition rates of the covariates' categories (such as between the rates of men and women).

Our model specification is evident from Table 4.5, which shows overall class shifts (all class moves, and all upward and downward moves). It emerges that mobility is hardly related to occupational category. Where it is significant, the sign of the effect is opposite to what the optimistic post-industrial perspective would predict: for the entire sample, both upward and downward class transitions are more common in the traditional occupations than in the services. This difference has increased, as indicated by the stronger effect for the younger cohorts (born between 1940 and 1956). When upward and downward moves are considered separately, occupational sector is significant only for upward mobility among young cohorts. Again, the service sector offers inferior rather than superior mobility opportunities.

The rate of mobility has generally increased over time, such that individuals belonging to younger birth cohorts are more likely to change class during their working lives than those belonging to older cohorts. There is evidence of a successive increase across the cohorts, so that individuals born in the 1950s show the highest mobility rates of all.[16] This holds true not only for class shifts in general, but also for upward and downward transitions considered separately. These results are in line with the optimistic version of post-industrial theory. However, the more recent changes (indicated by the difference between the two youngest cohorts) suggest that downward mobility accounts for the major part of the increase in the shift rate.

As for education, university attendance has a positive impact on general and upward class transitions, and a negative effect on downward moves. Secondary schooling has a similar but weaker influence. There are signs of a growing dependence of mobility on education. Schooling appears to matter somewhat more among the young cohorts for general and upward moves, but less for down-

Table 4.5   *Hazard rate models (Cox partial likelihood regression) of general, upward and downward class transitions until 1981 predicted by birth cohort, education, sex, occupational sector, age and number of previously held occupations, among employees in Sweden born 1920–56*

	Any move		Upward move		Downward move	
	All cohorts	Young cohorts	All cohorts	Young cohorts	All cohorts	Young cohorts
Cohort						
1930–9	.313		.451		(–.106)	
1940–9	.842		1.064		.459	
1950–6	1.252	.599	1.180	.337	1.206	.881
Occupational sector	–.211	–.308	(–.086)	–.284	(–.094)	(.020)
Education						
University	.678	.851	1.456	1.554	–.740	(–.568)
Secondary	.320	.447	.727	.829	–.440	(–.310)
Sex	(–.083)	(–.136)	–.361	–.414	.444	.488
Age	–.166	–.376	(–.054)	(.146)	(–.205)	–.906
(Age²)/10	.026	.066	(.009)	(.024)	.026	.163
N of previous occupations	1.208	1.457	1.090	1.364	1.242	1.527
Class						
I	–.359	(–.285)	–1.504	–1.571	–.944	–1.208
II	–.216	–.356	–.656	–.787	–.786	–1.188
III	.225	(.065)				
χ²	1648.82	947.16	1240.02	690.81	639.90	403.19
N	5,365	2,690	4,998	2,491	3,179	1,789

Unexponentiated regression coefficients and χ² values are given for the models. Non-significant estimates at the 95 percent level appear within parentheses.

For birth cohort, the reference category is the cohort born 1920–9; for education, the reference category is only compulsory schooling; for sex, the figures in the table are for women compared to men; for occupational sector, the figures in the table are for the service sector compared to the traditional sector; and for class, the reference category is either class I (columns 5 and 6) or class IV (columns 1 to 4).

ward shifts. Hence, as Gershuny's chapter on Great Britain also suggests, educational credentialism may in fact promote closure in the recruitment to top positions, although the evidence for this is not strong. As we saw earlier, women have lower upward transition rates than men, but higher rates of downward moves. These differences are of a roughly equal magnitude, so that sex has no significant impact on class mobility in general. The sex effects have changed very little (the coefficients are fairly stable across cohorts). If anything, they have become somewhat stronger. In short, the role of education has increased only slightly, and the ascriptive import-ance of sex has hardly declined. Taken together, these trends do not point to an increasingly meritocratic society.

Finally, we turn to an investigation of sectoral interaction effects in the determination of mobility, examining whether trends in mobility rates and the impact of education and sex vary by sector. The results are shown in Table 4.6.

With regard to mobility trends, the sectoral differences are generally small. All kinds of class shifts considered in the table have become more common over time. This is basically true regardless of sector, but the increase in mobility is slightly larger in the traditional occupations. These findings clearly weaken the optimistic post-industrial hypotheses.

The impact of education does seem to vary somewhat between sectors. University level education is a slightly more important determinant of mobility in the service sector, especially in the case of exits from unskilled jobs (class IV). The sectoral effect is, however, opposite for downward moves.

Sex has no significant influence in either sector on class moves in general, but women are disfavored within both occupational cat-egories with regard to downward as well as upward mobility. However, where interactions do appear, most clearly for exits from class IV, expectations of post-industrial theory are not fulfilled; that is, women are at a greater rather than lesser disadvantage in the service sector.

We may therefore conclude that the optimistic post-industrial perspective finds only weak support, and occasionally it is clearly rejected. On the positive side, the rates of class mobility have in most instances increased. However, upward and downward moves share this increase in roughly equal proportions. Indeed, in recent years downward moves have dominated. On the negative side from the post-industrial perspective, occupational sector has small and almost consistently non-significant effects on the rates of class transitions. Where sectoral effects do occur, they are mostly in the unexpected direction and increasing over time, such that prospects

Table 4.6 *Hazard rate models (Cox partial likelihood regression) of general, upward and downward class transitions and transitions out from the class of unskilled workers (class IV) until 1981 predicted by birth cohort, education, sex, age, number of previously held occupations and class among employees in Sweden born 1920–56, by occupational sector (traditional and service)*

	Any move		Upward move		Downward move		Out from class IV	
	Traditional	Service	Traditional	Service	Traditional	Service	Traditional	Service
Cohort								
1930–9	.337	(.250)	.457	.450	(.146)	(−.198)	.535	(.269)
1940–9	.901	.763	1.198	.883	.441	(.370)	1.346	.762
1950–6	1.382	1.217	1.343	1.158	1.245	1.177	1.731	1.593
Education								
University	.567	.797	1.322	1.688	−.931	−.662	.774	1.336
Secondary	.328	.345	.776	.724	−.427	−.526	.666	.486
Sex	(−.143)	(−.034)	−.400	−.412	.476	.616	−.256	−.500
Age	−.117	−.157	(−.039)	(−.010)	−.231	(−.223)	(−.035)	(.061)
$(Age^2)/10$	.018	.022	(.008)	(.000)	.032	(.025)	(.010)	(−.010)
N of previous occupations	1.109	1.213	.985	1.147	1.196	1.293	.847	1.087
Class								
I	−.597	(−.436)	−1.484	−1.608	(−.437)	−1.097		
II	(−.178)	(−.279)	−.656	−.785	(−.261)	−1.092		
III	.221	(.233)						
χ^2	1035.57	435.63	823.78	345.69	423.89	180.65	341.27	162.90
N	3,417	1,948	3,318	1,680	2,040	1,139	1,377	809

Unexponentiated regression coefficients and χ^2 values are given for the models. Non-significant estimates at the 95 percent level appear within parentheses.

For birth cohort, the reference category is the cohort born 1920–9; for education, the reference category is only compulsory schooling; for sex, the figures in the table are for women compared to men; and for class, the reference category is either class I (columns 5 and 6) or class IV (columns 1 to 4).

appear less beneficial in the service sector. The evidence with regard to achievement versus ascription, finally, is mixed. As a means of selection, education has become slightly more important, but gender inequality has, in some instances, also grown.

Summary and Conclusions

Our main question was whether, in Sweden, the advent of post-industrial society has fundamentally altered traditional, class-determined patterns of labor market inequality. Most of the empirical evidence leads us to say no. Stratification in Sweden remains heavily class-structured, despite the rise of the service industries, the public sector and the new 'post-industrial' occupations.

Social class, together with sex and age, is the main determinant of the quality of work and of wage differences. In Sweden, there are no indications of a distinct 'service proletariat' since the conditions of unskilled service workers are very similar to those of the traditional unskilled manual workers. In favor of post-industrial theories, however, we did find greater job autonomy and somewhat higher wages in the service occupations generally, along with a trend towards up-skilling in most occupational categories.

Our analyses of work-life class mobility have shown that sector divisions do not play an important role. As in Germany or Canada, mobility patterns are similar between manual and service workers. The two occupational categories are equally stable and there is a good deal of exchange between them. In Sweden, there is less mobility out from the unskilled service class than is the case in North America, but certainly more than in Germany – probably due to weaker educational barriers. Class mobility is only marginally related to occupational sector; and where there is an effect, its implication is typically that mobility opportunities are smaller in the service sector than elsewhere. Furthermore, differences between private and public sector employees tend to be to the disadvantage of the latter. More in accord with expectations of the optimistic post-industrial scenario, service industries seem to offer better prospects than traditional ones. Nonetheless, age and education remain the chief determinants of work-life class mobility. The analysis of longer-term trends showed an overall increase in mobility, but then this trend appears to be dominated by downward moves, and the sectoral variations are small.

On balance we would therefore have to conclude that class remains the fundamental force behind labor market inequality. How can we understand this finding? After all, it is not self-evident that class should be the dominant axis of stratification. I would like to point to four factors which I believe are important in this context. Three of these have a general relevance, while the fourth concerns Sweden specifically.

First, there is the issue of class definitions. The class structure may be seen as a structure of positions defined in terms of employment relations (Goldthorpe, 1987; Erikson and Goldthorpe, 1992). In its most simple version such a structure consists of three positions – employers, self-employed workers without employees, and employees. The differentiation within the latter category, which is the only one we have considered here, is contingent upon the relation between employers and employees. There are two basic types of such relations – the labour contract and the service relation (Goldthorpe, 1982). If the employer is able to exercise more or less direct control over the employee, a simple contract between the two parties by which labor power is exchanged for a wage will be a sufficient agreement. By contrast, if the employee works in a position with considerable autonomy, the employer must use other means than direct control to ensure responsible and loyal behavior by the employee. This typically requires more rewards than a wage. In exchange for time plus loyalty, employees in autonomous positions receive a salary plus a range of other rewards, such as career opportunities. This kind of service relation determines the conditions of most salaried employees (class I and II), while the labor contract is dominant among blue-collar workers (class III and IV).

If it is the nature of the employment relationship which explains inequality in job rewards, this should hold equally whether one works in the services or in the traditional economy. It might certainly be the case that service jobs are of a relatively autonomous character, and according to the empirical results above this is to some extent true for Sweden, but *in principle* they should not be more difficult than others to monitor. A worker in a hospital or a restaurant may be just as controlled as someone working on a building site or in a factory. Labor contracts and service relations are categories which are applicable to all work organizations, at least insofar as differential employment relations are motivated by efficiency considerations. This leads us to our second point.

The transformation of labor power (potential labor) to actual labor is the fundamental organizational problem for employers. In any organization operating under some kind of budget constraint, efficiency is a central concern, regardless of what constitutes its main activity. In the non-profit sector, say in public health care, this is less obvious. However, even taxes are ultimately scarce resources. In Sweden over recent years, central as well as local governments have introduced budgetary cuts and have begun to apply managerial principles taken from the private sector. Hence, the public sector has increasingly been subject to traditional efficiency concerns and, as a consequence, differences in organizational principles between sectors might very well be quite small.

Our third point has to do with skill. The skill content of a job is, with the employment relation, the most important feature in distinguishing classes. It is also a highly significant determinant of wages, and a constraining factor in the process of individual job mobility. There is no apparent reason why different industrial or occupational sectors should differ from each other in this regard. Skills are highly rewarded when they are costly to acquire and when their supply is restricted, regardless of employment sector. Since skill and class are closely connected (at least in the class model used here), it follows that class inequality which is due to variations in skill should not differ much between the sectors we have distinguished.

Finally, we should consider the impact of Swedish industrial relations and the solidaristic wage policy; unionization is not only very high (around 85 percent), but each union is also quite class-specific. At the national level, there are three dominant federations: the LO, organizing blue-collar workers (class III and IV), the TCO, organizing lower- and middle-level white-collar employees (class II) and a minor part of class I, and the SACO, representing salaried employees with academic degrees (the majority of class I). At least until the early 1980s, the distribution of job rewards was to a considerable extent determined through centralized negotiations between the employers' federations and the three national unions.[17] Thus, the negotiation system has been built around the class structure, rather than sectoral cleavages.

Wright (1980) once argued that occupational class schemes mapped technical rather than social relations of production, and that they therefore were badly suited to account for the generation of inequality. A similar critique may apply to the substitution of sectoral cleavages for class divisions in explanations of reward determination. It is not that job characteristics are invariant across industrial and occupational sectors. The point is that this variation may be largely technical rather than social in nature. Sectoral differences in work tasks are perhaps no more than that; employees in different sectors are, technically speaking, doing different things. But they may still be situated within the same kind of social relations, and this is probably crucial for their chances in the process of reward attainment.

Notes

I wish to thank Rune Åberg, Göran Ahrne, Robert Erikson, Gøsta Esping-Andersen, Johan Fritzell, Carl Le Grand, Jan Hoem, Aage Sørensen and Ryszard Szulkin for helpful comments on earlier drafts of this chapter.

1 In 1979–81, 24,432 individuals representative of the adult Swedish population were interviewed, with an average non-response rate of 15 percent. In the 1986–9 surveys, 25,118 individuals were interviewed, with a non-response rate of 21 percent. The number of respondents included in the analyses below is shown in the relevant tables. In several instances information is not available for all individuals, and the number of cases therefore varies. In general, if not otherwise stated, the reported results are based on all available respondents aged 18–65 who at the time of the interview were gainfully employed with a weekly working time of at least ten hours.

2 The occupational categories used here differ slightly from the ones in Chapter 1 and 2. First, we include only employees (the self-employed are excluded since both job rewards and mobility are most probably determined in quite a different manner for them as compared to the employees). Secondly, sales occupations are divided into a skilled and an unskilled category. Thirdly, not all engineers are treated as technicians; rather, those in jobs which require an academic degree are put in the category of professionals. The distinctions between employees and self-employed as well as the divisions of the groups of sales occupations and engineers are based on the socio-economic categorization (SEI), used by Statistics Sweden.

3 This class schema is based on pragmatic rather than theoretically elaborate considerations. In essence, the occupations are divided into one white-collar and one blue-collar segment, each in turn divided into one upper and one lower stratum. Not all relevant and available information on the occupations is used here, however. Most importantly, we have in most cases simply used the NYK (Nordic occupational classification) occupational titles, which resemble the international ISCO codes, in order to make the schema comparable with the schemata of other countries included in the present study. In the Swedish data, a very useful classification is the SEI code of occupations, which permits more reliable categorizations according to the skill requirements of different jobs. With some exceptions (see note 2 above), we have refrained from using this information for the sake of comparability. As a consequence, our class schema is less precise than it might have been, and the degree of class inequality of different kinds reported below is most probably underestimated.

4 Physical demands is a summated index (range 0 to 5) based on interview questions about whether the job involves heavy lifting, daily sweating, inappropriate work postures, one-sided work movements and exposure to shakings and vibrations.

5 Independent factors in the analysis are class, the three sectoral dichotomies, sex, age (five categories) and education (three categories). Similar analyses are made for each of the characteristics in Table 4.1, as reported below.

6 Stimulating work is measured by the question 'Is your job such that you have large possibilities to learn new things?' (yes/no).

7 Autonomy is a summated index (range 0 to 6) based on interview questions about the degree of personal influence of the respondent on the planning of his/her work tasks, on the level of his/her work pace, and on his/her working hours.

8 Wage is measured in Swedish kronor (SEK), in constant (1989) values. There is

no direct measure of wage level available in the data. Wage/hour has been estimated by $w=y/(z*52)$, where w is hourly wage, y is income from work during the year of the interview and z is the normal number of hours worked each week. The information on y is taken from tax registers, while z is based on interview data. Within each of the ten different occupational categories, employees with an estimated wage level below the 10th percentile or above the 99th percentile have been excluded from the analysis, in order to avoid unreasonably low or high wage values.

9   Only results for 1986–9 will be displayed. If not otherwise stated, estimates for 1979–81 are approximately similar. The wage variable is the natural logarithm of hourly wage. For an analysis of different functional forms of earnings and wages, see Petersen (1989), who concludes that the logged hourly wage rate is to be preferred in most cases.

10   Since age is an imperfect indicator of experience, it is likely that some part of the sex effect is due to differences in experience between men and women. However, Swedish data from other sources also reveal substantial wage inequality by sex, even when controlling for experience in better ways than are possible in the present analyses (see, e.g., Le Grand, 1991).

11   With regard to the private/public sector divide, the same kind of pattern is revealed, that is, broad sectoral similarities and slight interaction effects (not shown in Table 4.2). Thus, the wage differential between skilled and unskilled workers is larger in the public than in the private sector, while sex inequality is larger in the private sector, and wage is more dependent upon age in the public sector. In addition, service occupations are relatively better-paid in the public than in the private sector. Overall, however, the two sectors are quite similar in their wage determination patterns.

12   A majority of the respondents interviewed in 1979 were interviewed again in 1986 or 1987; similar panels are available for 1980/1988 and 1981/1989.

13   Sørensen and Tuma (1981) use earnings and status instead of class as indicators of job rewards, in line with the practice of much American empirical work on stratification. The class variable is in some sense, of course, a comparatively crude measure in relation to more detailed continuous scales. Nevertheless, it makes particular sense to use it in the present context; that is, when mobility is conceived of as transitions between classes. It might also be argued that class is a more comprehensive indicator of total (pecuniary and non-pecuniary) rewards, at least more so than earnings. In fact, wage level of the starting position is a generally non-significant predictor of mobility in the analyses performed below, and has therefore not been included in the final models.

14   Age is measured at the start of each occupation, while education is measured at the time of the interview. It would, of course, have been preferable to use information on educational histories, but such information was not collected in the surveys.

15   In addition, immigrants are excluded from the analyses, since a large part of their work-life mobility has taken place outside Sweden.

16   I have elsewhere (Tåhlin, 1993) analyzed trends in work-life class mobility using other data and other methods, and come to a different conclusion. For a sample of employees in industrial firms and the public sector in a Swedish city, there was hardly any trend towards increased mobility during recent decades as reflected by cohort comparisons. This difference in results could be due to a whole range of differences in research design between the two analyses. One such potentially

important difference is that the conclusion of no change was based on analyses of mobility from age 25 onwards. Indeed, when the same starting point is used in the present case (instead of age 18), the significant increase in mobility between the two youngest cohorts disappears, and becomes practically zero for upward moves. More conclusive evidence on the issue of mobility trends is desirable, and is actually underway in the 1991 Level of Living Survey (recently carried out by Statistics Sweden and researchers at Stockholm University).

17   As earlier underlined, this character of the bargaining system is probably an important explanation of why structural factors other than class (such as characteristics of firms or industrial sectors) are relatively insignificant reward determinants in Sweden as compared to, for instance, the United States. (For data on the US, see, e.g., Krueger and Summers, 1988; for data on Sweden other than those reported here, see Le Grand, 1989; and for a general discussion of structural factors influencing labour market inequality, see Kalleberg and Berg, 1987.) What has occurred during the 1980s in Sweden is that the local (establishment) level has become more important in negotiations, but the extent of this change, and the consequences of it, are still mostly unexplored issues.

5

Is There a New Service Proletariat?
The Tertiary Sector and Social Inequality
in Germany

*Hans-Peter Blossfeld, Gianna Giannelli and
Karl Ulrich Mayer*

During the last fifty years, the Federal Republic of Germany has
experienced a rapid change in occupational distribution and a shift
in employment from the primary to the secondary sector, and from
the secondary to the tertiary sector (e.g. Erikson and Goldthorpe
1985; Müller, 1985; Goldthorpe, 1987; Haller 1989; Mayer et al.,
1989). Although Germany thus shares with the other countries
included in this book the main trend of change towards a post-
industrial society, it is very different in the way this change is
realized through societal institutions and job mobility. In particular,
during their life-course German workers change jobs much less
frequently than workers in other industrialized countries (Carroll
and Mayer, 1986), and if they move, they do so along relatively
shielded job sequences and mobility chains (Blossfeld, 1987b).
Thus, in Germany, change in the occupational structure is to a large
extent a consequence of the influx of young workers and the
retirement of old workers so that the succession of generations
becomes the primary factor in the restructuring of occupations
(Blossfeld, 1989).

Several factors may be responsible for this specific type of
mobility and change in the German occupational structure. First,
for over 100 years, Germany has had a tripartite system of schools –
Volksschule, Realschule or *Mittelschule,* and *Gymnasium* – which
rigidly determines entry into the class and status system at almost all
levels (Mayer et al., 1989). Secondly, Germany has developed a
highly regulated system of vocational training dating back to the
conflicts between the traditional crafts and a free trade system in the
mid-nineteenth century (Lundgreen, 1980–1). This vocational
training system is a link between the general educational system and
the labor market and creates specific job trajectories and mobility

regimes. In particular, the high level of job stability enjoyed by Germans is to a large extent a consequence of this specific vocational training system. Thirdly, the organization of work within German firms tends to be much less differentiated than in other industrialized countries (Maurice et al., 1980). As a result, there are far fewer types of positions or 'empty places' to which employees can move. Fourthly, almost all work organizations with ten or more employees practice internal codetermination (Streeck, 1984). In each firm, a Works Council composed of employee representatives has strong consultative powers regarding the hiring, firing and suspension of employees. The effect of such practices is to make involuntary termination of employment uncommon, especially for the period observed in this study (Carroll and Mayer, 1986: 325). Fifthly, Germany was among the first to combat the organized labor movement through the introduction of a paternalistic welfare insurance system in order to defuse potential industrial conflict (Flora, 1976; Alber, 1982). Within the insurance system, manual workers and white-collar employees were tied to different public insurance companies. As a consequence, white-collar employees became a specific social category, which even within the private sector increasingly modeled itself according to the prototype of the civil servant in regard to age-graded payment, promotion and careers (Kocka and Prinz, 1983). Finally, in the 1960s and 1970s, the German welfare state allowed an increasing number of workers to move into early retirement with sufficiently high pensions and thus offered the labor market a less conflictual way of shedding workers from declining industries undergoing occupational restructuring (Mayer and Müller, 1986).

Given these specific German institutions and practices and the rapid changes that have taken place in the occupational structure in West Germany since World War II (Blossfeld, 1989; Mayer et al., 1989), it would be interesting to examine whether we can detect the emergence of a *new service proletariat* in the Federal Republic. That is, whether there is an emerging service proletariat of a significant quantitative size, mutually differentiated in its labor market chances from the traditional worker proletariat (see Esping-Andersen, this volume), and trapped in a vicious cycle of under-privilege over the life-course (Giddens, 1973).

Using data from the German Life History Study (Mayer and Brückner, 1988) and the German Socio-economic Panel (Hanefeld, 1987), we will analyze the educational and occupational careers of men and women over the last fifty years.[1] We will describe (1) to what extent men and women from successive birth cohorts enter unskilled service jobs; (2) how far this entry pattern is connected with the specific structure of the German educational system; (3) whether the proportions of unskilled service workers is stable over the later job career for men and women from different birth cohorts; and (4) how employment in unskilled service jobs is related to other occupational groups, unemployment and family work. We will begin by discussing several hypotheses on the service proletariat and its specific conditions in Germany and then report the results of our analyses.

Theoretical Perspectives on a Service Proletariat in Germany

Unskilled Services as Social Class
A systematic theoretical treatment of a service proletariat is notably absent from the literature on social inequality and social mobility. Available class-theoretical conceptions have focused on the worker–owner division and have distinguished classes along the authority dimension characteristic for industrial capitalism (see Esping-Andersen, this volume). The most widely used class schemes in empirical analyses – developed by Wright (1979, 1989) in a Marxist tradition and by Goldthorpe (1987) from a neo-Weberian point of view – thus do not differentiate between industrial and post-industrial class positions.

In a world which is increasingly characterized by post-industrial employment, however, these traditional conceptualizations of social class may not only lose their analytical value, but may also miss important new trends of social inequality in modern societies. In his recent work (see the introduction to this book), Esping-Andersen has therefore advocated a differentiation between jobs based on the logic of what he calls the 'fordist' versus 'post-fordist' division of labor.

If we accept Esping-Andersen's theoretical reasoning here that unskilled service workers live in a very specific world of work, characterized by a 'post-fordist' logic, then, following Weber (1978), we can ask to what extent the service proletariat in Germany forms a new social class by sharing a specific labor market position, that is, a typical pattern of job mobility between a larger number of occupational categories (Mayer and Carroll, 1987). Esping-Andersen's position would be strengthened if we could detect a mobility pattern for the service proletariat that differs qualitatively from that of other occupational groups, especially from the 'fordist' unskilled manual jobs and the 'fordist' unskilled commercial and administrative jobs. It should be a mobility pattern that derives from the specific 'location' of the service proletariat in the total structure of the occupational system and influences the movement into and out of the unskilled service class (Carroll and Mayer, 1986; Mayer et al., 1989: 226).

From the perspective of class formation, however, it is important that such an emergent service proletariat also reflects the tendency to 'hold' its members over time, so that it can form a stable and permanent class core that gives content to a unique demographic identity (Mayer and Carroll, 1987; Featherman et al., 1989). Membership of the service proletariat should therefore be highly stable across the working life. An emerging service proletariat as a social class should constitute an absorbing state with only few exits. Only under such conditions can the unskilled service class become a more thoroughgoing context for adult socialization and for differential allocation of socioeconomic and personal welfare (and, by extension, for children born to parents in this class: Featherman et al., 1989: 89).

Unskilled Services and Change in the Occupational Structure

The quantitative importance of any new service proletariat in the post-industrial society is naturally dependent on the type of job expansion within the tertiary sector and the skill requirements incurred by such expansion. If Braverman's (1977) low-skill hypothesis is correct, the modernization process should lead to an increasing number of unskilled service jobs over time, whereas were Bell's (1976) thesis of the growing service elite to be true, we should find a stable or even declining proportion of people employed in unskilled services.

In principle there are two ways in which changes in the occupational structure and shifts from the primary to the secondary and from the secondary to the tertiary sector can take place (Janossy, 1966). On the one hand, changes in the occupational structure can intensify work-life mobility and force people to move to other jobs. Because jobs in the unskilled service sector are easy to enter and because new entrants are soon on an equal footing with experienced employees, unskilled service jobs are likely to be turned to for second careers (Kaufmann and Spilerman, 1982). The service proletariat should therefore have an over-representation of older workers coming from declining occupations. Furthermore, in Germany such job shifts to the service proletariat can particularly be expected if general educational attainment is low (Blossfeld, 1989; Featherman et al., 1989). On the other hand, changes in the occupational structure can be brought about by generational change

(Ryder, 1965): the new entrants into the labor market will then take up new jobs, while workers leaving the labor market simultaneously leave obsolete ones. This type of change is, of course, particularly important for the expansion of new highly skilled jobs (e.g. computer scientists, engineers and professionals) in which a lengthy and up-to-date training is a prerequisite for job performance (Blossfeld, 1989). Unskilled service jobs may also be filled by young people entering the labor market. There are, however, two different interpretations of this type of youth employment which are crucial for the service proletariat as a new social class.

Unskilled Services as 'Youthful Stopgap Jobs'   The first interpretation is based on the notion that unskilled service jobs are to a large extent 'youthful stop-gap jobs' (Oppenheimer, 1990). They appeal especially to young people who have not yet committed themselves to a career or who for other reasons seek intermittent employment (Kaufmann and Spilerman, 1982). After a certain time, these young people make up their minds, enter a career line and ultimately end up at very diverse occupational destinations. Thus, working in unskilled service jobs bears little relation to the 'adult' occupational career, and employment in these jobs will provide almost no clues as to a person's long-run socioeconomic well-being. In her analysis for the United States, Oppenheimer presents empirical evidence that 'stopgap jobs exhibit low retention rates over a five-year period and the great majority of leavers move to career or career-entry jobs' (1990: 29).

Unskilled Services as Jobs in the Secondary Labor Market   The second interpretation is based on Doeringer and Piore's (1971) hypothesis of the dual labor market. The basic idea is that the labor market consists of two basic types of jobs, depending on whether employers invest in the training of employees (primary labor market) or refrain from doing so (secondary labor market). The primary market offers 'relatively high-paying, stable employment, with good working conditions, chances of advancement and equitable administration of work rules; and the . . . secondary market [is] decidedly less attractive in all of these respects' (Piore, 1969: 102). Because secondary labor market jobs are dead-end jobs that have no links with career ladders and institutionalized internal labor markets, there is no coherent career sequence. Therefore, dualists argue that workers become trapped in secondary labor markets, leading to a low level of mobility out of such markets. Entry into unskilled service jobs at the beginning of the job career will therefore confine mobility mainly to unskilled service jobs or other unskilled job categories across the working life.

Vocational Training and Unskilled Services in Germany
A recent analysis of labor market segmentation, however, has shown that in Germany internal labor markets are less responsible for labor market barriers than they are, for example, in the United States (Blossfeld and Mayer, 1988). Instead, labor market segments in Germany are much more the result of qualification barriers. Germany, in contrast to other Western industrial countries, particularly the United States, has a highly developed system of vocational training. This system has the following characteristics: (1) it normally combines theoretical learning in school with practical experiences at the workplace; (2) it provides highly standardized learning conditions for well-defined occupational categories; (3) it leads to a strong differentiation between unskilled and semi-skilled workers on the one hand and the occupationally trained workers on the other; and (4) it gives trained workers the opportunity to climb the job ladder, for example, as master craftsmen, technicians, semi-professionals, skilled administrators, managers, and often as technical college engineers (Blossfeld, 1990, 1991). Thus the labor market in Germany is strongly segmented according to qualifications and access to jobs across the working life is based mainly on training certificates. People without completed vocational training who enter unskilled service jobs at the beginning of their job career therefore have virtually no chance of a career or access to skilled positions later on in life (Blossfeld, 1989).

It is true that some skilled workers move to unskilled and semi-skilled positions after they have completed vocational training (Hofbauer, 1983), but in comparison with other countries, such as the United Kingdom and the United States, this type of downward occupational mobility is rare in Germany and upward mobility is the general pattern (König and Müller, 1986; Blossfeld and Mayer, 1988). Hence, the proportion of skilled people who move down to unskilled jobs, and hence to unskilled service jobs, should be very limited in our analysis.

Again, in comparison with countries such as the United Kingdom and the United States, the German vocational training system also allows a large number of young people to make a smooth transition from the general educational system to the employment system because the vocational training system feeds directly into the job system (Blossfeld, 1989, 1990, 1991; Hamilton, 1990). Germany therefore experiences the messy nature of the transition process from the educational system to the labor market, lasting several years and being characterized by a high level of job insecurity, job experimentation, and frequent job change to a far lesser degree (Hamilton, 1990). Hence, compared to the findings of Oppenheimer (1990) for the United States, stop-gap employment should only be of minor importance for German unskilled service work and mobility out of unskilled service jobs to career and career-entry jobs should be rare.

The main question for the German service proletariat will therefore be whether the mobility patterns of unskilled service workers do in fact differ from the mobility patterns of unskilled manual workers and unskilled commercial and administrative workers. That is to say, must we add a 'fordist' and 'post-fordist' division of work to the basic division of unskilled and skilled work in Germany?

Sex-specific Employment and Unskilled Services
Finally, in understanding unskilled service jobs it is important to differentiate between men's and women's work (Blossfeld, 1987a). According to Beck-Gernsheim and Ostner (1978), the division of labor into male and female occupations is based on a matching process of sex-specific interests and company-specific strategies of employment. They argue that women interested in employment tend to prefer occupations in which they can use already acquired skills, such as support, care, education and empathy for the needs of others. Consequently, female job choices tend to be concentrated on activities in the service field. Because these sex-specific occupational aspirations are anchored not only in subjective dispositions but also in firm-specific employment interests, occupational decisions create a very stable process of sex-specific occupational selection. Beck-Gernsheim (1976) therefore predicts that the proportion of women will increase in those occupational fields where, as a consequence of technical innovation and occupational change, the contents and modes of operation are closer to the 'female culture'. Therefore, the more household activities and household services are integrated into the market process (Willms-Herget, 1985), and the more new jobs are created in the service economy, the more the occupational structure of each younger cohort of women will shift away from manual occupations to the new service jobs (Blossfeld and Huinink, 1991).

Compared with men, however, not only are women assumed to be more willing to start their working life in hierarchically lower jobs (because of their lower levels of educational attainment and lower career and competitive orientations), but they are also assumed to be found more frequently in secondary labor market jobs, especially dead-end service jobs, as a consequence of sex-specific discrimination (Beck-Gernsheim, 1976).

Results

Entry into First Job
We will begin our analysis with a description of inter-cohort changes in the first jobs for men and women. Table 5.1 shows a clear sex-specific pattern of entry into first employment for all birth cohorts. Men are centered on production occupations and women on service and administrative occupations. Across cohorts, women show a greater movement into the tertiary sector. For men, employment in the production sector declines from about 76 percent (cohort 1926–30) to about 67 percent (cohort 1951–5),[2] while for women this occupational field decreases from about 36 percent (cohort 1926–30) to about 16 percent (cohort 1951–5). Conversely, for the same cohorts, women show an increase in service and administrative positions of 7.7 percentage points and 12.2 percentage points, respectively; for men we observe an increase of 6.9 percentage points and 2.3 percentage points.

Table 5.1 also highlights that the shift across cohorts from relatively unskilled production and service jobs to skilled service and administration occupations at entry into the labor market is more pronounced for women. Thus, at entry into the occupational system, the occupational chances of women relative to those of men improve across cohorts. This change in women's occupational chances corresponds to an obvious decline in the proportion of unqualified women (Blossfeld, 1989). The declining disadvantage of women at entry into the job market may thus be closely connected with the improvement in education across cohorts (Blossfeld, 1987a).

The results in Table 5.1 are more in accordance with Bell's prognosis than with that of Braverman, at least as regards first-entry occupations. Bell predicted that more technical and specialized knowledge would be required of working people as we enter the post-industrial society. The growth of unskilled jobs, which Braverman expected, and which was to have led to a polarization of the occupational structure, has not occurred, at least not for new entrants.

If we look specifically at the unskilled service jobs for birth cohorts 1926–30 and 1951–5, then we observe a more or less constant proportion of about 3 to 5 percent for men and a declining proportion (from about 19 percent to about 10 percent) for women. Hence, as far as labor market entry is concerned, we cannot say that this group would become increasingly important as regards Germany's development towards a post-industrial society this is in line with the results of the other studies in this book).

Occupational Career

Next, we consider whether the proportions of unskilled service workers show a decreasing, increasing or stable development across the job career for men and women from different birth cohorts. Figures 5.1 to 5.6 describe the educational and occupational career of men and women from three birth cohorts and are based on a combination of the German Life History data and the German Socio-economic Panel data. The German Life History data are used to describe the educational and occupational careers of the cohort 1929–31, 1939–41, and 1949–51 until 1981; that is, up to the ages 50, 40 and 30, respectively. The German Socio-economic Panel data are used to extend these graphs up to the ages 57, 47 and 37, respectively, to cover changes in the 1980s.

In each of these six figures, age is depicted on the x-axis. For every month, we counted the distribution of states within the educational and occupational system as well as relevant types of non-employment (family work, unemployment and retirement). (See Appendix for key.) Then we cumulated these proportions for each month and joined the points to get a picture of the changes of the distribution over the life-course.[3] Thus it is possible to use the x-axis to trace all transitions between different parts of the educational and occupational system in terms of net changes and to compare job structures across cohorts and between the sexes.

As an example of how to read the cumulative figures, let us first examine the educational and occupational history of men born between 1929 and 1931 (Figure 5.1). The figure shows that at the age of 10, 79 percent of these men were attending a lower secondary school (HS), 11 percent were attending middle school (MR) and 10 percent were attending upper secondary school (AB). The figure then shows how this cohort gradually left the general educational system. Thus, almost all the lower secondary school pupils had left school by about the age of 15, middle school students left school between the ages of 16 and 17, and the school-leaving age for most of the upper secondary school students was between 18 and 20 years. A small number of men between the ages of 14 and 20 had begun vocational training but did not complete it (BO). The highest percentage of men who also completed vocational training (BA) was 46 percent at age 17. Finally, 8 percent to 10 percent of these men attended university between the ages of 19 and 28 (UN).

Table 5.1   *Changes in the structure of first jobs for men and women from successive birth cohorts, Germany (percent)*

Sex	Occupational group	Birth cohort						
		1926–30	1931–5	1936–40	1941–5	1946–50	1951–5	1956–60
Men	*Production*	*76.2*	*82.5*	*81.2*	*70.8*	*69.1*	*66.9*	*75.0*
	Agricultural occupations	11.5	13.6	9.6	4.5	1.8	3.2	2.5
	Unskilled manual occupations	12.3	11.8	12.6	10.3	6.7	4.3	7.7
	Skilled manual occupations	48.8	54.8	55.2	49.4	53.5	50.0	57.8
	Technicians	2.2	1.8	2.2	4.5	5.7	7.2	4.8
	Engineers	1.4	0.5	1.6	2.1	1.4	2.2	1.2
	Services	*12.8*	*8.9*	*9.5*	*17.7*	*12.8*	*19.7*	*14.4*
	Unskilled services	3.1	2.7	3.6	4.5	1.8	5.4	7.7
	Skilled services	3.5	0.5	0.5	2.9	5.3	4.0	3.4
	Semi-professions	1.8	2.0	0.8	2.5	1.4	3.5	0.9
	Professions	4.4	3.7	4.6	7.8	4.3	6.8	2.4
	Administration	*11.0*	*8.6*	*9.3*	*11.5*	*18.1*	*13.3*	*10.6*
	Unskilled commercial and administrative occupations	3.5	3.6	3.8	3.3	5.0	4.3	4.6
	Skilled commercial and administrative occupations	7.0	5.0	5.2	7.4	12.4	8.6	5.8
	Managers	0.5	0.0	0.3	0.8	0.7	0.4	0.2
	Total	100.0	100.0	100.0	100.0	100.0	100.0	100.0
	N	227	221	366	243	282	278	583

Table 5.1 *continued*

		Birth cohort						
Sex	Occupational group	1926-30	1931-5	1936-40	1941-5	1946-50	1951-5	1956-60
Women	*Production*	*36.4*	*39.8*	*29.7*	*25.7*	*17.1*	*16.5*	*20.0*
	Agricultural occupations	11.7	7.6	5.3	1.1	1.5	0.7	2.2
	Unskilled manual occupations	13.8	19.1	15.0	13.0	5.8	5.5	4.8
	Skilled manual occupations	8.8	11.0	7.3	7.2	5.8	5.5	8.0
	Technicians	1.3	1.7	2.0	4.0	4.0	4.4	4.7
	Engineers	0.8	0.4	0.1	0.4	0.1	0.4	0.3
	Services	*35.1*	*36.2*	*36.0*	*29.5*	*45.9*	*42.8*	*38.4*
	Unskilled services	19.2	19.5	21.6	14.1	17.8	10.3	14.8
	Skilled services	4.6	4.4	5.0	5.1	10.0	12.7	10.1
	Semi-professions	10.0	10.6	6.7	7.8	13.1	12.5	10.0
	Professions	1.3	1.7	2.7	2.5	5.0	7.3	3.5
	Administration	*28.5*	*24.0*	*34.3*	*44.8*	*37.0*	*40.7*	*41.6*
	Unskilled commercial and administrative occupations	15.8	16.8	19.3	24.9	21.2	22.0	23.3
	Skilled commercial and administrative occupations	12.7	7.2	15.0	19.5	15.8	18.7	18.3
	Managers	0.0	0.0	0.0	0.4	0.0	0.0	0.0
	Total	100.0	100.0	100.0	100.0	100.0	100.0	100.0
	N	240	236	300	277	260	273	601

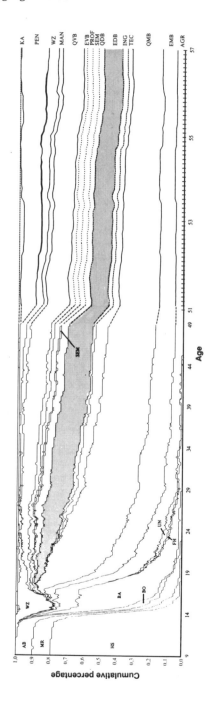

Figure 5.1   *Educational and occupational history of men, Germany (birth cohort 1929–31)*

For key to abbreviations for all figures, see Appendix at the end of the chapter

A more careful scrutiny of the distribution of this cohort at the age of 16 also shows that 18 percent were in the general school system, and 42 percent were in the vocational training system. The remainder had already left the educational system. Most of these were working in agriculture (15 percent) (AGR), unskilled manual occupations (5 percent) (EMB) and unskilled service jobs (2 percent) (EDB). The direct transition from the educational system to the employment system (i.e. without vocational training) that occurred in the immediate postwar period was thus associated with entry into unskilled or agricultural jobs. In addition, a large percentage of persons of this age were not employed (WZ) due to the consequences of the war (displacement, imprisonment, unemployment, etc.).

Let us now analyze the development of the proportion of men and women in unskilled service jobs by age. The proportion of this occupational group is shaded in Figures 5.1 to 5.6 to make it easier to follow their percentage across the life-course. At first, we focus on people born between 1929 and 1931 who have been followed up between the ages of 9 and 57 (Figures 5.1 and 5.2). There are marked differences between men and women. The proportion of men in unskilled service occupations rises continuously up to the age of 40 and then stabilizes at a relatively high level of about 14 percent. This means three things: (1) unskilled services are not youthful stop-gap jobs because the percentage is not high for the younger age groups with a subsequent decline (this is quite contrary to the situation in the United States and Canada as reported in this volume, Chapters 7 and 8); (2) unskilled services are not very important for the elderly because the percentage should then rise at higher ages, say after the age of 50 (Germany is also unique in this respect compared to other countries included in this volume); and (3) unskilled jobs are attractive to middle-aged workers, coming from other jobs. Later on we will show which occupational groups these middle-aged workers come from in more detail. As far as women in unskilled service jobs are concerned, their proportion at first increases to a level of about 17 percent at the age of 19 and then decreases to a level of about 8 percent at age 30. It seems that women in this occupational group interrupted employment particularly because of family work. This point will be made clearer in later steps of the analysis.

If we compare the development of the proportion of unskilled service jobs across cohorts (Figures 5.1 to 5.6), we can see that it declines for all ages and both sexes (see also Sørensen and Blossfeld, 1989).

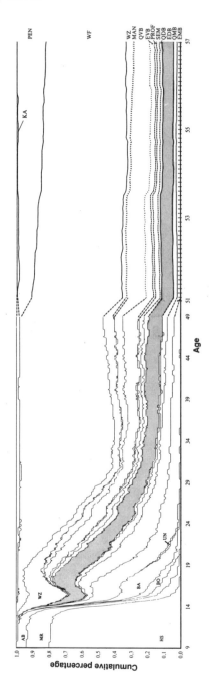

Figure 5.2   *Educational and occupational history of women, Germany (birth cohort 1929–31)*

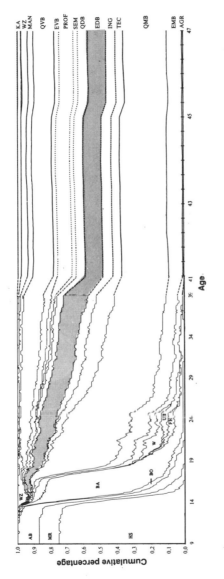

Figure 5.3   *Educational and occupational history of men, Germany (birth cohort 1939–41)*

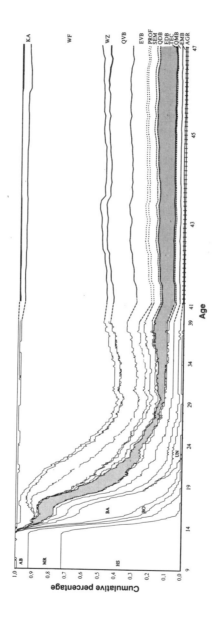

Figure 5.4   *Educational and occupational history of women, Germany (birth cohort 1939–41)*

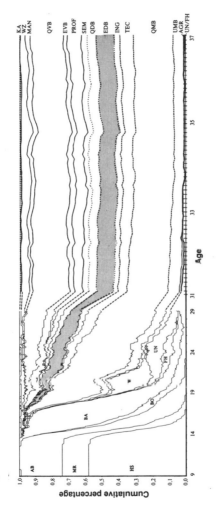

Figure 5.5 *Educational and occupational history of men, Germany (birth cohort 1949–51)*

126 *Changing classes*

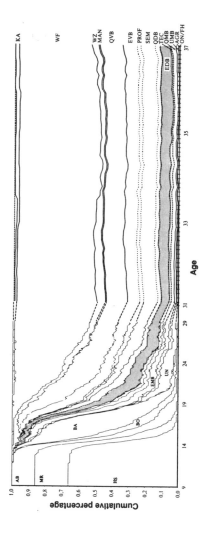

Figure 5.6 *Educational and occupational history of women, Germany (birth cohort 1949–51)*

Entry into the Labor Market and Vocational Training
As discussed in the theoretical part of this chapter, there are several studies which show that the German educational system leads to a strong differentiation between unskilled and semi-skilled workers on the one hand and the occupationally trained workers on the other. Thus, we examine the question of how employees with varying vocational qualifications are related to the various occupational groups, and especially to the unskilled jobs, at their point of entry into the employment system, that is, upon entry into their first job.
Table 5.2 shows that the majority of workers with no vocational

Table 5.2 *Vocational qualification and entry into the German labor market (first job) (percent)*

		Highest vocational qualification	
First job	All	No vocational qualification	Vocational training or master craftsman	*Abitur*, professional college degree or university degree
Unskilled jobs	*38.0*	*78.9*	*32.8*	*11.8*
Agricultural occupations	5.6	13.8	4.3	1.3
Unskilled manual occupations	10.1	25.1	7.5	3.0
Unskilled services	10.1	28.6	6.5	3.5
Unskilled commercial and administrative occupations	12.2	11.4	14.5	4.0
Skilled jobs	*56.0*	*21.1*	*65.9*	*57.3*
Skilled manual occupations	30.1	11.5	39.9	13.3
Technicians	3.6	0.1	3.3	8.7
Skilled services	5.1	2.1	6.0	4.2
Semi-professions	5.8	2.7	3.7	17.5
Skilled commercial and administrative occupations	11.4	4.0	13.0	13.6
Highly skilled jobs	*6.0*	*0.0*	*1.3*	*30.9*
Engineers	1.2	0.0	0.1	6.9
Professions	4.5	0.0	1.2	22.2
Managers	0.3	0.0	0.0	1.8
Total	100.0	100.0	100.0	100.0
N	3,695	696	2,376	623

qualification (78.9 percent) enter unskilled jobs, only 21.1 percent enter skilled jobs and none enter highly skilled jobs. Of those with a vocational qualification, 65.9 percent enter the labor force in skilled jobs, 1.3 percent in highly skilled jobs, but 32.8 percent are employed in unskilled jobs. This pattern concurs with Hofbauer's (1983) finding that a significant fraction of workers with vocational qualifications are subsequently employed in unskilled jobs. The most highly qualified employees are almost exclusively employed in skilled (57.3 percent) or highly skilled (30.9 percent) jobs. Table 5.2 thus verifies the thesis that qualifications acquired in the vocational training system are very important for entry opportunities in the West German labor market and help to segment the market – at least so far as entry into the occupational system is concerned.

If we now take a closer look at the unskilled services in Table 5.2, then we see that most of the individuals who enter the labor market without vocational training are employed in this group (28.6 percent), while the chance to enter unskilled service jobs is very small for beginners with vocational training (6.5 percent) and *Abitur*, professional college degree or university degree (3.5 percent). Entry into the service proletariat in Germany is therefore especially closely linked with having no vocational training (this is at variance with the studies for the United States and Canada included in this book).

However, the importance of vocational training actually increases throughout the job career, as shown in Table 5.3. In this table, highest vocational training and the type of employment at the beginning of the year 1988 (the year of the last available wave from the Socio-economic Panel) is cross-classified. For the people with vocational training, the proportion working in unskilled jobs (32.7 percent) is about the same as for the first job (32.8 percent) and the proportion of people with *Abitur* or higher educational qualifications decreases from 11.8 percent to 7.4 percent. Even if some people without vocational training manage to move up to skilled jobs (the percentage increases from 21.1 percent to 33.0 percent) and highly skilled jobs (the percentage increases from 0.0 percent to 1.4 percent), more than 65 percent still work in unskilled jobs.

If we compare Tables 5.2 and 5.3, we can observe that, as regards unskilled jobs, only one occupational group increases over the career: unskilled service jobs (from 10.1 percent to 14.4 percent). We also observe that the percentage of people without vocational training increases further for this occupational group. This means there is an increasing accumulation of unqualified workers across careers (the result reported for the United States in this volume is the opposite). However, the percentage of individuals with

Table 5.3 *Vocational qualification and employment at the beginning of 1988, Germany (percent)*

Job at the beginning of 1988	All	Highest vocational qualification		
		No vocational qualification	Vocational training or master craftsman	Abitur, professional college degree or university degree
Unskilled jobs	*32.3*	*65.6*	*32.7*	*7.4*
Agricultural occupations	2.2	4.5	2.1	0.7
Unskilled manual occupations	7.5	13.9	8.0	1.4
Unskilled services	14.4	34.9	13.4	3.1
Unskilled commercial and administrative occupations	8.2	12.3	9.2	2.2
Skilled jobs	*56.2*	*33.0*	*63.9*	*48.9*
Skilled manual occupations	20.3	16.5	27.1	2.5
Technicians	4.8	0.8	5.6	5.1
Skilled services	5.6	2.9	6.5	4.7
Semi-professions	6.4	1.3	4.0	17.4
Skilled commercial and administrative occupations	19.1	11.5	20.7	19.2
Highly skilled jobs	*11.5*	*1.4*	*3.4*	*43.7*
Engineers	3.4	0.3	0.6	14.1
Professions	5.6	0.8	1.1	23.1
Managers	2.5	0.3	1.7	6.5
Total	100.0	100.0	100.0	100.0
N	2,708	375	1,780	553

vocational training has also risen in unskilled service jobs over the working life (from 6.5 percent to 13.4 percent).

Job Mobility between Occupational Groups

Let us now consider the question of how mobility between the occupational groups develops over the job career. Does the service proletariat in Germany form a new social class by sharing a specific labor market position, that is, a typical pattern of job mobility between a larger number of occupational categories? Table 5.4, which shows the opportunities of moving from first job to the job at the beginning of the year 1988, tries to give an answer to this question.

First, Table 5.4 reveals a quite uniform pattern along the main

Table 5.4 *Mobility from first job to the job at the beginning of 1988, Germany (outflow proportions, percent)*

Job at the beginning of 1988		Unskilled jobs				Skilled jobs					Highly skilled jobs		
		AGR	UMB	EDB	EVB	QMB	TEC	QDB	SEM	QVB	ING	PROF	MAN
Unskilled jobs		*80.6*	*67.7*	*75.4*	*60.6*	*25.7*	*5.8*	*18.1*	*6.2*	*11.8*	*0.0*	*0.0*	*0.0*
Agricultural occupations	AGR	44.7	0.6	0.6	0.0	0.5	0.0	0.0	0.0	0.0	0.0	0.0	0.0
Unskilled manual occupations	UMB	12.6	38.9	7.9	1.1	7.6	2.9	4.3	0.0	0.8	0.0	0.0	0.0
Unskilled services	EDB	21.4	21.0	57.8	15.6	14.0	0.0	11.7	5.3	5.7	0.0	0.0	0.0
Unskilled commercial and administrative occupations	EVB	1.9	7.2	9.1	43.9	3.6	2.9	2.1	0.9	5.3	0.0	0.0	0.0
Skilled jobs		*19.4*	*32.3*	*24.6*	*36.7*	*68.7*	*67.7*	*81.9*	*82.5*	*80.8*	*6.3*	*21.7*	*14.3*
Skilled manual occupations	QMB	7.8	14.4	6.1	2.2	52.3	5.9	10.6	0.0	0.6	0.0	0.0	0.0
Technicians	TEC	2.9	4.8	1.0	1.7	5.4	55.9	0.0	0.0	0.8	6.3	0.0	0.0
Skilled services	QDB	1.9	3.0	4.2	1.7	4.5	0.0	60.7	1.8	0.7	0.0	0.0	0.0
Semi-professions	SEM	0.0	0.0	4.2	4.4	1.0	0.0	3.2	73.7	1.2	0.0	15.1	0.0
Skilled commercial and administrative occupations	QVB	6.8	10.1	9.1	26.7	5.5	5.9	7.4	7.0	77.5	0.0	6.6	14.3
Highly skilled jobs		*0.0*	*0.0*	*0.0*	*2.7*	*5.6*	*26.5*	*0.0*	*11.3*	*7.4*	*93.7*	*78.3*	*85.7*
Engineers	ING	0.0	0.0	0.0	0.0	2.9	13.2	0.0	0.0	1.6	84.4	0.9	0.0
Professions	PROF	0.0	0.0	0.0	0.0	1.3	5.9	0.0	11.3	1.7	3.3	71.7	0.0
Managers	MAN	0.0	0.0	0.0	2.7	1.4	7.4	0.0	0.0	4.1	6.0	5.7	85.7
Total of the employed in 1988		100.0	100.0	100.0	100.0	100.0	100.0	100.0	100.0	100.0	100.0	100.0	100.0
N of the employed in 1988		103	167	165	180	777	68	94	114	246	32	106	7
Unemployment[a]		10.4	6.2	10.3	6.3	5.0	2.8	5.1	3.4	3.9	0.0	1.0	0.0
In the family[b]		25.9	31.6	44.6	46.1	5.4	26.0	38.2	38.0	25.2	3.0	10.9	0.0

For key to abbreviations, see Appendix.
[a] As a proportion of the number of people employed and unemployed at the beginning of 1988.
[b] As a proportion of the number of people employed and in the household at the beginning of 1988.

diagonal: the more skilled the occupational group, the greater the tendency to be immobile. Thus, for unskilled jobs we find that between 38.9 percent and 57.8 percent of the individuals remain stable, for the skilled jobs these proportions are between 52.3 percent and 77.5 percent, and for the highly skilled jobs the proportions are between 71.7 percent and 85.7 percent. In general, mobility between each of the unskilled, skilled and highly skilled occupations is quite high and mobility across these occupational skill barriers is low.

We also observe a high degree of interchange between technicians and engineers, between semi-professions and professions, and between skilled commercial and administrative occupations and managers. Esping-Andersen's division between 'fordist' and 'post-fordist' jobs seems therefore to make sense for the skilled and highly skilled positions.

However, if we look at the unskilled jobs then the mobility pattern is less structured along the 'fordist' – 'non-fordist' division of labor. People starting out in unskilled jobs end up at very diverse occupational destinations. Most of them move to other unskilled jobs. As far as unskilled service jobs are concerned, they are the preferred destination of people starting out in agricultural jobs (21.4 percent) and unskilled manual jobs (21.0 percent). The percentage of people starting out in unskilled commercial and administrative jobs and then moving to the unskilled service jobs is again quite high (15.6 percent). Conversely, people who started their working life in unskilled service jobs to a large extent end up in unskilled manual jobs (7.9 percent) and unskilled commercial and administrative jobs (9.1 percent), even if the proportion of these occupational groups is declining across cohorts and over the working life.

In Germany, unskilled service jobs again prove not to be 'youthful stop-gap jobs' because the proportion of people who had their first employment in this job and then stay is the highest (57.8 percent) among the unskilled jobs (agricultural occupations 44.7 percent, unskilled manual occupations 38.9 percent and unskilled commercial and administrative jobs 43.9 percent). The percentage of people starting their career in unskilled service jobs and then moving to skilled and highly skilled jobs is smallest among the unskilled occupations (24.6 percent) (with the exception of agricultural occupations at 19.4 percent). Thus, in Germany the great majority of unskilled service leavers do not move to career or career-entry jobs as was postulated by the 'youthful stop-gap job thesis' (Oppenheimer, 1990). Instead, in Germany service jobs seem to be part of a pool of secondary jobs and people who enter these jobs at the beginning of their career are to a large extent confined in their mobility to unskilled service jobs and other unskilled job categories. Table 5.4 also shows that the percentage of unemployed people (with 10.3 percent) among the people who begun their career in unskilled service jobs is the highest compared to all occupational groups (again with the exception of agricultural occupations: 10.4 percent). Finally, the unskilled service jobs are to a large extent women's jobs (in this respect, the results for Germany resemble those for Sweden). This can be seen in the exceptionally high percentage of beginners in unskilled service jobs who have left the labor force to undertake family commitments during the time of the interview in 1988 (44.6 percent). This figure underlines earlier findings (see Figures 5.1 to 5.6): many (unqualified) women are increasingly employed in unskilled service jobs around the age of 20 and then move out of these jobs to undertake family commitments.

Because unskilled service jobs are a growing job category over the life-course – with a declining percentage across birth cohorts – we should finally answer the question: from which occupational groups do these employees come? Table 5.5 gives the composition of unskilled service workers at the beginning of 1988 by first job. We observe that most of these workers come from 'fordist' jobs. Manual workers account for the greatest share (44.5 percent). The proportion who first worked in skilled manual occupations is very high (33.7 percent) and is the strongest group within the unskilled service workers. This means that there is a close relationship between manual occupations and unskilled service jobs in terms of mobility. This clearly is not in accordance with Esping-Andersen's thesis that manual workers and unskilled service workers have very little in common. The opposite is true. Unskilled service jobs and unskilled manual jobs are very closely inter-connected (see Table 5.5).

Summary and Conclusion

The purpose of this chapter has been to give an answer to the question of whether or not there is a new quantitatively significant service proletariat emerging in the Federal Republic of Germany which is mutually differentiated in its labor market chances from the traditional worker's proletariat, and trapped into a vicious cycle of underprivilege over the life-course.

Our analysis shows that, across cohorts, there is a more or less constant proportion of men and a strongly declining proportion of women who entered an unskilled service job as the first job. Across cohorts, the percentage of men and women employed in unskilled

Table 5.5 *Mobility into the job at the beginning of 1988 from the first job, Germany (inflow proportions, percent)*

First job		Job at the beginning of 1988											
		Unskilled jobs				Skilled jobs					Highly skilled jobs		
		AGR	UMB	EDB	EVB	QMB	TEC	QDB	SEM	QVB	ING	PROF	MAN
Unskilled jobs		*92.3*	*57.8*	*55.7*	*69.8*	*9.8*	*14.2*	*14.7*	*11.6*	*25.1*	*0.0*	*0.0*	*11.1*
Agricultural occupations	AGR	88.5	8.1	6.8	1.4	1.7	1.0	1.7	0.0	2.0	0.0	0.0	0.0
Unskilled manual occupations	UMB	1.9	40.4	10.8	7.7	5.1	8.2	4.3	0.0	4.9	0.0	0.0	0.0
Unskilled services	EDB	1.9	8.1	29.4	9.7	2.1	2.0	6.1	5.4	4.3	0.0	0.0	0.0
Unskilled commercial and administrative occupations	EVB	0.0	1.2	8.7	51.0	0.9	3.0	2.6	6.2	13.9	0.0	0.0	11.1
Skilled jobs		*7.7*	*42.2*	*43.3*	*29.6*	*90.2*	*83.8*	*83.6*	*76.0*	*72.8*	*56.2*	*28.7*	*57.7*
Skilled manual occupations	QMB	7.7	36.7	33.7	18.1	86.7	42.4	30.4	6.2	12.4	36.0	9.3	24.4
Technicians	TEC	0.0	1.2	0.0	1.3	0.9	38.4	0.0	0.0	1.2	14.0	3.7	11.1
Skilled services	QDB	0.0	2.5	3.4	1.3	2.1	0.0	49.8	2.3	2.0	0.0	0.0	0.0
Semi-professions	SEM	0.0	0.6	1.9	0.6	0.0	1.0	1.7	65.2	2.3	0.0	12.0	0.0
Skilled commercial and administrative occupations	QVB	0.0	1.2	4.3	8.3	0.5	2.0	1.7	2.3	54.9	6.2	3.7	22.2
Highly skilled jobs		*0.0*	*0.0*	*0.0*	*0.6*	*0.0*	*2.0*	*1.7*	*12.4*	*2.0*	*43.8*	*71.3*	*31.2*
Engineers	ING	0.0	0.0	0.0	0.0	0.0	2.0	0.0	0.0	0.0	42.2	0.1	4.4
Professions	PROF	0.0	0.0	0.0	0.0	0.0	0.0	1.7	12.4	2.0	1.6	71.2	13.3
Managers	MAN	0.0	0.0	0.0	0.6	0.0	0.0	0.0	0.0	0.0	0.0	0.0	13.5
Total		100.0	100.0	100.0	100.0	100.0	100.0	100.0	100.0	100.0	100.0	100.0	100.0
N		52	161	320	155	497	99	115	129	314	64	108	45

For key to abbreviations, see Appendix.

service jobs at each age is also declining. Thus we cannot say that this occupational group would become increasingly important as Germany moves towards a post-industrial society. In this respect Germany is very similar to the other countries analyzed in this book.

There is, however, an important and sex-specific employment pattern in unskilled service jobs over the life-course (see also Hannan et al., 1990). For men, the proportion in unskilled service jobs rises continuously from the school-leaving age up to the age of about 40, and then stabilizes. This means three things: (1) unskilled service jobs in Germany are not youthful stop-gap jobs because the percentage should then be high for younger age groups and subsequently decline (in this respect Germany differs from the United States and Canada as shown in this volume); (2) unskilled service jobs in Germany are obviously less important for elderly workers because the percentage of employment in these jobs should then rise for higher age groups (this differs from the findings for the other countries in this book); and (3) unskilled service jobs in Germany constitute a dumping ground for middle-aged workers coming from other – frequently declining – occupations. For women, we find a different pattern across the life-course. Their proportion at first increases from the school-leaving ages to their early twenties and then decreases. This means that women in this occupational group interrupted their employment particularly due to family commitments.

The 'youthful stop-gap jobs' analogy does not apply well to the German case, partly because mobility out of unskilled service occupations is very low and, partly, because those who actually are mobile rarely move into skilled positions. Instead, in Germany, these jobs are part of a secondary labor market. The importance of vocational training certification in Germany is a major reason why unskilled job entrants rarely pursue career jobs.

In addressing Esping-Andersen's distinction between 'fordist' and 'post-fordist' jobs, our analyses suggest that it may be valid for the skilled positions, but not for unskilled jobs. In Germany there is a great deal of mobility between categories of unskilled employment. In fact, the greatest share of those working in unskilled service jobs in 1988 came from manual occupations, including skilled manual jobs. Hence, unskilled service jobs can be regarded as a 'collecting vessel' for redundant manual workers.

In summary, the internal composition of unskilled services in Germany is far more heterogeneous than the traditional manual working class. It is unlikely to develop into a new and distinct service proletariat.

Appendix

AB   = Upper secondary school
AGR   = Agricultural occupations
BO, BA = Vocational training
EDB   = Unskilled service jobs
EMB   = Unskilled manual jobs
EVB   = Unskilled commercial and administrative jobs
FH   = Polytechnic
HS   = Lower secondary school
ING   = Engineers
KA   = Unknown
MAN   = Manager
MR   = Middle school
PEN   = Retirement
PROF = Professions
QDB   = Skilled service occupations
QVB   = Skilled commercial and administrative jobs
SEM   = Semi-professions
TEC   = Technicians
UMB   = Manufacture
UN   = University
WF   = Household work
WZ   = Unemployment

Notes

1 A detailed description of the data bases and the classification of occupations can be found in Blossfeld et al. (1991).

2 The 1956–60 cohort is not comparable because, in 1988, the year of the last available panel wave, many men were still attending college or university.

3 We only give educational and occupational histories for individuals who, during the time of observation in the German Life History Study or the German Socio-economic Panel, held at least one occupation.

6

Post-industrial Career Structures in Britain

Jonathan Gershuny

The Question

What does the changing distribution of jobs in Britain mean for life-chances? Given the emergence, over the last fifty years, of a 'post-industrial' society in which the industrial proletariat is a declining minority of the labor force, and service jobs replace manufacturing, can we identify some new and distinctively post-industrial patterns in people's careers? This chapter investigates recent historical changes in the pattern of movement from job to job during working lives. It demonstrates some dramatic shifts in the pattern of career stratification that are corollaries of the post-industrial job structure in Britain.

My starting point is a paradox. We are accustomed to view the cross-sectional structure of employment in a society – the distri-bution of occupations and other locational characteristics of employment (such as ownership and management responsibilities) at any one point in history – as the major determinant of life-chances and the class structure. If there are so many manual or high-level service jobs in 1990, we tend to think loosely of the society as containing just that many members of the proletariat or the service class. And if the numbers of such jobs increases over historical time, we may want to infer that the size of the class has increased similarly. But considered more carefully, it emerges that the number of people who happen to possess particular occupational characteristics at one historical point has in fact no necessary implications for the pattern of stratification in a society.

What is important is not the number in each occupation at any one time, but rather the individuals' *trajectories through various occupations over time*. Of course, if the typical trajectories remain unchanged while numbers in one particular occupation increase, the overall size of the class associated with the growing occupation may itself increase. But this is by no means necessary. If individuals tend to spend a period in some 'intermediate' occupation, before proceeding to a longer term occupational destination, then, if the duration of the intermediate period lengthened somewhat, the intermediary occupational category could well increase as a proportion of all employment without any substantial consequences for the growth of an associated class.

Consider (to take a pertinent though somewhat artificial example) short-order cooks in fast-food joints. Suppose we find that the number of such jobs has increased over recent decades. Let us assume that these jobs are badly paid, stressful, insecure, have no career progression since few skills are accumulated, are particularly prone to industrial injury, are not pensionable, and so on. Clearly we might recruit sad high-school non-graduates to these jobs, who spend the next decades alternating between them and spells of unemployment: undoubtably an underclass. But does the growth in the number of greasy-spoon jobs *necessarily* imply a concomitant growth of a new underclass of service sector peons?

Let us suppose further that, in our lands of opportunity, postgraduate places in the medical schools and law and business faculties of the great universities are increasingly open to talented people, irrespective of their class of origin. Those from less-advantaged backgrounds must find jobs to pay their way through graduate school; some of them work in McDonald's. Our example suggests that a proportion of the next generation of senior professionals are currently short-order cooks. If the graduate schools have become increasingly open to bright children from poorer families, then the increasing number of low-skilled service jobs may indicate not the growth of a service underclass but a growing mobility into the top reaches of an elite service class.

Of course, the average short-order cook of 1993 is not a corporate lawyer in 2003 (though, to get a little ahead of the exposition, he or she is not very likely to be a short-order cook in 2003 either: there are other groups than students who might spend short spells in such jobs, among them women in a phase of intermittent employment alternating with full-time care of small children). The point is, however, simply that the growth of classes is in principle independent of the growth of occupational categories.

This seemingly paradoxical example is in fact just the converse of the rather more familiar case of a historical increase in the proportion of jobs in a high-status employment category without an improvement in chances of social mobility. Where once an occupation was recruited from formally unqualified workers who acquired skills informally (the watchmaker who repaired spectacles bought a box of lenses from a travelling salesman and learned optometry empirically) or from previously unqualified workers who acquired formal certification by part-time study or night-school course after they entered the workforce, it now demands formal qualifications of the sort provided by the mainstream educational system. The occupation is entered at the begining of the working life rather than part-way through it; the numbers in the occupation may perhaps increase, but those individuals in the occupation spend a larger proportion of their working lives in it, and opportunities for mobility into the occupation in the course of a working life accordingly diminish. (And, though this is not part of the story of this chapter, those in the higher-level occupations can best afford to buy better education for their children, so the diminished intra-career mobility accompanies a diminished inter-generational mobility.)

Clearly, therefore, in questions of stratification we are concerned with individual life-trajectories, with the specific sequences of particular jobs held by individuals during their careers, and not with the current population distribution of jobs. The distribution of jobs does not, in fact, tell us anything necessary about post-industrial class structure.

While the economic structural context of what follows is therefore the nature of the latest phases of industrial development, its subject is not the change as shown by successive cross-sectional distributions of occupations in Britain but rather the implications of the longitudinal evidence of individuals' occupational careers for the emergence of new and distinctively post-industrial patterns of stratification.

And certainly the discussions of the British data do not arbitrate in any general way between the various views of post-industrial society set out in the introduction to this book. What emerges, in the following discussion, is a view of how the evolution of Britain's particular occupational structure relates to these models. The picture developed below can be summarized quite simply.

Most important, is the growth of mid-career barriers to entry to the professional and technical occupations, and the increasing importance of formal educational qualification or certification as means of access to these jobs. The contrast drawn by Blossfeld, Giannelli and Mayer in this volume (Chapter 5) between the importance of qualifications in Germany and Britain is certainly still true; but the difference is declining. We see, in what follows, a marked contrast between successive age-cohorts in these occupations: the most recent British age cohort contains much less within-career upward occupational mobility than the previous: the short-order-cook-to-brain-surgeon model has now even less relevance than it had previously.

But the declining opportunity for within-career mobility into the high-end service occupations does not point directly to career immobility in low-level service occupations. Mobility into and out of these jobs remains high within the occupational career, and indeed appears to have risen substantially for women in the successive age cohorts. In common with the findings of the German, Canadian and US contributions to this collection, the low-level service occupations in Britain do not appear to have distinct class-like characteristics: they are not retentive, and do not have consistent membership from year to year. They show markedly more mobility than other sorts of low-end jobs; time spent in these occupations is often a relatively brief interlude in a career spent mostly elsewhere.

The focus of this chapter is on how British occupational groups are constituted from individuals' careers, rather than on the careers themselves. So what is presented concentrates on the previous histories of those in particular occupations at particular historical points, rather than on their subsequent destinations (i.e. inflow rather than outflow statistics). But in fact the same story emerges from both sorts of British statistics (which indeed matches in general terms the results from the other countries in this collection); decreasing within-career opportunities for upwards mobility into what the introduction termed the 'post-industrial hierarchy'; movement into 'management' as the major remaining opportunity for within-career 'upwards' movement; and, for men a constant, and for women an increasing, opportunity for circulation amongst the various sorts of relatively low-level jobs in the manufacturing and service sectors. A dualistic society, perhaps, but with no evidence of the emergence of a new, low-level, specifically service-related class.[1]

British Data on Occupational Careers

Until recently most sociological discussion in the United Kingdom has concentrated on inter-generational rather than intra-generational mobility, and this focus is reflected in a shortage of data: we have nothing to rival, for instance, the German cohort study. There was some life history data, collected by government departments for administrative purposes during the mid-1970s and early 1980s (the 1975 National Training Survey, the 1980 Women and Employment survey). Both of these have been used by academic social scientists, but the former does not have continuous data covering the entire working life of its respondents, and while the latter has received some sustained academic attention, most notably in a series of publications by Shirley Dex (1984a, 1984a, b), its general usefulness is limited by the fact that it includes only women.

Matters are now improving. Since December 1990, researchers have had limited access to the Longitudinal Study data, linking individual records from the 1971 and 1981 Population Censuses with administrative information on births and deaths. There is the British Panel Study, whose first wave went into the field late in 1991, which plans to collect life and work history data in its second wave. And there are plans for a new household survey which will have recalled life event data as its main focus.

But for the moment, the best British source of general information on the events of the life-course comes from the 1986 Social Change and Economic Life (SCEL) survey. Between one-third and one half of the resources of this survey were devoted to collecting detailed life and work history data for its 6,000 working-age respondents. It is, however, not a national random population survey. Its sample is random, but drawn from addresses in six 'travel-to-work areas' (and therefore has a mix of urban and rural respondents) in regions of England and Scotland with widely varying economic characteristics. In what follows, I shall use evidence from SCEL as giving a general indication of the impact of economic change on the working lives of people in Britain. We have no grounds for thinking that the lives described in the data are unrepresentative, but nevertheless the sample is not a nationally representative one.

Fixed Interval versus Event Data

Work histories are collected as series of 'events'. These 'events' are changes in the nature of employment; they are essentially *irregular* in form: the more filled the life is with incidents and eventualities, the more event records are required to describe it. So, though two lives may have the same extent in historical time, the length of their conventional life history records may be very different. This obviously greatly complicates the analysis. Since the events that make up a life are evidently not all of equivalent status, for any one individual let alone between different individuals, we cannot simply calculate statistics by adding up events. The general solution to this problem, as provided by the social science literature (Allison, 1984; Blossfeld et al., 1989; Yamaguchi, 1991) is to shift the focus of analysis from the individual to the event. Each event has its own characteristics (including its duration and its position in middle or the end of the life-course). The subject in most sociological event history analysis, the 'case', is the event not the individual.

But though we *collect* and *store* the data this way, it is not inevitable that we have to *analyze* the data this way. Life-course data in the form of a series of changes of state that pass above a particular threshold of significance nevertheless describe a continuous stream of occupation locations. The representation of the stream of occupational locations is more parsimonious if we only register changes, but the parsimony imposes costs in the form of the irregular durations and the censoring of events, which in turn leads to difficulties in analysis.

An alternative way of representing that stream is to sample it at fixed intervals. As long as the frequency of the sampling is sufficiently large relative to the frequency of change in the characteristics of the stream, we lose no information. For the issues of occupational position covered in this chapter, a yearly sampling frequency is quite sufficient. The sampling procedure means a loss of parsimony in the representation of life histories but it greatly simplifies the analysis. In particular it means that we no longer have the problems of variable duration events and censoring (though of course we still have to deal with the fact that our respondents have lived differing lengths of time).

By reorganizing the data in this way, we can re-establish the individual as the 'case'. This enables much more straightforward analysis. It becomes possible, for example, to explain individuals' occupational status or prestige at one point in time by their positions at previous points in time using standard regression techniques. But this chapter will concentrate on even more basic descriptive analyses, using a yearly sampled version of the SCEL data to examine individuals' occupational careers.

Occupational Change in Aggregate Terms

The baseline against which we must investigate occupational careers is the change in the overall occupational structure of employment. In principle we should start by presenting cross-sectional occupational data for the successive decades since the respondents to the SCEL survey entered the workforce. Unfortunately this sort of evidence is not available. The system of occupational classification used in each Population Census is not a constant, and changed radically between 1961 and 1971, and there are no consistent and detailed survey series for British occupational structure before the mid-1970s.

But instead, we can use the information contained in the work histories themselves. This source of evidence does, however, pose a problem. Even assuming that the six travel-to-work areas are reasonably representative of the whole working population in 1986, our sample will nevertheless be *grossly unrepresentative of the past*:

it will exclude those of the working population of 1976 who were more than 50 years old, those of 1966 who were more than 40 years old, and so on. The further back we look at the occupational distribution, using our retrospective data, the more the picture is biased towards younger workers.

One way of dealing with this is progressively to restrict the comparisons as we look further backwards. Thus, we could compare the occupational distributions of all those below 50 years for 1976 and 1986, below 40 years for 1966 to 1986, and so on. In what follows, however, we use the somewhat equivalent but slightly more complex procedure of plotting occupational structure by both the stage in the working life and the point in historical time (which allows us to make mental projections, continuing the age/occupation curves into the future, as the best-available basis for guesses about the post-1986 occupational distributions for the younger age cohorts).

This procedure relies on the use of pseudo-entry cohorts. The German life history study has real birth cohorts, taking a series of single entry years spaced at intervals of one decade. This sampling strategy has the consequence that quite clear contrasts may be drawn between successive cohorts. In our case, the sample was not stratified by birth year, so our respondents from each decade cohort are spread evenly across that decade; nevertheless, in what follows, I discuss averages for decade groups. People of the same age enter the workforce at different times, depending on their schooling: I have chosen (for a reason which will become apparent) to order the analysis by date of entry to the workforce rather than date of birth. Throughout the cohort group includes all those who entered the workforce in a given decade, which gives each cohort a constant number in the workforce during the whole of the period covered.

Figures 6.1 to 6.6 summarize each year in employment for each entry cohort and sex. For the purposes of this first summary, I have taken the eleven occupational categories in the Esping-Andersen classification, and reduced them further into six broader groups, each of which show rather similar patterns of cross-sectional change.

The group in Figure 6.1 is a combination of the professional, semi-professional, technical and high-skill service occupations. For both men and women the curves shift regularly upwards in successive cohorts: plainly these jobs are substantially increasing as a proportion of the workforce; the overall growth for these groups is really quite remarkable. We should also note that within each sex and cohort, the proportion in these occupations increases reasonably regularly with the length of time in the workforce. Even if the

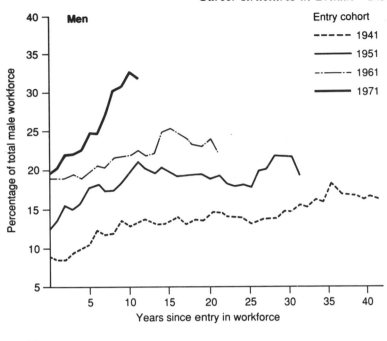

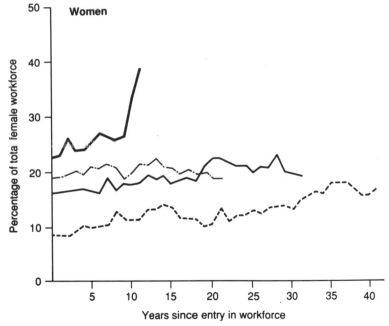

Figure 6.1 *Professional and technical occupations, SCEL sample, UK*

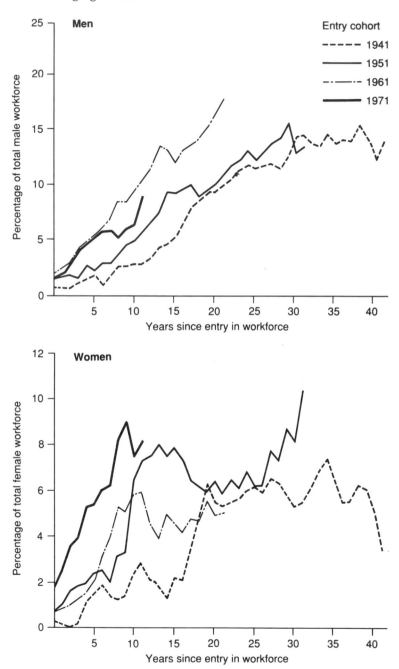

Figure 6.2   *Managers, SCEL sample, UK*

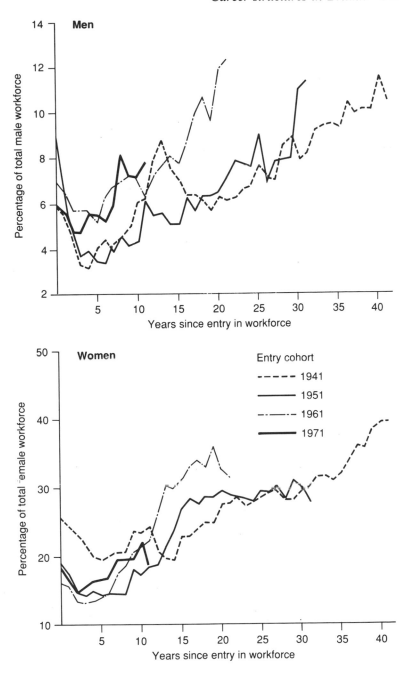

Figure 6.3   *Sales and unskilled service occupations, SCEL sample, UK*

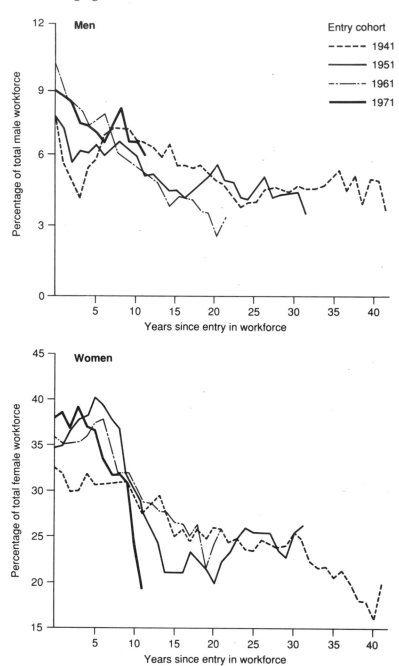

Figure 6.4   *Clerical occupations, SCEL sample, UK*

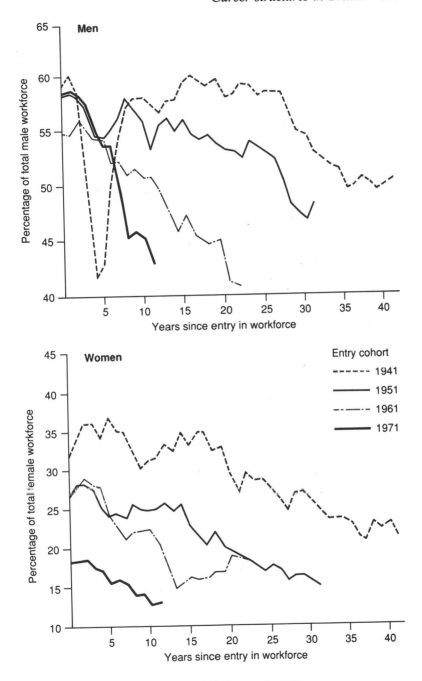

Figure 6.5   *Manual occupations, SCEL sample, UK*

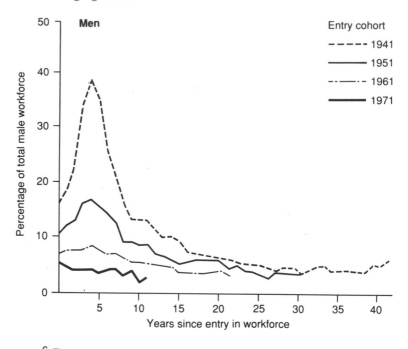

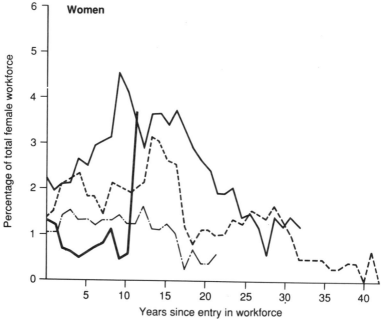

Figure 6.6   *Primary, military, etc. occupations (men), 'other'*
occupations (women), SCEL sample, UK

curves for the youngest cohorts level off in the future, and subsequent cohorts show no further upwards shift, this evidence suggests that that the overall proportion of the workforce in these high-level jobs will rise above 30 percent for both men and women in coming decades. (Note, however, that the *pseudo*-cohort method means that estimates for the final points for each entry cohort in Figures 6.1 to 6.6 are increasingly distorted as a result of the falling number of respondents on which the estimates are based.)

The second group, managers (Figure 6.2), shows the same sort of progressive increase through the working life, though the progression here is very much steeper, with very few in the category at the begining of the working life. Again, the curves shift upwards over time, indicating an increase in the total in these jobs; the growth is rather smaller and less regular here than in the broad professional group.

The combined group of sales and unskilled service workers (Figure 6.3) once more shows the same two features: an uneven upwards progression through the life-course, and an (in this case rather weaker) upwards shift between successive entry cohorts. In this broad occupational category, women clearly predominate: around 30 percent of the women are in this broad category after fifteen years in work, as against 6 to 8 percent of men. (Note the sharp downwards trend in the early years in this sector. In part this is a result of the unskilled service and shop-work characteristic as an easy-to-come-by first job, perhaps reflecting earlier casual work experience while still at school. But for the men, there is another explanation, which will emerge when we discuss the plot for manual workers.) The clerical workers (Figure 6.4) show no very clear pattern of shift between the successive entry cohorts, but for each cohort this occupation employs a regularly decreasing proportion with the length of time in the workforce. Clerical work is again a strongly female category.

The manual workers (Figure 6.5) provide a picture which is pretty much the reverse of the broad professional group: the older the worker, the less likely to be in a manual occupation, and for any given number of years in the workforce, the more recent the entry to the workforce the less likely to be in a manual job. We see a really striking dip in the proportion of men employed in the manual sector in the early years in the workforce. In the 1941–50 cohort, the proportion drops from around 60 percent in the first years, to hardly more than 40 percent in year 5, rising again to nearly 60 percent by year 10. This is a reflection of military service: a majority of British boys in the 1940s left school at the age of 14 and spent a few years in employment before they were old enough to enter the armed forces.

(Conscription was at the age of 18, for an indefinite period in wartime and for two years thereafter, then reduced to one year, and finally abolished in the mid-1950s; girls were not conscripted.) We see a lesser version of this same phenomenon for the 1951 to 1960 entry cohort, reflecting the shorter period of conscription and its subsequent abolition. It disappears for the subsequent cohorts.

The influence of military conscription emerges more clearly when we consider the final pair of plots (Figure 6.6) which put together primary occupations, failures of classification, and the armed forces. The women's plot here averages 2 percent of the workforce, and most of the variation in it is statistical noise. The men's plot, by contrast, is quite clear. Primary occupations, over the period covered by our life histories, declined from around 6 percent to around 3 percent of all employment. The 38 percent of the male 1941–50 entry cohort in this occupational group at the 5-year point thus clearly represents military service. This interruption in the work lives of young men in the earlier cohorts is of some importance in our later discussion.

The overall picture of occupational change that emerges from these figures is quite clear. Managerial, professional and technical occupations, and also the unskilled service and sales occupations, increase as a proportion of all employment though the life-course, and also show a tendency to increase, age-for-age, through success-ive entry cohorts. Clerical workers show a declining proportion through the life-course, though a rough age-for-age constancy between cohorts. Manual workers overall show decline both through the work-life and across cohorts.

This picture is of successive cross-sections. It tells us about overall levels of employment at successive points in time for the different levels of work experience. It provides the background of employ-ment structure: we might wish to see it as describing the stock of jobs out of which people construct their careers. It tells us nothing directly, however, about individuals' careers. The changing stock of jobs may be reflected directly in individuals' life-chances. If, to continue with my previous example, the growth in low-skilled services means the increase in the size of the group which spends its working life in low-skilled service jobs, then we have evidence of some sort of service underclass; otherwise, we have a quite different phenomenon, a transitional occupational category, which serves to lubricate individuals' transitions into and out of the workforce, and between more permanent occupational locations.

Where Do Current Occupation Groups Come From?

One very straightforward way to describe careers is to group people according to their occupation at some particular point in time, and then find some means of characterizing the previous occupational histories of each of the groups. There is a wide variety of alternative means of characterization, including numbers and frequency of changes, the particular nature of changes (i.e. counts of changes between specified pairs of occupations) and the historical sequence of transitions of a given nature. But one particular advantage of the fixed interval representation of the work history data, is that, while all the information on transitions and sequences is preserved, it is also very easy to derive information on aggregate durations in particular occupations over the life-course. The empirical argument of this chapter depends on characterizing individuals' occupational histories in terms of totals of time spent in the various occupations.

Table 6.1 lays out 'occupational time budgets' (the term is derived from Featherman et al., 1989; the direct origin of this and the following tables is, however, from techniques used in analyzing conventional day or week time budget diaries). For this and the following tabulation, the 1941–60, and the 1971–86 entries to the workforce have been treated as single cohorts.

The matrices summarize the whole working lives of each of the three cohorts. So the entry 5.6 in the first cell tells us that 5.6 percent of the working life of this cohort consisted of managerial employment of men who were managers at the survey date of 1986. Reading further along this column, we see that 1.5 percent of the working life of this cohort consisted of clerical employment of men who were managers in 1986, and 3 percent was skilled or unskilled manual employment of the 1986 male managers. The row total 13.4 gives the proportion of the working life of this cohort which belongs to the 1986 managers – which, more simply, is the proportion of the cohort in managerial jobs in 1986. The column totals, by contrast, give the aggregate of time spent by the cohort in each occupation throughout their working lives. So the difference between the column totals and the equivalent row totals indicates in a rather conservative manner the change in the size of employment in the various occupations of members of each cohort, over the working life of that particular cohort.

We can see, by comparing the diagonal elements of these matrices with the appropriate row totals, that some sorts of occupational employment are more stable than others. Only 42 percent (i.e. 5.6/13.4) of the work-life of the 1986 managers in the 1941–60 age cohort was spent in managerial work. By contrast, 70

Table 6.1 *Occupational time budget: whole male sample, UK (percent of all cohort time in occupation)*

Final occupation	Managerial	Professional	Semi-professional	Technical	Skilled service	Unskilled service	Clerical	Sales	Skilled manual	Unskilled manual	Primary, other	% in final occupations
Entry cohort 1941–60												
Managerial	5.6	0.7	0.3	0.5	0.3	0.2	1.5	0.7	1.1	1.9	0.6	13.4
Professional	0.2	3.6	0.1	0.5	0.1	0.0	0.2	0.2	0.3	0.9	0.3	6.4
Semi-professional	0.1	0.3	2.4	0.3	0.1	0.0	0.1	0.2	0.7	0.4	0.1	4.5
Technical	0.2	0.2	0.0	1.9	0.1	0.0	0.1	0.0	0.5	0.6	0.3	3.9
Skilled service	0.1	0.0	0.0	0.0	1.6	0.1	0.0	0.1	0.4	0.4	0.2	2.9
Unskilled service	0.1	0.0	0.0	0.0	0.3	2.0	0.1	0.2	0.4	1.8	0.7	5.6
Clerical	0.2	0.1	0.0	0.1	0.1	0.0	2.9	0.1	0.3	0.6	0.2	4.6
Sales	0.2	0.0	0.0	0.1	0.1	0.0	0.2	1.5	0.3	0.8	0.1	3.3
Skilled manual	0.2	0.3	0.0	0.1	0.1	0.2	0.0	0.1	10.4	2.6	0.8	14.9
Unskilled manual	0.7	0.6	0.0	0.3	0.4	0.5	0.3	0.5	3.0	27.1	3.4	36.9
Primary, other	0.0	0.0	0.0	0.1	0.0	0.0	0.0	0.0	0.1	0.5	2.7	3.6
Whole cohort	7.7	5.9	2.8	3.9	3.2	3.0	5.5	3.5	17.4	37.6	9.4	100
Entry cohort 1961–70												
Managerial	7.1	1.0	0.1	0.8	0.4	0.1	2.3	1.0	1.3	2.0	0.5	16.5
Professional	0.2	6.6	0.1	0.6	0.1	0.0	0.4	0.1	0.9	0.6	0.2	9.7
Semi-professional	0.1	0.1	4.1	0.0	0.0	0.1	0.2	0.1	0.2	0.4	0.3	5.6
Technical	0.1	0.2	0.1	2.6	0.0	0.0	0.2	0.0	0.6	0.4	0.0	4.2
Skilled service	0.0	0.0	0.0	0.0	2.0	0.1	0.0	0.0	0.1	0.7	0.1	3.0
Unskilled service	0.3	0.1	0.0	0.0	0.1	1.7	0.1	0.2	0.5	1.1	0.3	4.4

Table 6.1 *continued*

Final occupation	Managerial	Professional	Semi-professional	Technical	Skilled service	Unskilled service	Clerical	Sales	Skilled manual	Unskilled manual	Primary, other	% in final occupations
Clerical	0.3	0.1	0.1	0.1	0.1	0.0	2.1	0.0	0.2	0.4	0.0	3.5
Sales	0.6	0.2	0.0	0.3	0.1	0.1	0.3	2.4	0.4	1.1	0.1	5.5
Skilled manual	0.1	0.2	0.0	0.0	0.1	0.1	0.1	0.1	9.3	3.0	0.2	13.2
Unskilled manual	0.2	0.6	0.0	0.2	0.2	0.7	0.3	0.5	2.9	24.0	1.7	31.3
Primary, other	0.0	0.1	0.0	0.0	0.0	0.1	0.1	0.0	0.1	0.3	2.3	3.0
Whole cohort	9.1	9.2	4.5	4.7	3.2	2.9	6.1	4.4	16.3	34.0	5.7	100
Entry cohort 1971–87												
Managerial	3.8	0.5	0.1	0.2	0.0	0.1	0.7	0.4	0.5	0.6	0.1	6.9
Professional	0.2	8.2	0.2	0.4	0.0	0.0	0.6	0.1	0.3	0.4	0.1	10.5
Semi-professional	0.0	0.1	4.6	0.0	0.0	0.0	0.0	0.0	0.1	0.1	0.0	5.0
Technical	0.0	0.3	0.0	4.9	0.0	0.0	0.1	0.1	0.3	0.7	0.0	6.6
Skilled service	0.2	0.0	0.0	0.0	2.2	0.1	0.2	0.0	0.1	0.0	0.1	2.9
Unskilled service	0.0	0.1	0.0	0.0	0.0	1.9	0.0	0.2	0.4	0.7	0.1	3.5
Clerical	0.1	0.1	0.0	0.1	0.0	0.1	5.3	0.0	0.1	0.4	0.0	6.2
Sales	0.3	0.2	0.1	0.0	0.0	0.0	0.3	2.1	0.3	0.4	0.1	3.9
Skilled manual	0.1	0.1	0.0	0.2	0.0	0.0	0.1	0.2	14.2	2.0	0.1	17.1
Unskilled manual	0.2	0.3	0.2	0.5	0.2	0.5	0.6	0.4	1.9	29.0	0.9	34.5
Primary, other	0.0	0.0	0.1	0.0	0.0	0.1	0.0	0.0	0.1	0.3	2.3	2.8
Whole cohort	4.8	10.1	5.2	6.3	2.4	2.9	8.0	3.5	18.2	34.6	3.9	100

Because of rounding, columns and rows do not always sum precisely.

Table 6.2 *Occupational time budget: whole female sample, UK (percent of all cohort time in occupation)*

Final occupation	Managerial	Professional	Semi-professional	Technical	Skilled service	Unskilled service	Clerical	Sales	Skilled manual	Unskilled manual	Primary, other	% in final occupations
Entry cohort 1941–60												
Managerial	2.7	0.1	0.2	0.1	0.1	0.3	1.4	0.8	0.2	0.4	0.0	6.4
Professional	0.0	0.8	0.2	0.0	0.0	0.0	0.3	0.2	0.0	0.1	0.0	1.6
Semi-professional	0.1	0.1	8.5	0.0	0.2	0.7	1.0	0.3	0.1	0.5	0.0	11.5
Technical	0.0	0.0	0.1	0.7	0.0	0.1	0.0	0.3	0.0	0.0	0.0	1.1
Skilled service	0.1	0.0	0.0	0.0	1.4	0.6	0.2	0.3	0.0	0.3	0.0	3.0
Unskilled service	0.1	0.1	0.6	0.0	0.3	8.8	2.1	1.6	0.3	2.8	0.2	16.9
Clerical	0.6	0.2	0.3	0.1	0.3	1.5	20.5	1.1	0.1	1.2	0.2	26.3
Sales	0.3	0.0	0.2	0.1	0.1	0.9	0.9	4.1	0.1	0.9	0.0	7.6
Skilled manual	0.0	0.0	0.1	0.0	0.1	0.3	0.2	0.2	2.3	0.7	0.1	3.9
Unskilled manual	0.1	0.0	0.3	0.0	0.2	2.6	0.7	1.1	0.5	14.3	0.2	20.1
Primary, other	0.0	0.0	0.1	0.0	0.0	0.3	0.1	0.0	0.0	0.2	1.1	1.8
Whole cohort	4.2	1.4	10.5	1.2	2.8	16.1	27.3	9.7	3.6	21.5	1.8	100
Entry cohort 1961–70												
Managerial	1.7	0.1	0.1	0.0	0.2	0.2	0.8	0.5	0.1	0.3	0.0	4.0
Professional	0.1	1.4	0.1	0.0	0.0	0.0	0.1	0.1	0.0	0.1	0.0	1.9
Semi-professional	0.1	0.0	10.6	0.1	0.1	0.8	0.8	0.2	0.0	0.6	0.0	13.3
Technical	0.0	0.0	0.0	1.3	0.0	0.1	0.3	0.1	0.0	0.1	0.0	1.8

Table 6.2 *continued*

Final occupation	Managerial	Professional	Semi-professional	Technical	Skilled service	Unskilled service	Clerical	Sales	Skilled manual	Unskilled manual	Primary, other	% in final occupations
Skilled service	0.0	0.0	0.1	0.0	2.8	0.2	0.2	0.2	0.0	0.2	0.1	3.9
Unskilled service	0.2	0.1	0.4	0.2	0.2	7.1	1.5	1.0	0.3	2.4	0.2	13.6
Clerical	0.7	0.1	0.6	0.3	0.2	1.7	24.9	1.4	0.2	1.1	0.1	31.2
Sales	0.2	0.1	0.3	0.1	0.3	0.8	1.4	4.6	0.1	0.8	0.0	8.6
Skilled manual	0.0	0.0	0.0	0.0	0.1	0.3	0.1	0.2	1.1	0.5	0.0	2.3
Unskilled manual	0.1	0.1	0.3	0.0	0.1	2.0	0.8	0.9	0.4	13.3	0.1	18.1
Primary, other	0.0	0.0	0.1	0.0	0.0	0.1	0.2	0.1	0.0	0.2	0.7	1.3
Whole cohort	3.1	1.8	12.5	1.9	4.0	13.4	31.2	9.2	2.2	19.4	1.2	100
Entry cohort 1971–87												
Managerial	3.9	0.1	0.2	0.0	0.1	0.3	1.3	0.6	0.0	0.2	0.0	6.7
Professional	0.1	2.5	0.1	0.2	0.0	0.1	0.7	0.1	0.0	0.1	0.0	3.9
Semi-professional	0.1	0.0	14.7	0.0	0.1	0.9	0.6	0.3	0.0	0.3	0.0	17.1
Technical	0.0	0.0	0.0	2.0	0.0	0.0	0.3	0.0	0.0	0.0	0.0	2.4
Skilled service	0.0	0.0	0.0	0.0	2.3	0.1	0.2	0.1	0.0	0.1	0.0	2.7
Unskilled service	0.0	0.0	0.3	0.0	0.2	5.7	1.0	0.3	0.2	0.5	0.0	8.2
Clerical	0.4	0.2	0.5	0.0	0.2	1.1	29.2	0.8	0.1	0.4	0.1	33.1
Sales	0.1	0.1	0.1	0.0	0.1	0.6	0.9	6.6	0.1	0.7	0.0	9.3
Skilled manual	0.0	0.0	0.0	0.1	0.1	0.1	0.1	0.1	1.9	0.4	0.0	2.8
Unskilled manual	0.1	0.0	0.2	0.1	0.1	0.5	0.3	0.7	0.2	11.1	0.0	13.1
Primary, other	0.0	0.0	0.0	0.0	0.0	0.0	0.0	0.0	0.0	0.0	0.6	0.7
Whole cohort	4.7	2.9	16.1	2.4	3.3	9.3	34.6	9.5	2.5	13.8	0.9	100

Because of rounding, columns and rows do not always sum precisely.

percent of the work-life of the 1986 skilled manual workers in this cohort was spent in skilled manual work (and a further 17 percent of the work-lives of this group was spent in unskilled manual work). Table 6.2 provides the equivalent information for women

We cannot use these tables to investigate historical change, since the successive cohorts have lived different distances through their working lives. But we can, simply by inspecting these tables, gain a view of relative career stabilities of the various occupational groups.

Before we do so, however, we should both add some information, and simplify the presentation. Tables 6.1 and 6.2 give the total of time in various occupations: we could amplify these tables by further sub-dividing to indicate both the sequential positions of jobs and the nature of the transitions into and out of them. The whole career total of time spent by the 1986 managers in managerial jobs could for example be sub-divided according to whether the employment concerned was a first job after entering the labor force, or a managerial job following previous employment in some other occupation and itself followed by work in some other occupation, or a spell of managerial work that continued until 1986. (These and many other variations may be computed routinely within a standard statistical package such as SPSS by manipulation of the fixed-interval work history representation.)

For the moment, however, I have simply extended the analysis of Tables 6.1 and 6.2 by sub-dividing the occupational time in the major diagonal cells into time spent by individuals who have spent their whole working lives in their 1986 occupations, and time spent in their 1986 occupations by those who have at some point in their careers worked in some other occupations. Thus, of the 3.6 percent of the 1941–60 cohort's working lives that consists of 1986 professionals' time in professional jobs, 0.8 percent is time spent by those who have had their whole working lives in professional jobs, and 2.8 percent is time spent in professional jobs by those who have at some point in their career worked in some other occupation.

Tables 6.1 and 6.2 are too large to be readily assimilable even before we split the diagonal cells in this way. So we should also summarize the off-diagonal elements. In Table 6.3, the first two columns for each cohort represent the proportions of the aggregate working life-times of those in each 1986 occupation who have been in those occupations throughout their careers ('immobile'), and the proportions spent in those occupations by people who have had some other work at some point (i.e. the other diagonal or 'stable'). The third column sums those of the off-diagonal cells of the Table 6.1 and 6.2 rows which relate to time in managerial, professional, semi-professional and skilled service occupations ('high-level service' occupations). The fourth sums the off-diagonals relating to unskilled services, sales and clerical work ('low-level service' occupations). And the fifth column sums the off-diagonals relating to skilled and unskilled manual occupations and others ('manual' occupations).

In Table 6.3, the eleven occupational groups may be seen as falling into three broad categories. There is the category of career-stable occupations that would in most cases qualify for Goldthorpe's service class (i.e. relatively autonomous work practices, well-paid and prestigious) – professionals, semi-professionals, technicians, skilled service workers – in which for both men and women the total of the two diagonal entries is in general well above 50 percent of the row total. There is a second group, consisting of occupations which show, for both men and women, similar or even higher levels of career stability but with generally lower levels of prestige, autonomy and pay, consisting of the clerical, manual and primary/residual group.

And there is a third group, the managerial, unskilled service and sales occupations. For men, these show much lower career stability; the diagonal entries for these three occupational categories only rise above the 50 percent level for the 1971–86 entry cohort, and are well below those for the other occupational categories in each cohort. For the managerial group this is virtually a matter of definition, since, in the Esping-Andersen classification, 'managers' includes (on the grounds of the difficulty of differentiation), in addition to those with some vocational managerial qualification, all those whose occupational designation includes the word manager; those with managerial functions without formal management education must either have acquired managerial skills 'on the job' or through some form of in-service training. Unsurprisingly, for this reason, we find that the 1986 female managers have rather similar occupational time-budgets to their male counterparts. But the relatively low diagonal proportion for male sales and unskilled service workers is not a matter of definition. Men could in principle have specialized careers in these occupations: they mostly do not do so.

The picture for women is rather different. Cohort-for-cohort, they have markedly higher levels of career specialization than do men in these two occupations in 1986. For the 1941–60 entry cohort, the total of the two diagonal proportions for men and women in unskilled service occupations were, respectively, 0.35 and 0.52, and in sales occupations, 0.45 and 0.54; for the 1971–86 cohort the equivalent diagonal proportions were 0.56 and 0.69, and 0.55 and 0.70. Women are nearly as likely to specialize in these two occupations as they are to specialize in skilled manual work (though

Table 6.3   *Whole life occupational time allocation, UK (proportions of time in occupation)*

Occupation in 1986	Entry cohort														
	1941-60					1961-70					1971-86				
	Immobile	Stable	High-level service	Low-level service	Manual	Immobile	Stable	High-level service	Low-level service	Manual	Immobile	Stable	High-level service	Low-level service	Manual
Professional															
Men	0.12	0.44	0.13	0.06	0.25	0.34	0.34	0.10	0.05	0.17	0.49	0.30	0.08	0.06	0.08
Women	0.18	0.33	0.15	0.29	0.05	0.52	0.23	0.07	0.14	0.04	0.29	0.34	0.10	0.23	0.03
Semi-professional															
Men	0.09	0.43	0.16	0.06	0.26	0.33	0.41	0.05	0.06	0.15	0.70	0.22	0.03	0.02	0.03
Women	0.33	0.41	0.04	0.17	0.05	0.42	0.37	0.02	0.14	0.05	0.64	0.23	0.02	0.10	0.02
Technical															
Men	0.05	0.44	0.13	0.03	0.35	0.16	0.45	0.10	0.05	0.24	0.33	0.41	0.06	0.03	0.17
Wmen	0.21	0.44	0.11	0.16	0.07	0.24	0.45	0.04	0.22	0.04	0.64	0.20	0.02	0.14	0.00
Skilled service workers															
Men	0.10	0.47	0.04	0.06	0.34	0.24	0.42	0.02	0.04	0.28	0.35	0.40	0.06	0.10	0.09
Women	0.10	0.38	0.04	0.36	0.12	0.36	0.37	0.03	0.15	0.08	0.67	0.18	0.00	0.12	0.03
Managers															
Men	0.01	0.41	0.13	0.18	0.27	0.02	0.42	0.14	0.20	0.22	0.11	0.44	0.11	0.17	0.17
Women	0.00	0.43	0.09	0.39	0.10	0.05	0.38	0.09	0.38	0.10	0.16	0.43	0.05	0.33	0.03

Table 6.3 *continued*

Occupation in 1986	Entry cohort														
	1941–60					1961–70					1971–86				
	Immobile	Stable	High-level service	Low-level service	Manual	Immobile	Stable	High-level service	Low-level service	Manual	Immobile	Stable	High-level service	Low-level service	Manual
Unskilled service workers															
Men	0.02	0.33	0.08	0.06	0.51	0.04	0.34	0.13	0.07	0.42	0.13	0.43	0.04	0.05	0.36
Women	0.05	0.47	0.07	0.22	0.19	0.07	0.46	0.08	0.18	0.21	0.31	0.38	0.06	0.16	0.09
Sales workers															
Men	0.04	0.41	0.13	0.07	0.35	0.00	0.43	0.20	0.07	0.30	0.12	0.43	0.15	0.09	0.21
Women	0.06	0.48	0.09	0.23	0.13	0.12	0.41	0.11	0.26	0.10	0.36	0.34	0.05	0.16	0.09
Clerical workers															
Men	0.20	0.42	0.12	0.03	0.23	0.23	0.38	0.20	0.02	0.18	0.58	0.27	0.06	0.02	0.07
Women	0.37	0.41	0.06	0.10	0.06	0.46	0.34	0.06	0.10	0.04	0.66	0.22	0.04	0.06	0.02
Skilled manual workers															
Men	0.19	0.51	0.05	0.02	0.23	0.36	0.34	0.03	0.02	0.24	0.54	0.28	0.02	0.02	0.13
Women	0.16	0.44	0.06	0.15	0.20	0.12	0.36	0.07	0.23	0.23	0.20	0.48	0.05	0.12	0.15
Unskilled manual workers															
Men	0.19	0.55	0.06	0.04	0.17	0.34	0.43	0.04	0.05	0.15	0.54	0.30	0.04	0.04	0.08
Women	0.26	0.46	0.03	0.22	0.03	0.27	0.46	0.03	0.21	0.02	0.58	0.27	0.03	0.11	0.01
Primary and other workers															
Men	0.43	0.33	0.06	0.02	0.17	0.33	0.43	0.05	0.06	0.12	0.41	0.39	0.03	0.02	0.14
Women	0.25	0.35	0.05	0.22	0.12	0.14	0.37	0.06	0.26	0.16	0.60	0.29	0.00	0.11	0.00

these diagonal proportions do still remain below those for women in most other occupations).

Historical Change in Men's Career Patterns

Tables 6.1 to 6.3 utilize virtually the whole of the data set to give us as comprehensive an overview as is possible of careers of men and women in the eleven Esping-Andersen categories. We have been able to compare occupation with occupation, and men with women, but only within the entry cohorts. Obviously, those in the more recent entry cohorts have shorter total working lives, so a given proportion of their working lives spent in one particular occupation has a quite different meaning to that of the same proportion spent by a member of an older entry cohort. So, for example, we can make nothing of the fact that the diagonal proportion of the working lives of women in sales occupations rose from 0.54 for the 1941–60 entry to 0.70 for the 1971–86 entry; this might easily represent, say, an identical set of duration-related probabilities of transition to and from the occupation for the two cohorts.

But if we are willing to sacrifice some of the data set, we can get at least a partial view of change in occupational careers. The coefficients in Tables 6.4 and 6.5 are calculated in a similar way to those of Table 6.3, but with a crucial difference: the final occupational groupings relate not to the respondents' occupations in 1986, but to their occupations after fifteen years in the workforce (and the occupational time budgets and immobility indicators also relate to these first fifteen years of work). This, incidentally, is the reason for organizing the analysis on the basis of respondents' entry to the workforce rather than age. If we had to truncate the cohorts at a given age, then the various occupations would, because of their rather different ages at the end of full-time education, have had significantly different lengths of working lives, and the time budgets for the different occupational groups would have been incommensurable. (Readers should also note that these tables now cover only the first three decade entry cohorts from 1941: obviously, the later cohorts have not completed the necessary fifteen years in employment.)

Table 6.4, therefore, allows us to compare occupational stability in successive male entry cohorts. Consider first the column showing the proportion of each occupation's work-time budget coming from men who were immobile in their fifteenth-year occupation category throughout all their fifteen years in employment. The three broad

Table 6.4   *Proportions of first fifteen years in occupations,* men, UK

Occupation after 15 years	Entry cohort	Immobile	Stable	High service	Low service	Manual
Professional	1941–50	0.11	0.44	0.14	0.02	0.30
	1951–60	0.13	0.43	0.13	0.08	0.21
	1961–70	0.37	0.25	0.14	0.05	0.19
Semi-professional	1941–50	0.09	0.34	0.12	0.07	0.37
	1951–60	0.09	0.50	0.20	0.05	0.16
	1961–70	0.50	0.25	0.06	0.06	0.13
Technical	1941–50	0.08	0.36	0.16	0.03	0.37
	1951–60	0.04	0.49	0.11	0.02	0.34
	1961–70	0.22	0.39	0.08	0.08	0.24
Skilled service	1941–50	0.08	0.48	0.05	0.04	0.35
	1951–60	0.11	0.45	0.04	0.08	0.33
	1961–70	0.32	0.26	0.04	0.08	0.30
Managerial	1941–50	0.00	0.44	0.10	0.18	0.27
	1951–60	0.01	0.39	0.15	0.18	0.27
	1961–70	0.03	0.41	0.13	0.23	0.20
Unskilled service	1941–50	0.03	0.34	0.04	0.07	0.52
	1951–60	0.00	0.32	0.15	0.04	0.49
	1961–70	0.05	0.33	0.09	0.11	0.42
Sales	1941–50	0.09	0.33	0.16	0.08	0.35
	1951–60	0.00	0.46	0.12	0.07	0.35
	1961–70	0.00	0.44	0.13	0.09	0.34
Clerical	1941–50	0.14	0.46	0.16	0.03	0.22
	1951–60	0.28	0.36	0.09	0.03	0.24
	1961–70	0.25	0.44	0.13	0.04	0.15
Skilled manual	1941–50	0.08	0.56	0.07	0.03	0.26
	1951–60	0.31	0.44	0.04	0.01	0.20
	1961–70	0.41	0.31	0.03	0.02	0.24
Unskilled manual	1941–50	0.15	0.60	0.04	0.03	0.18
	1951–60	0.22	0.50	0.07	0.04	0.17
	1961–70	0.43	0.35	0.05	0.05	0.12
Primary, other	1941–50	0.46	0.36	0.02	0.01	0.16
	1951–60	0.38	0.30	0.10	0.04	0.18
	1961–70	0.28	0.43	0.06	0.06	0.18

groupings we found in Table 6.3 emerge here with great clarity.[2] The professional, semi-professional, technical and skilled service categories all show substantial increases in the proportion of their time budgets accounted for by immobile individuals. The three male occupation groups with low career stability in Table 6.3 all retain their very low immobility coefficients, and show no tendency to increase them. Male clerical and manual workers, who had relatively high levels of career stability in Table 6.3, again show relatively high and in two of the three cases quite steeply rising immobility coefficients.

Why, given that the other ten occupational categories conform so well to our expectations from Table 6.3, does the immobility coefficient for the eleventh, the 'primary and other' category tumble so sharply? I was initially inclined to explain this by the very sharp reduction in numbers employed in the primary sector over the period. But of course this should lead to a relatively constant immobility coefficient (on the assumption that the numbers leaving the occupation are relatively constant for each cohort). An alternative answer may relate to the reduction in the size of the British career military establishment during the first two decades of the period; sixteen-year engagement of 'boy soldiers' was a common pattern of military service.

The previously mentioned ending of military conscription in Britain may in turn explain part of the apparently increasing immobility in some of the other occupational categories. We saw previously that, in the first two decade cohorts, those occupations with a relatively young age of entry to the workforce were quite substantially affected by a temporary drain of young workers during their period of military service. That drain of 18-year-olds, in an occupation whose modal age of entry was 14 in 1950, will substantially reduce the immobility coefficient.

This on its own may explain away part of the striking growth in immobility among manual workers. But for the professional, semi-professional and technician categories, this will interact with another process: the growing importance of qualifications derived from the formal educational system for gaining entry to these occupations. At the begining of the period, large parts of all three of these occupational groups in Britain maintained 'apprentice-type' entry systems – dentists and lawyers, as well as social workers and engineering technicians and nurses, could enter these occupations directly, without tertiary-level qualifications, and often without completed secondary education. So while the drain to conscription clearly depressed the immobility coefficient among these occupations for the first and to a lesser degree the second entry cohort (where many would enter the occupation well before they were due for military service), subsequently the drive to professionalization (which emphasized formal educational qualifications) raised both the age of, and the barriers to, entry to these occupations. The particularly fast growth in the immobility coefficients between the two later cohorts presumably reflects the explosively fast growth of tertiary education in Britain between the late 1950s and the early 1970s.

This very rapid growth in the career immobility coefficients is partly, and in one of the four occupational groups concerned, largely, counterbalanced by a decline in the 'other diagonal' category. One might therefore be tempted to dismiss this growth in requirements for qualifications as simply a status inflation effect. But consider the implications of this growth for individuals' life-chances. While there is still an apprentice-type entry route for an occupation, it is in principle possible to enter it from other occupations. But where entry is limited by a requirement for formal educational qualification, and the educational system assumes a single continuous period of full-time education, to be completed prior to entry to the workforce, entry from other occupations rather than direct from the educational system becomes more difficult. This consequence is seen with great clarity in Table 6.4. The 'manual' proportion of the work-time budget of the fifteenth-year professionals falls from 0.30 for the 1941–50 entry, to 0.19 for the 1961–70 entry; for semi-professionals, from 0.37 to 0.13; for technicians, from 0.37 to 0.24. 'Upward mobility' from the manual occupations into these higher-status occupations has been severely curtailed.

Three of the four occupational categories that we placed in the high-level career-stable group as a result of Table 6.3 thus emerge from Table 6.4 as showing substantial increases in career stability over historical time, and consequentially declining opportunities for career mobility. The fourth, skilled service occupations, shows a rather smaller change over this period (but the onward march of professionalization may well produce less career mobility in this group for later cohorts).

The group of occupational categories that we previously categorized as lower grade but career stable similarly shows increasing career stability over time. The sum of the two components of the diagonal for male clerical workers rose from 0.60 to 0.69, for skilled manual workers from 0.64 to 0.72, and for unskilled manual workers from 0.75 to 0.78. And the occupational categories that emerged previously as having relatively low levels of career stability show a striking consistency in this coefficient over time. The total of the two diagonal components for male managerial workers remains just about constant at 0.44 for the three cohorts. For unskilled service workers the sum is 0.37 for the first cohort, falls to 0.32 for the second, and rises again to 0.38 for the third; for sales workers it increases marginally from 0.42 for the first to 0.44 for the third cohort. Notice that for the managerial category, the high proportion from manual and low-level service occupations hardly falls: the proportions of the working life of the fifteenth-year male managers spent in these job categories was 0.45 for the 1941–50 entry cohort, and 0.43 for the 1961–70. This is, in our data, the only remaining substantial route for upwards social mobility. And the growth in professional management education in Britain over the last two decades may serve to close off even this route.

Historical Change in Women's Career Patterns

Women in higher-grade occupations show, with some exceptions, a parallel increase in the immobility coefficients (see Table 6.5). Among professional workers, the extraordinary growth in the proportion of professional women who spend the whole of their first fifteen years of employment in the professions (from 0.13 to 0.62) perhaps reflects an interaction between the general strain towards educational qualification, and the extra determination required for women to achieve entry into employment which maintained (at least until recently) informal bars against their entry. Skilled service work also shows an increase in the immobility coefficient (albeit from a very low 0.16 in the first cohort to something around the male average level of 0.46 for the most recent cohort).

But for the other two categories, semi-professionals and technicians, the growth in immobility is rather less regular (rising from 0.42 to 0.62 and then falling again to 0.48 for the former, and from 0.32 to 0.67 to 0.29 for the latter). It may be connected with the very considerable overall increase in women's rate of participation in paid work (particularly marked for middle-class women from the mid-1950s): perhaps some women who initially entered the workforce in jobs below the level that would be expected for men with equivalent formal qualifications in the expectation that they would leave the labor market subsequently decided to remain and seek career advancement.

And, just as for men, the two components of the diagonal together show regular increases through the cohorts: the professional women's diagonal coefficient rose from 0.64 to 0.76; that of semi-professional women rose from 0.76 to 0.83; of women technicians from 0.62 to 0.71; and of women in skilled services from 0.66 to 0.75. And upwards mobility from manual jobs and (much more important for women than for men) from the lower-skilled service occupations fell in proportion. Mobility into each of these occupational categories is in fact rather more restricted for women than for men.

Table 6.5   *Proportions of first fifteen years in occupations, women, UK*

Occupation after 15 years	Entry cohort	Immobile	Stable	High service	Low service	Manual
Professional	1941–50	0.13	0.51	0.04	0.21	0.12
	1951–60	0.48	0.31	0.01	0.15	0.04
	1961–70	0.62	0.14	0.07	0.13	0.04
Semi-professional	1941–50	0.42	0.34	0.01	0.17	0.04
	1951–60	0.62	0.22	0.02	0.09	0.05
	1961–70	0.48	0.35	0.01	0.13	0.04
Technical	1941–50	0.32	0.30	0.00	0.23	0.15
	1951–60	0.67	0.19	0.05	0.09	0.00
	1961–70	0.29	0.42	0.06	0.21	0.02
Skilled service	1941–50	0.16	0.50	0.02	0.30	0.02
	1951–60	0.28	0.39	0.04	0.17	0.12
	1961–70	0.46	0.29	0.01	0.20	0.04
Managerial	1941–50	0.00	0.38	0.02	0.36	0.24
	1951–60	0.03	0.39	0.09	0.44	0.04
	1961–70	0.05	0.38	0.11	0.33	0.13
Unskilled service	1941–50	0.35	0.36	0.03	0.12	0.15
	1951–60	0.08	0.48	0.07	0.12	0.25
	1961–70	0.08	0.44	0.11	0.19	0.17
Sales	1941–50	0.47	0.31	0.02	0.14	0.06
	1951–60	0.30	0.40	0.08	0.12	0.10
	1961–70	0.22	0.38	0.08	0.17	0.15
Clerical	1941–50	0.70	0.19	0.03	0.04	0.04
	1951–60	0.62	0.23	0.04	0.06	0.05
	1961–70	0.59	0.25	0.05	0.07	0.03
Skilled manual	1941–50	0.21	0.43	0.02	0.17	0.16
	1951–60	0.32	0.30	0.08	0.12	0.18
	1961–70	0.24	0.27	0.05	0.24	0.20
Unskilled manual	1941–50	0.57	0.27	0.01	0.13	0.03
	1951–60	0.47	0.34	0.02	0.13	0.03
	1961–70	0.39	0.38	0.03	0.18	0.02
Primary, other	1941–50	0.22	0.49	0.01	0.11	0.18
	1951–60	0.39	0.32	0.04	0.15	0.11
	1961–70	0.16	0.39	0.06	0.26	0.14

The pattern for women managerial workers is rather similar to that of men in this occupation: a rather limited rise in the diagonal sum, from 0.38 to 0.43, coupled with a rather high (though somewhat declining) rate of recruitment from low-level service and manual occupations. Again, in our data, this represents a surviving avenue of upwards mobility which may prove to have been blocked for later entry cohorts by the march of 'professional management'.

As we suspected from Table 6.3, women in the unskilled service and sales occupations have rather different career patterns to those of men. For the first cohort, quite unlike men, these two occupations showed considerable career stability, with a diagonal sum of 0.71 for unskilled service workers and 0.78 for sales workers (where the male equivalents were 0.37 and 0.42 respectively). The explanation for the difference is clear from Figure 6.3: these were (and to a lesser degree still are) largely female-segregated occupations, just as domestic service was for earlier generations of women. Those few men in these occupations did not, for this reason, consider them to be career locations (as evidenced by the very small proportion of 'immobile' time for these men). And, again in contrast to men, these occupations show substantial declines in career stability through the cohorts (though the diagonal coefficients for the 1961–70 cohort, 0.52 for unskilled services, 0.60 for sales, are still substantially above the male equivalents of 0.38 and 0.44).

This declining career stability for women in sales and unskilled services mirrors similar declines in career stability for the fifteenth-year women manual workers. Those women in the skilled manual category (whose diagonal sum fell from 0.64 to 0.51) show a divergence from men in this category, whose diagonal sum rose over the three cohorts (from 0.64 to 0.72). Unskilled women manual workers have a small decline in their diagonal sum, from 0.84 to 0.77, in this case converging with that of male unskilled manuals whose fifteen-year career stability index rose from 0.75 to 0.78.

So the overall picture of change for women is in part similar and in part dissimilar to that for men: substantial increases in career stability for the higher-level occupations (which means decreases in the possibility of upwards mobility during the working life); high (but, unlike men, declining) career stability in clerical and unskilled manual work; lower (and, again unlike men, declining) career stability for unskilled services, sales and skilled manual occupations; and managerial work remaining (at least until the most recent entries to the labour market) the sole potential route for substantial upward career mobility.

Post-industrial Careers in Britain

We can summarize the foregoing quite succinctly. We can envisage three distinct sorts of historical change in careers. Some occupations might follow *Pattern A*, in which we see, in successive cohorts, a growing career stability, but no growth in immobility. That is, people spend more of their first fifteen years in the fifteenth-year occupation even though their first job was not in that occupation. But rather more frequently we find *Pattern B*, in which, by contrast, there is a historically growing proportion of the occupational time accounted for by occupationally immobile people. In this case, the proportion of within-career entry is falling, at successive historical points, as more of the time in the occupation is spent by people who entered it at the begining of their working lives; this trend might be described as 'professionalization'. Contrasting with this is *Pattern C*, the converse historical trend: de-professionalization or de-skilling indicated in the tables by growth in the non-stable off-diagonal categories.

For men, we see the progress towards career immobility (i.e. Pattern B) in the professions, semi-professions, technicians and skilled service workers, and among the clerical and manual workers, and the relative mobility among managerial, unskilled service and sales workers. For women, we see a similar progress towards immobility for the higher-grade occupations (with the exception of the technician group, which shifts towards greater mobility between the 1951–60 and the 1961–70 cohorts – though the net change in this occupational category between 1941–50 and 1961–70 is still towards immobility) and a near constancy for the managerial group. But the remaining five women's occupational groups are becoming *more* mobile; though (with the important exception of unskilled manual workers) this is the opposite direction of *change* to men, it nevertheless represents something like a convergence in *absolute levels* of mobility with the equivalent male categories. (The growing divergence in career mobility between male and female unskilled manual workers appears from Tables 6.4 and 6.5 to reflect the greater availability of sales and service jobs to unskilled women.)

This quite compact summary of patterns of mobility, when combined with the pictures of the changes in the sizes of the various occupational groups given by Figures 6.1 to 6.6, provides us with the answer to the central question of the nature of the change in career stratification that has accompanied the post-industrial occupational structure in Britain.

The higher-status occupational groups, which comprise a growing proportion of all employment, show increasing career immobility for both men and women. The Daniel Bell-type service elite becomes more self-contained, recruiting direct from the educational system, and less dependent on flows from lower-status occupations. Given Bell's (1976) view of the centrality of theoretical knowledge, which, as it grows in importance for processes of production, serves to increase the power of the new service class, it is in a sense unsurprising that the older processes whereby people gained access to higher-level occupations by acquiring knowledge empirically in the course of their working lives should be supplanted by more formal educational processes. But there is nothing in this model that makes it necessary that this formal education should be completed *prior to the first entry into the workforce*: I shall return to this point in a moment.

Male manual manufacturing workers, a historically declining proportion of the working population, show a similar increase in career stability. We cannot explain this as a converse of the previous phenomenon, since the flow from higher- to lower-status jobs has (to judge from Tables 6.4 and 6.5) always been more limited than its converse. But we may assume that there has been a parallel growth of more formalized qualification for these lower-level jobs, reducing flows between the various categories of less-skilled manual and service occupations. (However, at least part of the difference between the first and second age cohort is an artifactual consequence of the previously mentioned ending of military conscription.) The proportion of manual jobs classed as skilled has increased relative to unskilled, so we cannot support at least the more simple-minded version of the Braverman de-skilling thesis; but perhaps the growing immobility of the two groups corresponds to a more sophisticated reading of it.

The low-skilled service and sales occupations are a small part of overall male employment (around 5 percent of male jobs after fifteen years in the workforce); the relatively high mobility of this group confirms its status as providing transitional employment – not, however, as in my optimistic parable at the beginning of the chapter, providing a staging post for transition into higher-level occupations, but rather leading to other low-level service or manufacturing industry jobs.

The declining career stability of all the lower-level female occupational categories may have some important implications for stratification. The largest and fastest growing group of employed women are in the low-skilled services and sales occupations, and though it does not appear that women are fixed in these locations, it is plain from Table 6.5 that we have a *circulation* of women among these various manufacturing and particularly service industrial jobs. And the decline in career stability among these groups over the cohorts we can study from the SCEL data suggests that the jobs involved are increasingly insecure, and do not bring even the limited benefits that come with a sustained career in one occupation.

The emerging pattern of career stratification in Britain may thus be summarized as follows: a service elite, growing both as a proportion of the workforce and in its career stability; management remaining, by the 1970s, the main route of upward career mobility (though we may suspect that the growth of formal management education may also cut away this route in the future); a male industrial proletariat, declining in size, but also increasing in career stability; and a growing female proletariat, decreasingly specialized as between manufacturing and services (though the SCEL materials we have examined do not provide any direct evidence for this, we may nevertheless infer that the increasing career mobility in this group corresponds to increasingly insecure conditions of employment). There is no evidence here of a specific low-level service class; rather, it appears that the low-skilled services form part of a more general pool of low-skill, low career stability jobs for women.

Some Implications

This picture plainly has some important implications for educational policy. I have argued that the logic of the increasingly complex nature of production in advanced societies may act, through a growing demand for formal educational qualifications, to reduce career mobility.

If the educational system worked so as to offer chances to children irrespective of their parents' advantages, this would not necessarily be a worrying development. But the system does not work this way in Britain (or anywhere else), nor, through fifty years of various forms of British educational policy largely designed to achieve such a pattern of opportunity, have we gained any clear idea of how it might be achieved. Parents' advantages are quite reliably reproduced in their children by the educational system. We have seen that in Britain, over this same fifty years, prospects of upward mobility *within* careers have also been quite strikingly diminished. Hence, overall life-chances for the worse-off part of society are also severely diminished.

Which brings us back to my starting point. The short-order cook/ corporate lawyer example with which I introduced this paper is clearly a possible route for upward occupational mobility. But in Britain over recent decades, it has happened with sharply diminishing frequency; British 'transitional' jobs are not part of an upward career trajectory. Such jobs can only facilitate upwards mobility where there is systematic, reliable and sustained institutional support for the acquisition of formal qualifications that goes well beyond the standard educational provisions for children and young adults. This support is, to judge from the evidence we have considered, lacking in Britain.

By recognizing parents' rights to choose their children's education, we necessarily reproduce patterns of advantage within the educational system. If we wish to improve life-chances without infringing these parental rights, we must therefore look to educational provisions later in life, once children are removed from their parents' immediate milieu and begin to formulate their own life plans. The logic of production in a post-industrial society advantages those with theoretical knowledge. Advantaged parents may be expected to give their children advantaged access to this early in their lives. We should therefore perhaps give priority to improving the access of the less advantaged to formal education later in the life-course. The cook is now less likely to become a lawyer in Britain than once was the case; there are some strong arguments for public policy to reinstate and promote this form of mobility.

A second major area of concern is the apparent emergence of increasing numbers of low-status, unstable careers for women. Explaining these goes beyond the scope of this chapter, but we may have a strong presumption that it relates, not to newly emerging features of the post-industrial occupational structure, but to the persistence of traditional household and family structures – specifically women's differential responsibilities for providing family care – in the context of women's increasing desire for formal employment. There are also clearly potential policy responses to this phenomenon: improved child-care provisions, extensions in rights for parental leave and parental job protection. These are all areas in which Britain lags considerably behind the other countries described in this volume.

Notes

1. The following account leaves aside the question of households' rather than individuals' locations in a system of stratification. Also, we do not discuss the role of unemployment in career patterns; I have discussed this at length in a separate article (Gershuny and Marsh, 1993). In the life history data discussed below, spells of unemployment are reclassified to the respondent's occupation in the last-held job.

2. We might parenthetically note that the consistency between the cross-sectional patterns that emerge from the fifteen-year and the whole-career coefficients suggests that we do not lose too much by truncating the data to give longitudinal comparisons.

7

Does Post-industrialism Matter?
The Canadian Experience

John Myles, Garnett Picot and Ted Wannell

Post-industrialism's New Class Structure?

During the 1980s, the downside of post-industrialism became a public issue in North America. As Canada and the United States began to come out of the Great Recession of the early 1980s, emergent employment patterns came in for considerable attention. In Europe, recovery was accompanied by stagnant or even negative job growth, bringing the new metaphors of 'jobless growth' and 'post-employment society' into the social science lexicon. In contrast, employment levels in North America rose strongly after 1983. The bad news was that much of this growth occurred in the low-wage segment of the service economy and manufacturing employment was comparatively stagnant. As a result, the 'McJobs' scenario – a picture of the future depicting a massive shift of employment out of well-paid manufacturing jobs into low-paying service employment – became increasingly popular in the press, among academics, in social policy circles and the labour movement. Summarizing two years of research on the service economy, the Economic Council of Canada, a semi-official 'think tank' that advises the Canadian government, painted a gloomy portrait of Canada's post-industrial labor market trends in a report entitled *Good Jobs, Bad Jobs* published in 1989, and with more detail in *Employment in the Service Economy* in 1991.[1]

Relative to the European experience, the service economy is not 'new' in North America. As Joachim Singelmann (1978) has shown, Canada and the United States did not follow the classical trajectory described by the Fisher–Clark thesis of employment shifts from primary to secondary and, subsequently, tertiary industries. The shift of employment from agriculture into goods and services occurred simultaneously. 'In both countries,' Singelmann concludes, 'the decline of agriculture led to a concomitant growth of transformative and service industries, with services overtaking the transformative sector by the turn of the century (1978: 1233). The employment share of the transformative sector (manufacturing, primary and construction) peaked at about one-half of total employment, in Canada during the 1950s and in the United States in the 1960s. These North American peaks occurred sooner and at lower levels than in Europe.

In view of this long experience with 'post-industrialism', why the concern now? Until the 1980s, the prevailing view of post-industrialism had been decidedly optimistic, closer to Daniel Bell's (1976) vision of the 'knowledge society' than Harry Braverman's (1974) gloomy picture of the next stage in the 'degradation of labor'. What had changed? First, the mid-1970s marked the end of the long postwar boom that brought rising wages and living standards to North American workers. In Canada, hourly wages and salaries peaked in 1976 and then fell, rising slowly during the recovery of the 1980s but not returning to the postwar highs of the mid-1970s (Economic Council of Canada, 1991: 137).

Compounding this development was the changing character of service sector growth. During the 1950s and 1960s, the shift to services had largely meant growth in public administration and the 'welfare state industries' associated with health, education and social services (Picot, 1986). Relative to traditional employment in goods production, these sectors provided a large number of 'good jobs' for both women and men. Changes in the industrial mix of employment were modest during the 1970s but accelerated once again in the 1980s. Two features of the recent changes drew particular attention. The first was 'de-industrialization'. Employment in manufacturing began to decline not just as a share of total employment but in absolute terms as well. Relative to previous recessions, the manufacturing jobs lost in the 1981–2 recession were slow to return. Not until 1989 did the manufacturing workforce at 2.1 million return to 1981 levels. It then fell dramatically during the 1990–1 recession, to 1.8 million by mid-1991. The second reason for concern was the changing character of service employment. Despite continued expansion in social and business services, consumer and retail services were becoming a major source of new employment, accounting for 341,590 of the 770,790 new jobs added to the economy between 1981 and 1989.

The reason for concern over this shift in employment patterns is highlighted in Figure 7.1, where we contrast the wage and skill profiles of seven industry sectors.[2] Business services, social services and public administration ('government') have comparatively few low-skill or low-wage jobs; consumer and retail services have a large number of both. In manufacturing, there are a large number of

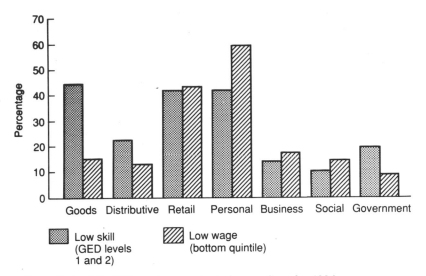

Figure 7.1 *Job skills and wages by industry, Canada, 1986*

Skills data: 1986 Census of Canada; wages data: Statistics Canada, 1986 Labour Market Activity Survey

unskilled jobs but comparatively few low-wage jobs. In services, by contrast, wages tend to follow skills.[3] Potentially, then, a massive shift of labor from unskilled manufacturing to unskilled jobs in services could mark the end of North America's high-wage working class. The 'working class' of industrial capitalism made up of unskilled *but* well-paid blue-collar workers is replaced by a low-skill *and* low-wage post-industrial working class in services.

In 1983, Bob Kuttner captured this imagery with the metaphor of the 'declining middle class.' De-industrialization and the shift to services, he argued, was leading to a polarization of the class structure between an elite of well-paid knowledge workers and a larger mass of unskilled service workers. The core of the traditional North American 'middle class' – high-wage workers in manufacturing, construction, utilities and transportation – was eroding and with it the social structure on which postwar social harmony had been constructed. The process of 'embourgeoisement' that brought suburban homes, automobiles and income security to working-class families in the 1950s and 1960s was over. But is it so?

We take up the answer to this question in four parts. The first two sections describe what is *not* happening. In the usual 'post-industrial' scenarios, the culprit invoked to explain the declining fortunes of North American workers is the changing employment mix that results from the shift from goods to services. In the first section, we ask whether the shift to services has brought into being a 'new service proletariat', a fraction of the working class who should be thought of as a post-industrial underclass whose life-chances are inferior to and whose material interests are different from those of the traditional working class of industrial capitalism. Based on somewhat limited evidence, our tentative answer to this question is no. As in the United States (see Jacobs, this volume), the Canadian results indicate that low-wage, low-skill jobs in services and sales are 'stop-gap jobs' that mainly serve as 'ports of entry' or 'launching pads' for new labor force entrants and 'ports of exit' for older workers. In the second section, we summarize results of our previous studies (Myles et al., 1988; Picot et al., 1990) on the role of the shift to services in altering the structure of wages and earnings in Canada. We conclude that while the structure of wages and earnings in Canada has become more polarized since the 1960s, the shift to services has *not* been the major motor driving this development. In effect, if the term 'post-industrialism' is used simply to describe changes in the occupational and industrial mix of employment then the answer to the question 'Does post-industrialism matter?' is 'not very much'! Relative to other economy-wide changes, the effects of industrial restructuring in this conventional sense are modest.

If the service economy is not the culprit it has been made out to be, what is? In the third section we will argue that the critics of restructuring have been looking in the wrong place with the wrong analytical tools. Restructuring can take place in two ways, not one: as a result of changes in the mix of occupations and industries or by restructuring *within* occupations and industries. It is the latter, not the former, that has been altering North American earnings patterns and life-chances. By looking only at shifts in employment *between* industries and occupations, much of the movement and restructuring is missed. Both Canadian and American studies of employment restructuring show that job losses and gains take place primarily through a redistribution of jobs among firms *within* rather than *between* industries (Baldwin and Gorecki, 1990; Davis and Haltiwanger, 1990). Inter-firm competition within industries results in the decline or death of some firms, and the expansion and creation of others. In this way, new jobs are created and wage structures are altered since wage rates in existing jobs are less likely to adjust to economic pressures than are wages in newly created jobs. The consequence of this restructuring is potentially even more serious than envisioned by the de-industrialization theorists. Inter-firm restructuring within industries has resulted in a more polarized distribution of wages and earnings *within all* industries and occupations, that is, in the economy as a whole.

Wage polarization in the 1980s has been compounded by the end of real growth in wages and earnings. In the fourth section, we show that the main result of these changes has been to alter substantially the 'mobility regime' of North American workers and their families. Relative to the experiences of the generations who entered the labor market in the quarter century following World War II, the path to 'upward mobility' for recent cohorts has become longer and harder.

A New Service Proletariat?

Whether or not low-wage service employment creates the potential for the emergence of a 'new class' or new class fraction in Western capitalism depends on several factors. As shown in Chapter 2, unskilled service workers still constitute no more than 10 to 12 percent of the labor force in most countries. However, when we add retail sales occupations, the majority of which are also low wage and low skill (see also Jacobs, this volume), the figure rises to about 18 percent of the Canadian labor force, 15 percent of men and 23 percent of women. Hence, as a share of total employment, the size of the low-wage service sector is substantial and growing. What remains at issue is whether these new 'servant jobs' are becoming the site for the formation of a new 'servant class'.

The answer to this question depends not on the size of the sector but rather on the nature of the temporal connection between a set of positions (unskilled service occupations) and the individual biographies of the people who fill them. Following Goldthorpe, Mark Western (1991) uses the term 'demographic class formation' to describe this link. Demographic class formation occurs when the individual biographies of the members of a class demonstrate a 'continuity of class content', that is, when 'they consist of people whose class membership endures over their lifetime and whose social relationships are largely confined within a given class' (Western, 1991: 62). Traditionally, most male blue-collar workers got their jobs as young men and spent all or a good part of their lives in the same job or circulating between a limited set of similar jobs. Since they spent most or a significant part of their lives in this 'class' they had an interest in its fate, they developed social bonds with other blue-collar workers, and formed unions and parties to pursue their collective interests. The question then is whether the post-industrial working class is like this. Or are the low-skilled, low-wage service jobs 'stop-gap' jobs, places which people 'pass through' on their way to somewhere else?

The ideal data for answering this question are life history data that allow for detailed reconstruction of individual biographies. Since there are no Canadian data of this sort we are forced to rely on indirect evidence of two kinds, cohort data for specific occupations over a twenty-year period and short-term (twelve-month) occupational exit rates for selected occupations.

In Table 7.1, we show the percentage of men in selected occupations (based on Esping-Andersen's classification shown in Chapter 2) by age for 1961, 1971 and 1981. The data are from the Decennial Census of Canada. The occupations are selected to contrast the traditional site of male working-class employment (unskilled and skilled manual occupations) with unskilled service and sales occupations. Together, these four broad categories accounted for 56 percent of male employment in 1981. The first five columns of each table divide the labour force into ten-year age groups so that cohort flows can be followed over time (by reading the diagonals of the table). The last two columns divide the younger workforce into narrower age bands (15–20, 21–6) simply to provide more detail on the age concentration of selected occupations.

It should be noted that these cohorts do not necessarily consist of the same people in the different time periods. These are not longitudinal data in which people are tracked through time. Thus, determining occupational mobility of individuals is not possible from this data set. Nonetheless, knowledge of the *proportion* of a cohort in a particular occupation and how that proportion changes as a cohort ages can provide valuable evidence on likely occupational flows. For example, the distributions in Table 7.1 indicate that unskilled service jobs have become increasingly important as a point of entry to the labor market for young men. Between 1961 and 1981, unskilled service occupations increased from 10.2 to 17.7 percent of all jobs held by 15- to 20-year-old males. Much of this may be the increase in part-time service sector employment among young males, but even if it is, one might expect this to lead to full-time unskilled service sector jobs for some. It is clear, however, that young men do not stay in these jobs for long. For men in their late twenties and early thirties, the percentage in unskilled service jobs is the same in the 1980s as it was in the 1960s despite the rising percentage of young men who begin in these jobs.

Historically, service occupations have also provided a 'port of exit' for older males who began their work-lives in more physically demanding blue-collar occupations (Melz, 1969). This pattern can be seen in Table 7.1 by inspection of the diagonals. Whereas only 5.3 percent of men aged 35–44 in 1961 were in unskilled services, by the time these men were aged 55–64, in 1981, 9.1 percent were employed in such jobs. But the declining significance of this pattern

Table 7.1 Percentage of employed men in selected occupations by age, Canada, 1961–81

	15–24	25–34	35–44	45–54	55–64	15–20	21–6
Unskilled service							
1961	8.1	4.6	5.3	7.3	10.6	10.2	5.7
1971	11.2	4.5	5.0	7.2	11.2	17.6	6.3
1981	11.9	4.5	3.9	5.5	9.1	17.7	6.3
Sales							
1961	8.2	9.5	11.21	11.7	9.8	8.2	8.0
1971	7.5	9.7	9.9	9.9	10.5	7.4	7.9
1981	7.5	8.5	8.7	8.8	8.6	7.4	7.8
Unskilled manual							
1961	33.0	28.9	26.7	25.7	26.2	33.5	30.9
1971	32.7	23.8	24.2	22.8	21.9	35.6	28.2
1981	28.8	22.6	19.6	20.9	19.2	28.2	28.2
Skilled manual							
1961	12.8	20.1	22.7	22.9	23.7	11.1	16.2
1971	11.9	17.8	21.4	21.5	19.9	9.1	15.3
1981	14.6	17.6	18.9	21.0	19.2	11.3	17.6

Source: Decennial Census of Canada

is also evidenced by the fact that the proportion of 55- to 64-year-old men in unskilled services actually declined from 10.6 to 9.1 percent between 1961 and 1981. For men aged 35–54, the proportions in unskilled service occupations have also declined over time. The percentage of 35- to 44-year-old men in these jobs fell from 5.3 to 3.9 percent between 1961 and 1981 and among 45- to 54-year-olds it declined from 7.3 to 5.5 percent. In sum, since the 1960s, unskilled service occupations have grown in importance as a point of labor market entry for men but the importance of such jobs over the remainder of the male adult life-course has declined. And as shown in the table, sales occupations declined in significance in all age groups.

As in the past, *the core working-class occupations for men continue to be skilled and unskilled manual jobs.* In 1981, 43.4 percent of 15- to 24- and 38.5 percent of 35- to 44-year-olds were in these occupations. Over time, there has been a shift in the mix of skilled and unskilled manual work, with a move towards more young men entering skilled jobs. The proportion of 15- to 24-year-olds in unskilled manual jobs fell from 33 to 29 percent over the two decades, while it rose from 13 to 15 percent in skilled manual jobs. Furthermore, as evident from both the cross-section and the cohort flows, the percentage of men in unskilled manual jobs declines early in the life-course and the percentage in skilled manual occupations rises until their forties. At least until the 1980s, then, the main effect of the shift to services was simply to postpone, not reduce, entry into traditional blue-collar jobs for men.

The patterns for women (Table 7.2) are even more striking. Here we contrast unskilled service and sales occupations with clerical work, the latter being the main source of 'working-class' jobs for women. Young women enter unskilled service jobs in larger numbers than young men but, remarkably, the percentage of women who begin their work-lives in such jobs has scarcely changed since the 1960s, rising from 22.9 to 24.5 percent among 15- to 20-year-old women and declining from 12.9 to 11.6 percent among women aged 21–6.

Moreover, the proportion of women in unskilled services declines quite quickly with age. In 1971 20 percent of women aged 15–24 were in unskilled service occupations. A decade later (1981) only 10 percent of these women (now aged 25–34) were in the same types of jobs. Although these are not necessarily the same women (since these are not longitudinal data which track individuals), the percentages indicate that, at the very least, one-half of these women had exited from unskilled service occupations by 1981. Finally, the proportion of women in unskilled services over the age of 25 has

Table 7.2 *Percentage of employed women in selected occupations by age, Canada, 1961–81*

	15–24	25–34	35–44	45–54	55–64	15–20	21–6
Unskilled service							
1961	18.7	14.8	17.3	18.8	26.0	22.9	12.9
1971	19.9	12.3	14.6	17.3	21.3	27.2	12.4
1981	18.3	10.3	12.2	14.2	16.8	24.5	11.6
Sales							
1961	8.6	8.7	14.8	16.7	13.1	11.3	5.3
1971	8.6	5.4	10.1	13.6	13.6	11.6	5.1
1981	10.2	6.3	8.7	11.0	11.9	13.0	7.2
Clerical							
1961	39.5	36.5	29.7	24.6	20.3	37.3	41.7
1971	40.2	37.5	34.6	33.2	28.5	36.3	43.1
1981	40.5	37.7	33.9	32.8	31.0	36.5	43.5

Source: Decennial Census of Canada

been falling since 1961, indicating that women are more likely to move out of these jobs in the 1980s than in the 1960s. Approximately 19 percent of all women aged 15–24 are found in unskilled service jobs in all three periods but the proportion of 35- to 44-year-old women in similar jobs fell from 17 percent in 1961 to 12 percent in 1981. As with young men, unskilled service jobs provide a significant number of entry-level jobs for young women, but the significance of such jobs over the rest of the life-course has declined, not increased, with time.

The cohort-specific patterns for women in sales occupations tell a similar story. Employment in sales has risen among young women but declined among middle-aged and older women. Instead, better-paying clerical jobs, always the main site of female employment, have increased in importance for middle-aged and older women.[4]

For both sexes, then, the evidence points away from a 'new service proletariat' scenario. As they have grown, unskilled service and sales occupations have become increasingly important as ports of entry to the labor market for young workers but not as permanent sites of life-time employment.

A second source of information on occupational mobility, this time true longitudinal data for a twelve-month period, leads to similar conclusions. The occupational 'exit rates' in Table 7.3 – the percentage of persons employed full-time in an occupation who have left the occupation at the end of a twelve-month interval – also highlight the transitional character of unskilled service jobs. As indicated by the age-specific patterns, there is enormous volatility in the youth labor market in general. Between one-third and one-half of people exit from the broad occupational classifications over a one-year period, depending upon the occupation. But young men and young women exit from unskilled service and sales occupations at higher rates (in the 50 percent range) than from other occupations (in the 35 percent range). Young men also leave clerical jobs in large numbers.

Table 7.3 *One-year occupational exit rates (percent), full-time employees, by age and sex, Canada, 1986–7*

	Women		Men	
	16–24	25–34	16–24	25–34
Unskilled service	52	32	43	28
Sales	50	37	49	25
Clerical	35	22	48	17
Skilled manual	36	38	35	17
Unskilled manual	33	22	38	23

Source: Statistics Canada, Labour Market Activity Survey

In short, in response to the question of whether the service sector is becoming increasingly important as a site for the formation of a new 'service proletariat' that recruits and maintains its members over an extended period of the life-course, the answer seems to be no. The result is not entirely surprising. Wage levels are among the best predictors of job exit and entry: workers, not surprisingly, leave low-wage jobs in pursuit of better-paying jobs and once in them will try to stay there (Picot and Baldwin, 1990; Morisette et al., 1992). Similarly, employers have little incentive to try to retain workers in jobs with minimal skill and training requirements. They will not introduce higher wage rates to retain workers if productivity resulting from the training and from specific knowledge is not forthcoming. It would seem that the high rate of growth of unskilled service and retail jobs is largely concentrated among the young; the proportion of older workers in these jobs has not been rising. A larger share of young workers now use such jobs to enter the labor market but the evidence suggests that exit rates are quite high as many move on to other types of employment.

What these results do suggest, however, is that the shift to services is resulting in a restructuring of the economic life-course. Young people's entry into better-paying occupations is being delayed and this period of 'apprenticeship' in low-wage services is likely to become longer as service employment rises. There is certainly good prima facie evidence for this conclusion. As we show in Figure 7.2, the relative wages of younger workers fell dramatically during the 1980s while the relative wages of older workers tended to rise. This change in the age–earnings profile can be traced to the late 1970s and is evident among both sexes and all regions of the country. The question remains, however, as to whether the shift to services accounts for this change. The answer to the question presupposes some understanding of the relation between the shift to services, 'de-industrialization', and wage structures more generally.

The Shift to Services and Changing Wage Structures: In Search of the Declining Middle

During the 1980s, the search for the declining middle began in earnest in both Canada and the United States. The debate was at once political, methodological and substantive. It was political because implicit in the de-industrialization thesis advanced by authors such as Bluestone and Harrison (1982) and popularized by Kuttner (1983) was a critique of the revival of the laissez-faire economic policies of the Reagan administration. If unleashing market forces was destroying America's 'middle class', then pre-

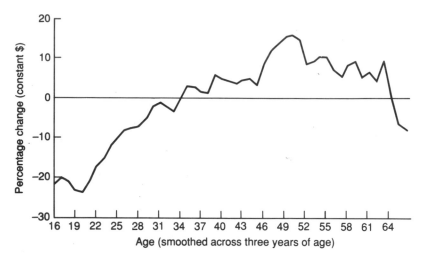

Figure 7.2   *Change in average hourly wages by age, Canada,*
1981–6 (1981 Survey of Work History and Statistics Canada,
1986)

sumably something else was called for, preferably an industrial
strategy that would save traditional wage patterns and living
standards. Following the release of the first major paper showing
that American earnings were indeed becoming more polarized
(Bluestone and Harrison, 1986), the debate turned to questions of
methodology requiring new solutions to a whole set of new technical
problems.[5]

As the technical issues were resolved, the facts of the matter, if
not the reasons for them, became widely accepted.[6] Our analyses at
Statistics Canada, for example, showed a shift of about 8 percentage
points out of the 'middle' earnings levels into the bottom (4.2
percent) and into the top (3.8 percent) of the distribution between
1967 and 1986 (Picot et al., 1990). Disaggregations of this pattern
indicate that most of this change occurred in the 1980s, that is, that
the trend was accelerating with time. But was post-industrialism/ de-
industrialization the culprit? Both Canadian and American analyses
soon showed that while changes in the industrial and occupational
structure were part of the story, their role was a minor one. Change
in the distribution of wages (and job skills) was occurring more
rapidly than could be explained by shifts in the mix of jobs among
industries and occupations.

During the 1980s, the service sector's share of full-time equivalent
jobs increased by almost 4 percentage points, rising from 66 percent
to 70 percent. This is almost as much of a shift as occurred in either

the 1960s or the 1970s. In principle, such shifts might account for the changing wage pattern but in fact their contribution was modest. In Canada, changes in industrial composition accounted for 13 percent of the total change in the wage distribution and only 11 percent of the growth in low-wage jobs during the 1980s (Myles et al., 1988). These and other results[7] are similar to those reported from comparable American studies (Lawrence, 1984; Tilly et al., 1987; Jacobs, this volume). In sum, little of the shift in wage or earnings distribution is accounted for by the changing industrial mix of employment.

What of changes in the occupational structure? One of the earliest (and, for sociologists, most important) lessons learned from the 'declining-middle' research is that changes in occupational structure are a poor guide to changes in wage and earnings distributions. In an early study, Neal Rosenthal (1985) ranked occupations by median earnings and showed that the proportion of jobs in low-paying *occupations* in the United States had declined between 1973 and 1982. From this he concluded that the proportion of low-paying *jobs* had also declined. McMahon and Tschetter (1986), however, soon demonstrated the fallacy underlying this conclusion: earnings distributions within occupations are not constant. The earnings distributions within occupations had shifted downward so that over this period there was an *increasing* proportion of low-paying jobs.

The extent to which changes in occupational structure can be misleading when drawing conclusions about wages and earnings can be shown by contrasting trends in wages and earnings with changes in the skill distribution of occupations. Changes in occupational structure have continued to favor high-skill over low-skill occupations (Boyd, 1990; Economic Council of Canada, 1991; Myles, 1988). Growth was especially high in managerial, professional and technical occupations right through the 1980s. However, changes in occupational mix, while significant, contribute rather little to change in wage and earnings structures. Between 1981 and 1986, occupational shifts accounted for only 19 percent of the change in the economy-wide wage distribution in Canada (Myles et al., 1988: 58).

The joint effect of changes in the industry and occupational mix accounted for only 22 percent of the total change in the distribution of wage rates in jobs during the 1980s (Myles et al., 1988: 61). All of these results proved to be robust irrespective of sex, age (though more on this below) or whether we considered all jobs or only those jobs held on a full-time basis (i.e. the growth in part-time employment has little to do with the changes observed here).

What of the youth labor market? As noted earlier, the shift to low-wage service occupations has had its main impact on the young and, since the 1970s, there has been substantial wage polarization between age cohorts. Does growing service employment among the young explain the shift in the age–earnings profile? The 1980s brought quite substantial shifts in employment patterns for both young men and young women away from higher-paying occupations into low-wage services and sales occupations. But as in the economy as a whole, these occupation and industry shifts explain only a modest share of the decline in youth wages. The percentage of young workers employed full-time who were earning less than $5.25 per hour increased by a remarkable 13.5 percentage points between 1981 and 1986 but only 2 percentage points was due to the changing industry mix of employment (Myles et al., 1988: 66).

In sum, wage restructuring was a major and defining feature of the Canadian economy in the 1980s but 'post-industrial restructuring' in the usual meaning of that term – the changing industry and occupational mix of employment – was not the principal motor driving this change. The point is not that the growth and decline in low- and high-wage occupations or low- and high-wage industries are of no significance. The McJobs scenarios (increasing numbers of jobs in low-wage services) that became so popular in the 1980s are real but they also distract us from more fundamental changes taking place.

The McJobs Scenario: What's Wrong With It?

The results summarized in the previous section clearly put the usual version of the McJobs phenomenon into question. But just what is wrong with this scenario? We will argue that accounts emphasizing the growth of low-wage consumer services as the 'motor' behind the changing wage distribution of jobs have mistaken the symptom for the cause. During the 1980s, wage polarization in Canada took the form of a rising wage gap between middle-aged and younger workers. The shift in the age–earnings profile, however, was an economy-wide pheonomenon: the downward shift in youth wages was characteristic of all industries and occupations. This shift was only more apparent in consumer services because of the large number of young people employed in this sector and the public visibility of such jobs.

Within consumer services, the share of jobs at the bottom of the wage distribution (paying less than $6.74 in 1986) held by workers aged 16–24 rose by almost 17 percentage points between 1981 and

1986. The pattern in consumer services, however, was evident in all sectors. The share of low-wage jobs among young, *full-time* workers increased by 13 percent in natural resources, 15 percent in manufacturing, 16 percent in construction, 13 percent in distributive services, 7 percent in business services, 15 percent in health, education and welfare and 14 percent in public administration.

Similar, though more modest, downward shifts also occurred among 25- to 34-year-olds *in all industry sectors*. In contrast, among older cohorts there was a general shift from lower to higher wage levels.[8] In effect, what was in fact an economy-wide trend (declining entry-level wages) became identified with one of its manifestations, low-wage employment in the expanding consumer service sector. The reasons for this error are not difficult to discern: young people make up a disproportionate share of employees in consumer sector jobs, which by their very nature are highly visible to the public.

Until recently, the deteriorating labor market position of young people in the North American labor market was the *locus classicus* for demonstrating Easterlin's thesis that one's fortune in life is a function of the size of one's birth cohort. As predicted, the earnings of young North American men and women began to decline when the large 'baby boom' cohorts entered the labor market in the 1970s (Welch, 1979). Not surprisingly, 'generational crowding' – the argument that declining youth wages were a result of intense wage competition resulting from the large number of young people in the baby boom cohorts – was soon advanced to account for North America's declining middle (Lawrence, 1984; Levy, 1988). This supply-side account is an optimistic one in the sense that if generational crowding accounts for wage restructuring we can expect things to return to 'normal' as the baby boom passes through the system. As we move from 'baby boom' to 'baby bust', the age–earnings profile should shift again in favour of younger workers.

To date, however, the 'birth and fortune' thesis has not been a good predictor of trends. Indeed, the wages of young people began an even more precipitous decline after the baby boom cohorts peaked in the mid- to late seventies in both Canada (Picot et al., 1990) and the United States (Lillard and Macunovich, 1988). As might be expected, the decline accelerated during the 'great recession' of the early 1980s but there has been little or no recovery since, despite the fact that the number of young people in the labor market declined throughout the 1980s.

If 'demography' does not hold the answer, there are two implications: first, the changes observed in the 1980s may be relatively permanent, and, secondly, to find the explanation we must look to the 'demand side' of the market. Having eliminated changes in occupational structure and industry composition (a demand-side account) as the driving force, where can we look? There are several contending, and not incompatible, explanations available. These demand-side accounts make no mention of the age-specific pattern of wage restructuring we have identified. They are, however, quite consistent with such an outcome. Typically, the effects of economic restructuring will appear among new labour market entrants, that is, among the young. Wage restructuring within firms (e.g. two-tier contracting) will begin among new employees who are not yet protected by seniority or tenure provisions. Inter-firm restructuring will have much the same results since new firms and industries ('greenfield plants') also draw their employees mainly from new labor market entrants. In short, changes that appear first in the 'youth' labor market are an indicator of tendencies that may soon work their way through the entire age structure.

According to Robert Reich (1989), wage polarization in the United States is a result of globalization and a new international division of labor. American employees in what he calls 'symbolic-analytic' services are competitive on a world-wide basis so their earnings have been rising. Symbolic-analytic services are based on the manipulation of information and include the work of lawyers, bankers, management consultants, research scientists, musicians and film producers, among others. Reich estimates that symbolic-analytic services account for 40 percent of America's GNP and 20 percent of jobs. In contrast, routine production workers – including routine clerical and manufacturing employees – are not competitive with foreign workers, so their earnings are falling. In short, the fordist strategy which created the paradox of a low-skill–high-wage labor force in North America is no longer working. As with other demand-side explanations, such shifts would be expected to show up first in the 'youth' labor market (among new job entrants).

There is now substantial evidence for a growing skill premium – using education as the indicator – in the United States (Blackburn et al., 1990), though no measure of how much of the overall change in the wage structure can be attributed to this fact. Canadian evidence is more ambiguous. Our Canadian results (Myles et al., 1988) show that educational credentials were no protection against the downward shift in wages in jobs held by younger workers during the 1980s. There was a net shift from higher to lower wage levels of 17 percent among post-secondary graduates between 1981 and 1986 compared to 22 percent among high-school dropouts. Others (Blackburn and Bloom, 1990) have also failed to find decreasing returns to education in the recent past in Canada.

We have also made a preliminary effort to test Reich's hypothesis by classifying occupations into four categories: information analysts (or symbolic-analytic jobs that include professors, scientists, engineers, lawyers, physicians, musicians, technical sales people, etc.), in-person services (secretaries, tellers, salespersons, waiters), routine production workers, and others. If Reich's thesis is correct, we would expect to see rising relative earnings among the information analysts, and a decline among routine production workers. But in fact *relative* mean annual earnings of both the information analysts and routine production workers (employed full time and full year) actually declined between 1971 and 1986. It was only among the as yet unanalyzed 'other' category that relative earnings rose. These are admittedly very preliminary results and the patterns anticipated by Reich may exist in those sectors of the economy most susceptible to globalization (e.g. manufacturing, business services), but for the economy as a whole the predicted pattern is still not evident.

A second account attempts to explain wage polarization in terms of a generic restructuring of the labor market as a whole. It is also the most pessimistic account since it suggests that in future not only will young workers start off at relatively lower wages than in the past but they can also expect slow growth in earnings over the life-course and lower total lifetime earnings as a result of a downward shift in the typical age–earnings gradient.

Bluestone and Harrison's (1989) description of the changing rules of the market exemplifies this viewpoint:

> Among the 'rule changes' we have in mind . . are erosion of the real minimum wage, the uneven diffusion of wage freeze and concession demands among firms, the growth of two-tiered wage systems, the transformation by employers of full time into part time jobs, and the continued outsourcing of production from work sites whose wage schedules are characterized by relatively high means and low variances (thanks in part to the presence of unions) to suppliers with wage distributions having on average lower means and higher variances.

What all of this points to is a general weakening in the bargaining power of labor over the whole of the labor market. A generic change in the structure of the labor market of this sort is consistent with the pattern of eroding youth wages since the effects will be most pronounced among new labor market entrants. Two-tier wage contracts that establish different pay scales for current and new employees are only the most obvious example. An increase in contracting out (outsourcing) also involves a shift from older, established firms to new firms with younger workforces. This account is more pessimistic than the others, since it suggests that lower entry-level wages are unlikely to be recovered later in the career. There is some anecdotal evidence for this view but traditional data sources derived from population or labor force surveys are clearly inadequate to the task. Instead, firm-level data that allow intra- and inter-firm changes in wages and earnings are required.

In one such firm-based study, Wannell (1991) has shown that part of the polarization in the wage distribution (notably the increase in low-wage jobs) is due to *intra*-industry restructuring in the form of a significant decline in average firm size. Small firms tend to have younger, less experienced, workforces, are less likely to be unionized, pay lower wages and offer fewer benefits than large firms (Morisette, 1991). Hence, an increase in employment in small firms, as observed over the 1980s, would tend to increase the number of low-wage jobs. This could occur because of rapid growth in sectors dominated by small firms (e.g. in consumer services or construction), or because of a decline in firm size in all sectors. The latter explanation is more significant. Inter-industry shifts – from sectors with large employers to sectors with small employers – played only a supporting role in this increase in small-firm employment. Although the shift to services accounted for most of the growth among the very smallest firms, it accounted for only about a third of the total down-sizing that took place in the 1980s. The shift of employment share to smaller firms occurred in all major sectors and was *more* pronounced in goods-producing than in service industries.

Similar shifts of jobs to small and medium-sized employers have been noted in the United States, the United Kingdom, the Netherlands and the Federal Republic of Germany (Brynjolfsson et al., 1989; Davis and Haltiwanger, 1990). Brynjolfsson et al. (1989) point to a 'post-industrial' interpretation of this development but one that differs from the conventional emphasis on changes in industry mix. New technologies and economic relationships, they argue, favor smaller units of organization by reducing economies of scale and reinforcing consumer demand for more heterogeneous products, eroding the cornerstone of mass production. New information technology reduces large firms' reliance on internal channels of supply by facilitating the use of external markets.

These accounts echo the themes of the recent literature on 'post-fordism' and 'flexible specialization' (Piore and Sabel, 1984; Cohen and Zysman, 1987). They highlight the fact that 'post-industrial' restructuring refers not only to *inter*-industry shifts from goods to service but also to *intra*-industry change in the kinds of goods and services produced and in the *way* they are produced, that is, in the organization of production. The cumulative evidence, in our view, indicates that the latter set of changes are exercising a greater impact on the distribution of wages, earnings and life-chances than the former.

If the 'flexible specialization' thesis is valid, the direction of change has not been the positive sort anticipated in much of that literature, where emphasis has been placed on the shift from semi-skilled mass production to more craft-like, skilled work. Occupational skill levels have risen over the postwar period (Myles, 1988; Howell and Wolff, 1988; Boyd, 1990; Economic Council of Canada, 1991), but despite rising skill levels, low-wage employment has grown faster than average or high-paying jobs.

As Mahon (1991: 318) points out, the fordist mass production model required high levels of mass consumption ensuring that workers' wages were high enough to consume what they produced. The 'craft revival' model, she points out, makes no such demands. Flexible specialization, as Piore and Sabel admit, could well flourish in a regime that resembles 'the old Bourbon Kingdom of Naples, where an island of craftsmen, producing for the court, was surrounded by a sub-proletarian sea of misery' (1984: 279). Emergent patterns in North America do resemble this 'Naples' model of post-industrialism but the division it is generating is distributed over the life-cycle: membership in North America's post-industrial 'sub-proletariat' appears to be a temporary condition associated with early stages of the economic life-course. What this points to is a shift in 'mobility regimes', a topic of long-standing interest to sociologists and one to which we turn next.

The Future of Upward Mobility

Throughout the 1980s, those concerned with emergent labor market patterns and the future of inequality focused their attention on the growing number of low-wage, low-skill service jobs. The basis for concern is real. The number of such jobs has been growing and relative wage rates in these jobs have been declining. It is premature to conclude that these trends will not result in the creation of a low-wage service proletariat in the future, but thus far, at least, the patterns we can observe do not point in that direction. If this were the end of the story, we might well conclude that the structure of life-chances in a post-industrial economy will be little different from that of the recent past. But this is not the case. Two important changes have taken place since the 1970s that have altered the economic life-course of North American workers. The first is the change in the age–earnings profile we have emphasized in this chapter. The second is the end to real growth in wages, earnings and incomes that we identified in the introduction. If the observed change in the age–earnings profile proves to be relatively permanent and we do not return to a period of significant real wage growth, the typical economic life-course of current and future generations will be significantly different from that of the postwar generations.

As Levy (1988) shows for the United States, structurally generated 'upward mobility' – between generations and over the life-course – took place at unprecedented levels in the postwar decades. But since the mid-1970s it has slowed considerably. The referent here is not occupational mobility, the traditional concern of sociologists, but economic mobility – the continuous improvement in living standards relative to one's family of origin and to one's starting point in the labor market. Levy begins with a few commonplace observations on American postwar economic history. From World War II until 1973 real wages and earnings grew at between 2.5 and 3.0 percent per year. Median family income (in constant dollars) increased by 42 percent between 1949 and 1959 and by 38 percent between 1959 and 1969. Some simple mathematics can tell us what that means in terms of inter- and intra-generational mobility. Levy (1988: 78–82) summarizes them in a few graphic examples:

- A young man who left home at age 18 in the 1950s would, by age 30, be earning about 15 percent more than his father had earned when the young man was living at home.
- In the 1950s a man who made the transition from age 40 to 50 would, on average, have realized a 34 percent increase in real income. During the 1960s, a similar passage from age 40 to 50 would have increased earnings by 29 percent. The 40 to 50 passage is used to illustrate what would happen in the absence of a promotion or occupational mobility since for most employees the big promotions are behind them by age 40.

In short, young people, and especially young men, who entered the labor force during the 1950s and 1960s began their work-lives on an economic escalator that raised living standards independently of any other form of mobility. With the end of real wage growth in the middle of the 1970s the escalator effect of real wage growth came to an end. Again the implications are obvious. Over the life-course, workers now experience the economic mobility embedded in age-graded earnings hierarchies but the multiplier effect of economic growth, the main source of 'upward mobility' (i.e. increasing standard of living), has been removed.

Crude estimates of the magnitude of this change for Canada are presented in Table 7.4, where we show the percentage change in

Table 7.4   *Percentage gain in cohort average wages and salaries by selected time periods, Canada*

	(1) Income gain for men passing from age			
	15–24 to 25–34	25–34 to 35–44	35–44 to 45–54	45–54 to 55–64
1951–61	90	62	48	38
1961–71	123	79	55	39
1971–81	90	34	10	−1
	(2) Income gain for men passing from age			
	20–6 to 27–33	27–33 to 34–40	34–40 to 41–7	41–7 to 48–54
1967–73	85	37	31	15
1973–81	58	13	1	−4
1981–8	41	9	5	−6
	(3) Income gain for women passing from age			
	20–6 to 27–33	27–33 to 34–40	34–40 to 41–7	41–7 to 48–54
1967–73	7	61	65	42
1973–81	32	59	68	28
1981–8	23	21	21	8

Sources: (1) Decennial Census of Canada; (2 and 3) Statistics Canada, Survey of Consumer Finances

average wages and salaries experienced during ten-year age transitions for different cohorts over the postwar period. The estimates are 'crude' in the sense that change in the average earnings for a cohort could be affected by changes in the labor force behavior of the cohort (e.g. hours worked) and by changes in the composition of the cohort (i.e. entry and exit of members of the cohort). Because of the rapid increase in female labor force participation, estimates for women are less meaningful and are shown only for the more recent time period.

The results in panel 1 show the sharp rise in real income for all age cohorts during the 1950s and 1960s and the impact of the end to real wage growth that began in the mid-1970s. Panels 2 and 3 show the change for three narrower periods that roughly correspond to: (1) the last years of the postwar boom (1967–73); (2) the period of stagflation between 1973 and 1981 leading up to the recession of 1982–83; and (3) the period just prior to recession and recovery between 1981 and 1988.[9] The slowdown in the rate of growth of earnings over the life-course is evident for all cohorts as we move from earlier to more recent periods, and, in the case of older men, becomes negative.

In sum, not only are young workers starting from a lower relative economic position in the labor market (as a result of the shift in the age–earnings profile), they have also lost the escalator of economic growth to bring them back to the living standards of their parents. One consequence, already evident, is the 'cluttered nest': young unmarried adults have been staying in (or returning to) their parental homes in ever growing numbers (Boyd and Pryor, 1989), reversing an earlier trend towards earlier home-leaving. For the young people who have entered the North American labor market since the 1970s, it is clear that the path to 'upward mobility' will be longer and harder than that of earlier cohorts.

Conclusion

Like many others, we began our explorations of post-industrialism in the mid-1980s in search of a 'new class structure'. Our results showed that Canadian wage and earnings distribution were polarizing but not for the reasons we had expected. Polarization was taking place between generations, not between industry or occupational sectors. The patterns we have noted here with respect to transitions in and out of the growing sector of unskilled service jobs point in the same direction: rather than a new class structure, post-industrialism appears to bringing about a new economic life-course.

The more difficult and speculative question is whether developments in the youth labor market are pointing us towards a more generic restructuring of the labor market as implied in our discussion of declining firm size. When restructuring occurs, the effects are more likely to show up among young workers than in the labor force as a whole. This is because the redistribution of jobs occurs largely through the relative decline of entry-level jobs in some firms and a relative abundance of entry-level jobs in others. There is some indication that a generic restructuring of the labor market is taking place but only the passage of time will teach us the extent and nature of its effects.

Notes

The views expressed in this chapter are the authors' own and not necessarily those of Statistics Canada.

We are grateful to Jill Quadagno, Jim Fendrich and members of the Florida State Political Economy Group for their critical comments on previous drafts.

1 Shortly after these studies were released the Economic Council also became a victim of changing times. The Council's demise was announced in the federal budget of 1992.

2   Skill levels are measured with the General Educational Development (GED) scale, one of a family of measures widely used in Canada and the United States to indicate skill requirements of detailed (four-digit) occupational categories. 'Low skill' refers to occupations with a GED score of 1 or 2 on a 6-point scale. While differing in detail, very similar inter-industry patterns are found using a wide variety of 'objective' and 'subjective' measures of occupational and job skill requirements (Myles, 1988; Myles and Fawcett, 1990). 'Low wage' jobs include all those with an hourly pay rate of $6.76 an hour or less in 1986 and roughly corresponds to the bottom quintile of the wage distribution. For full details see Myles et al. (1988).

3   Greater capital intensity, higher productivity and stronger unions in the goods sector may generate rents for these workers.

4   Using the same definition of 'low-wage' work as in Figure 7.1, the percentages of low-wage jobs in clerical, sales and service occupations are 23 percent, 37 percent and 49 percent, respectively (Myles et al., 1988: table A-14). The definition of service occupations in this study did not distinguish between skilled and unskilled.

5   One of the contributions of the debate was the development of a set of new methodological tools for studying wage and earnings distributions. Traditional inequality measures such as quintile shares, Gini, Theil, etc. do not answer questions about the size of the 'middle class' or of any other group. By definition, such measures treat the middle class as a fixed quantity (e.g. the middle third of the population) and ask whether its share of the pie is getting larger or smaller. Indeed, measured inequality in this traditional sense and measures of wage polarization can move in opposite directions. For a more complete discussion see Myles et al. (1988) and Wolfson (1989).

6   In Canada, the main evidence for these claims comes from three sets of studies. The first was conducted at Statistics Canada by the authors and presented in two reports (Myles et al., 1988; Picot et al., 1990). The second was also conducted at Statistics Canada, on behalf of the Economic Council of Canada (1991; see also Wolfson, 1989). Finally, a series of comparative Canada–US papers has been produced under the auspices of the Donner Foundation (see especially Blackburn and Bloom, 1990; Hanratty and Blank, 1990). Though differing in analytical emphasis, all three have produced similar results with respect to general trends and patterns. There has been an increase in the share of jobs at both the bottom and top of the wage distribution, with fewer in the middle. Although there has been increasing polarization of labor market incomes for individuals and families in both Canada and the United States, the distribution of total family income (after transfers and taxes) has been stable in Canada though not in the United States (Wolfson, 1989; Blackburn and Bloom, 1990; Hanratty and Blank, 1990). In effect, the 'welfare state' has managed to offset the effects of wage polarization in Canada but not in the US. For a review of American evidence see Frank Levy and Richard Murnane (1992).

7   Our analysis of earnings data for 1980 and 1985 from the Canadian Census confirm and reinforce these results. Only 10 per cent of the total change in the economy-wide earnings distribution was accounted for by changing industrial composition. For the 1970–80 period (again using Census earnings distributions) we were able to account for 28 per cent of the change among full-time, full-year workers.

8   Similar trends were evident when we examined age-specific wage patterns within occupations.

9   The time-points were selected in order to have comparable points in the business cycle. As a result some accuracy is lost in the cohort transitions: six years in the first interval, eight years in the second and seven years in the third. Whatever bias is introduced because of this works against the claim we are making here; that is, our estimates of the effect of the slowdown are conservative, since the longer time intervals for the later periods allow for more income growth.

8

Careers in the US Service Economy

Jerry A. Jacobs

The emergence of post-industrial society has raised important issues throughout the social sciences and humanities. What is distinctive about post-industrial political movements (Touraine, 1971; Offe, 1985; Melucci, 1989)? What can account for the development of postmodern architecture (Jencks, 1987) and deconstructionist literary analysis (Connor, 1989)? Do social and economic frameworks developed to account for industrial society provide sound guidance for understanding the nature and trajectory of post-industrial society (Bell, 1976; Block, 1990)?

In keeping with the theme of this volume, the organizing question for this chapter is whether an increasingly closed group of workers is developing at the low end of the service economy, possibly facing a deteriorating social position (Esping-Andersen, 1991). We attempt to answer this question for the United States in the period 1969–87 by addressing four specific subsidiary questions. (1) Did employment levels increase in this group of relatively undesirable jobs? (2) Did incomes of workers in these occupations decline, either absolutely or relative to those of other workers? (3) Did the age–earnings profile of this group level out? And (4) did career mobility out of such jobs become more difficult? Despite the extensive debate regarding the growth of inequality in the United States labor market (Levy, 1988; Burtless, 1990; Harrison and Bluestone, 1988; Jencks and Peterson, 1991), little attention has been paid to the basic question of whether the same individuals stay in the same occupations for long or short spells.

To foreshadow the results presented in more detail below, if the group in question is defined as workers in unskilled service occupations, the answer to three of these four questions in the United States is clearly negative.

First, employment in unskilled service occupations did not increase substantially. The proportion of the labor force employed in unskilled service occupations inched up between 1969 and 1987, from 11.77 percent to 12.08 percent of the labor force (see Table 8.1). Further, unskilled service workers declined as a fraction of consumer service industry employment. Unskilled service work in the United States is thus larger than in any of the other countries included in this study, but it is not a rapidly growing segment of the US labor force.

Secondly, annual earnings of unskilled service workers did fall in absolute terms between 1969 and 1987, and fell more than those of other workers. Yet this decline was due to three economy-wide trends: the deteriorating position of less educated workers, younger workers, and especially part-time workers (see Table 8.2). The decline in earnings relative to the economy as a whole was due to the concentration in unskilled service jobs of workers with these attributes (see Tables 8.3 and 8.4). The lower earnings of unskilled service workers than their manufacturing counterparts parallels findings reported in this volume for Canada, Norway and Sweden.

Thirdly, the age–earnings profile of unskilled service workers is quite flat, with little upward slope after age 25. Yet the shape of this trajectory improved slightly between 1969 and 1987 (see Table 8.5).

Finally, career mobility out of unskilled service occupations is very high for young employees, and increased slightly between 1971–2 and 1987–8 (see Tables 8.6 to 8.8). In this respect, the United States resembles the Canadian and Scandinavian cases more than Britain and Germany, although the mobility rates of different countries are not entirely comparable due to differences in data and methodology.

What distinctive features of the United States labor market might contribute to the particular configuration of its service economy? The majority of comparative research has focused on inter-generational mobility rather than career mobility (but see Kalleberg, 1988). Nonetheless, I suspect that several institutional arrangements are likely to be relevant here. The United States has a lower level of unionization, has a weaker connection between formal education and the labor market, and relies more heavily on part-time employment than many other countries.

Union membership declined from one-third of the non-agricultural labor force at its postwar peak to less than one-fifth of the labor force in 1987. Less than one in six workers in the private sector is a union member (US Bureau of Labor Statistics, 1988). Freeman and his colleagues have maintained that unions promote wage equality, and that the decline in union membership has been a significant factor in contributing to the growth in inequality. Blackburn et al. (1990) have estimated that about one-quarter of the growth in inequality in the returns to education is due to the decline in union membership during the 1970s and 1980s.

Unskilled service jobs are rarely unionized in the United States. As a result, benefits such as health-care coverage and pensions are much less evident in these jobs than in the rest of the economy. Further, since union membership tends to reduce turnover (Freeman and Medoff, 1984), the higher rate of mobility from unskilled service jobs in the United States may be due in part to the low rate of unionization. Unfortunately, data on union membership are not included in the Current Population Survey the same month as data on mobility, so the impact of unionization on mobility patterns cannot be directly assessed here.

A second distinctive feature of the US labor market is the lack of formal connections between work and school, particularly at the level of secondary education. Rosenbaum and Kariya (1989, 1991) have noted that employers do not inspect the grades of job applicants with high school degrees or less formal education. They complain that this undermines the ability of schools to induce co-operative behavior on the part of non-college-bound students. Osterman (1980) has shown that the relatively weak connection between work and primary and secondary education has been an enduring feature of the US social structure throughout the twentieth century. It has been suggested that this institutional weakness results in relatively high youth unemployment (Freeman and Holzer, 1986). I am suggesting the same institutional weakness may account for the relatively high rate of early career mobility in the United States which is typical of employment in unskilled service jobs.

A third distinctive feature of unskilled service work in the US labor market is the relatively high concentration of part-time workers in this group of occupations. Comparative data indicate that the United States has a higher level of part-time employment than most industrial countries, but follows Norway, England and Sweden in this respect (Thurman and Trah, 1990). The disproportionate representation of part-time workers in unskilled service work is responsible for its low and declining wages and is associated with its high rate of career mobility. Explicitly comparative research will be needed to assess the role these arrangements play in accounting for the distinctive outcomes in the United States.

This chapter examines trends in the United States in service industry employment during the 1970s and 1980s. We first consider the growth in service employment, and then turn to the question of who is engaged in unskilled service jobs. We examine earnings and mobility in turn.

The Growth of the Service Economy in the United States 1969–87

A sample of 127,125 individuals surveyed in the 1970 Census were assigned 1980 occupation and industry codes in conjunction with the 1980 Census (Priebe, 1985; see also Treiman et al., 1988). This double coding enables us to compare 1970 with 1988 using the same (1980 Census) definitions of occupation and industry. These data obviate the need for imprecise adjustment of occupational and industry categories. Data for 1988 were obtained from the March 1988 Current Population Survey, a survey of 117,849 individuals. The earnings apply to the previous year, so that the 1988 data provide information on 1987 earnings, and the 1970 data provide information on 1969 earnings. For consistency, industry and occupation data also refer to 1969 and 1987. Thus all results refer to either 1969 or 1987, with the exception of the career mobility analyses, which compare mobility during the 1971–2 period with mobility during the 1987–8 period. The CPS data can be utilized for short-term mobility analyses, as they include a one-year retrospective question concerning occupational and industrial mobility.

For the analysis of earnings, the 1970 Census and 1988 CPS data sets were merged in order to create a pooled cross-sectional time series (with two time points). The earnings measure employed is the total annual wage and salary earnings of the individual. (Note that occupational differentials as well as the sex gap in earnings are somewhat larger for annual, as compared with hourly, earnings.) In the multi-variate analysis of earnings, the log of earnings is the dependent variable. Individuals with zero or negative earnings are excluded from the analysis.[1] This analysis examines whether occupational differentials in earnings have changed during this period.

The trends in the size and composition of the service economy depend a great deal on what groups are included in the service economy, and also on whether industry or occupation is taken as a defining characteristic of service employment. Service *industries* employ professionals, managers and clerical workers as well as such service workers as repair technicians and bartenders. As we will see, only a part – albeit a significant part – of service *industry* employment is comprised of service *occupations*. Trends in *industrial* distributions produce a bifurcated pattern, with growth in both the most and least desirable sectors of the economy. However, if the focus is on *occupational* trends, as is the case for the majority of this paper, recent trends in the United States have been generally favorable. In order to understand these different aspects of the same trends, Table 8.1 presents a cross-classification of major industries and occupations for the experienced civilian labor force for 1969 and 1987. (It should be noted that these data are coded in a manner designed for international comparability and thus differ from the conventional major occupation and industry definitions.)

Employment in the US labor force is composed of two-fifths services, one-quarter manufacturing and one-quarter distribution (retail sales, wholesale trade and transportation and utilities), with the remaining 7 percent divided between government administration (other than the provision of services), agriculture and mining. Within the service economy, social services (19.77 percent of employment) led in size, followed by business services (12.24 percent of employment) and consumer services (7.39 percent). When the three groups are combined, services have substantially surpassed manufacturing in employment, which represented just under one-quarter (24.61 percent) of employment in 1987. Even when mining and agricultural employment are added to manufacturing, this combination of primary and secondary production still represented less than a third of the contemporary labor force.

In extensive analyses conducted for this project which are too detailed to be included in this chapter, I found that employment in consumer services resembles retail sales in many key respects, while differing substantially from both social services and business services. Consumer service and retail sales industries are both characterized by young, part-time workers with relatively low education and high rates of turnover, while social services and business services employ older, better-educated workers on a full-time basis with much greater career stability. In short, these findings indicate that consumer services and retail sales, together comprising one-quarter of US employment in 1987, represent the bottom end of the emerging service economy. In contrast, social services and business services, together representing nearly one-third of employment in the United States, do not represent the specter of deteriorating employment opportunities that some pessimists ascribe to service employment. Moreover, the social services resemble public administration more than they do business services. Consequently, a potentially more useful summary of employment by industry in the United States would be as follows: one-quarter social services (including public administration), one-quarter retail distribution (consumer services and retail sales), one-quarter manufacturing, one-tenth business services and one-tenth wholesale distribution (wholesale trade, transportation and utilities), with the remaining 4 percent divided between agriculture and mining.

How have these employment patterns changed since 1969? As is well known, the share of manufacturing employment in the United

Table 8.1 *Occupational distribution of employment by industry, USA, 1969–87 (percent)*

	Consumer service	Retail sales	Social service	Public admin.	Business service	Manufacturing	Whole-sale	Utility/Transport	Agri-culture/other	Mining	Total
Managers											
1987	9.19	5.83	7.73	11.22	16.47	9.18	7.10	8.67	2.40	9.19	8.94
1969	6.08	6.43	4.97	7.77	13.38	5.27	9.54	4.60	0.66	5.40	6.13
Change	+3.11	−0.60	+2.76	+3.45	+3.09	+3.91	−2.44	+4.07	+1.74	+3.79	+2.81
Professions – high											
1987	5.01	1.93	11.30	14.07	14.16	7.66	2.26	7.93	2.30	14.38	7.88
1969	3.62	2.03	10.52	12.49	11.97	6.08	2.66	5.51	2.36	8.90	6.40
Change	+1.39	−0.10	+0.78	+1.58	+2.19	+1.58	−0.40	+2.42	−0.06	+5.48	+1.48
Technicians											
1987	0.42	0.23	3.96	3.82	3.54	3.26	0.86	2.95	0.76	5.41	2.53
1969	0.24	0.09	2.95	3.40	3.24	2.99	0.61	1.57	0.31	2.80	2.07
Change	+0.18	+0.14	+1.01	+0.42	+0.30	+0.27	+0.25	+1.38	+0.45	+2.61	+0.46
Professions											
1987	7.95	0.09	33.89	2.90	0.86	0.19	0.14	0.30	0.00	0.00	7.60
1969	7.34	0.12	38.24	1.51	0.73	0.14	0.09	0.27	0.02	0.10	7.03
Change	+0.61	−0.03	−4.35	+1.39	+0.13	+0.05	+0.05	+0.03	−0.02	−0.10	+0.57
Skilled services											
1987	24.65	10.10	5.65	24.16	1.03	1.14	1.87	8.05	0.89	4.08	6.72
1969	24.04	7.07	3.90	25.04	0.95	1.00	2.18	9.58	0.96	4.50	5.59
Change	+0.61	+3.03	+1.75	−0.88	+0.08	+0.14	−0.31	−1.53	−0.07	−0.42	+1.13

Table 8.1 *continued*

	Consumer service	Retail sales	Social service	Public admin.	Business service	Manufac- turing	Whole- sale	Utility/ Transport	Agri- culture/ other	Mining	Total
Unskilled service											
1987	30.65	17.85	15.34	5.51	9.99	3.79	5.20	9.02	12.96	2.76	12.08
1969	38.47	17.73	18.06	7.50	7.09	4.32	6.17	8.73	5.92	2.40	11.77
Change	−7.82	+0.12	−2.72	−1.99	+2.90	−0.53	−0.97	+0.29	+7.04	+0.36	+0.31
Clerical											
1987	7.82	7.24	19.05	32.45	33.82	9.17	17.44	27.47	3.84	14.72	15.97
1969	6.22	8.89	18.02	33.33	41.50	9.96	20.50	31.97	1.16	9.80	15.94
Change	+1.60	−1.65	+1.03	−0.88	−7.68	−0.79	−3.06	−4.50	+2.68	+4.92	+0.03
Sales											
1987	4.97	42.48	0.68	0.85	15.44	3.19	40.60	4.23	0.43	1.91	12.70
1969	4.77	40.02	0.80	1.08	16.13	3.22	30.11	2.00	0.48	0.80	10.58
Change	+0.20	+2.46	−0.12	−0.23	−0.69	−0.03	+10.49	+2.23	−0.05	+1.11	+2.12
Skilled manual											
1987	4.09	2.62	1.16	2.89	2.37	28.47	4.25	8.63	0.62	13.08	9.25
1969	4.40	3.19	1.52	3.97	2.91	26.85	7.62	10.62	0.41	18.40	11.66
Change	−0.31	−0.57	−0.36	−1.08	−0.54	+1.62	−3.37	−1.99	+0.21	−5.32	−2.41
Unskilled manual											
1987	5.05	11.60	1.22	2.11	2.27	33.69	20.04	22.76	2.88	34.45	13.93
1969	4.70	14.41	0.90	3.87	2.00	39.70	20.41	25.15	2.75	46.90	19.53
Change	+0.35	−2.81	−0.32	−1.76	+0.27	−6.01	−0.37	−2.39	+0.13	−12.45	−5.60
Agriculture/other											
1987	0.20	0.03	0.03	0.02	0.06	0.27	0.24	0.00	72.92	0.00	2.40
1969	0.13	0.02	0.12	0.04	0.12	0.48	0.11	0.01	85.97	0.00	3.30
Change	+0.07	+0.00	−0.09	−0.02	−0.06	−0.21	+0.13	−0.01	−13.05	+0.00	−0.90

States declined sharply during this period, from over one-third to just under one-quarter of the labor force. This decline, along with a slight loss of employment share in utilities and transportation, was matched by an increase in service and sales employment. Business services were the fastest employment gainers, followed by social services, retail sales and finally consumer services. The growth in the more desirable sectors of the service economy (social and business services) was thus more than twice as large as the growth in the less desirable retail sales and consumer service industries. In supplemental analyses not shown here, I have found that social and business services have been the engine of employment growth among full-time and full-year workers, while retail sales and consumer services absorbed most of growth in part-time and part-year employment (see Jacobs, 1991, for details).

Not surprisingly, the occupational composition of industries varies widely. Unskilled service occupations are concentrated in the consumer service industry, and are less evident in social and business services. Managers, professionals and technicians comprised over half of social-service employment, with an additional third represented by lower-status professionals. One third of business-service employees were managers and high-status professionals, and one-third were clerical workers. In contrast, over half of workers in the consumer service *industry* were employed in skilled and unskilled service *occupations*. The occupational distribution in all of the service industries differs from manufacturing, where three-fifths of employees were skilled or unskilled manual workers.

Given our focus on unskilled service workers, a significant result in Table 8.1 is the very modest growth of employment in this group of occupations. There was less than one-third of one percent increase in employment in unskilled service work during the 1969–87 period. The pattern across industries was highly uneven. Unskilled service work showed clear increases in two industries – business services and agriculture – while showing substantial declines in others – consumer services, social services and public administration. On the basis of these data, it is hard to conclude that there is a rapidly growing post-industrial proletariat comprised of unskilled service workers in the United States. There has just not been enough growth in the size of this group to provide the basis for any dire predictions about the post-industrial class structure.

Overall, the occupational structure continued to edge slightly upward during the 1969–87 period. All of the white-collar occupations increased their share of employment, while all of the blue-collar occupations lost employment share. Management (+2.81

percent), professionals and technicians (+2.51 percent), sales (+2.12 percent) and skilled and unskilled service (+1.44 percent) occupations grew, while skilled manual (−2.41 percent) and especially unskilled manual (−5.60 percent) occupations continued to decline.

One must combine sales employment with unskilled service work in order to see any appreciable growth in the less desirable white-collar occupations during this period. As we will see, there are a number of striking similarities in attributes and career patterns of sales and unskilled service workers. But even so, the combined change represents less than 3 percent growth in employment share over a twenty-year period. Thus, the growth of the service economy is much more evident in the industrial analysis than in the occupational analysis. Even combining skilled and unskilled service work, the occupational changes evident during the 1970s and 1980s were modest. The industrial changes, in contrast, were much sharper.

This chapter touches only indirectly on the question of the contribution of industrial restructuring to the recent growth of inequality in the United States. There is a lively, ongoing debate on this question among economists and sociologists in the United States. The current state of this discussion indicates that while de-industrialization is undoubtedly implicated in the growth of inequality, it explains only a modest proportion – perhaps one-quarter to one-third – of the growth of inequality in recent years (Loveman and Tilly, 1988; Grubb and Wilson, 1989; Blackburn et al., 1990). The data in Table 8.1 help to explain why the fallout of industrial restructuring has not been even greater: industrial shifts over the last twenty years have been substantially larger than the associated occupational shifts. In other words, the expectation that industrial restructuring would generate a massive reordering of social inequality rests on the assumption that occupational structure follows the industrial distribution of jobs. The results in Table 8.1 show that this relationship is much less direct and more complex. Modest occupational upgrading continued in the face of substantial industrial shifts. Since industrial shifts did not produce significantly deteriorating occupational shifts, they have not had as large an impact on wage inequality as might have been expected. Direct industrial effects on wages, unmediated by occupational composition, do exist, as we will see, and these effects are responsible for the contribution of restructuring to the growth in wage inequality in the United States. But the impact of these changes has been modest.

The occupational data are consistent with the relatively optimistic view that expansion in the higher-status components of the occupational structure will permit continued upward inter-generation and career mobility to overshadow downward mobility. The patterns of industry growth suggest a more mixed picture, since growth is evident in services at both the low end (consumer service and retail sales industries) and the high end (social and business services). A third, more pessimistic view of the changing opportunity structure focuses on the stagnant earnings opportunities, which I examine below. A complete appraisal of the dynamics of opportunity should ideally incorporate these partially disparate trends.

The Changing Demographics of Unskilled Service Employment

Table 8.2 documents the demographic composition of unskilled service workers for 1969 and 1987. Data for the labor force as a whole are provided as a convenient reference point. Unskilled service workers are disproportionately female, yet women's over-

Table 8.2   *Attributes of incumbents by occupation, USA, 1969–87 (percent)*

	Unskilled service workers		Total labor force	
	1987	1969	1987	1969
N	10,045	14,674	81,004	125,509
Female	51.0	48.6	46.8	37.9
Black	14.0	20.1	8.4	9.0
Education				
Mean (years)	(11.5)	(10.1)	(12.8)	(11.6)
Less than high school	35.3	60.4	18.5	38.2
High school graduates	42.7	30.6	39.7	35.6
Some college	16.9	7.7	20.4	13.4
4+ years college	5.0	1.2	21.5	12.9
Age				
Mean (years)	(36.0)	(40.7)	(37.6)	(39.8)
16–24	30.0	22.7	19.1	18.9
25–34	23.9	15.8	27.8	21.1
35–44	17.6	18.0	23.8	20.8
45–54	12.7	20.3	15.4	21.2
55–64	10.8	16.8	10.3	14.1
65+	5.0	6.4	3.6	4.0
Full time	60.0	69.7	78.1	81.6
Full year worked	55.7	58.3	68.8	66.9

representation in unskilled service work did not increase between 1969 and 1987. In 1987, the proportion of females in unskilled service work exceeded the labor force as a whole by just over 4 percent, whereas in 1969 the differential was just over 10 percent. Indeed, the level of sex segregation across occupations declined slightly, whether measured across broad or narrow occupational groups or across industries.[2]

Blacks were slightly over-represented in unskilled service employment in 1987, but for Blacks as well as women the concentration in this area declined. Racial segregation fell for the labor force as a whole at a modest rate between 1969 and 1987, with an especially rapid decline in segregation among part-time workers.[3] These patterns held for both Black men and Black women. The principal sex difference among Blacks is that Black women were under-represented among part-time workers (in both 1969 and 1987) while Black men remained slightly over-represented among part-time workers (see Jacobs, 1991, for a more detailed discussion of race and gender issues).

Although the educational credentials of unskilled service workers rose between 1969 and 1987, they remained over a year behind the rest of the labor force in years of schooling completed. Unskilled service workers were almost twice as likely to be high school dropouts as the rest of the labor force by 1987, compared with 1.6 times as likely in 1969. Employees with no more education than a high school diploma comprised a much smaller portion of the US labor force in 1987 than in 1969, due to the retirement of earlier cohorts with less education. Yet those with limited educational credentials became relatively worse-off, as they were increasingly concentrated in low-end service jobs, jobs whose incomes fell during this period (Blackburn et al., 1990).

The United States resembles Canada and the Scandinavian countries in the youthfulness of unskilled service workers, in sharp contrast to their middle-aged counterparts in Germany and Britain. New entrants to the labor force (those aged 16–24) were increasingly over-represented in unskilled service work in the United States by 1987. Whereas in 1969, unskilled service workers were slightly older than the labor force as a whole, by 1987 they were slightly younger. Young workers' over-representation in unskilled service employment increased substantially between 1969 and 1987. In 1987, 30 percent of unskilled service workers were under age 25, compared with less than 20 percent of the labor force as a whole. Unskilled service workers were also over-represented at the other extreme of the age distribution, those aged 65 and over.

The increasing concentration of the young in low-end service employment is crucial for our appraisal of the career dimension of service employment. The over-representation of the young in low-end service jobs implies that such undesirable jobs are for many a way-station to other, more desirable positions rather than a final career destination. Clearly many individuals are able to escape the low-end trap by the time they are in their late twenties and early thirties. Their ability to exit is undoubtedly conditioned by their educational attainment, sex and race. A key question, then, is whether the rates of exit are increasing or decreasing over time, both overall and for particular subgroups of the population.

In analyses not shown here, I found that retail sales workers resemble unskilled service workers in a number of key respects. Both groups are disproportionately female, young, part-time workers with limited formal education. In contrast, unskilled manual workers are less likely to be female, young and are much less likely to work part time and part year. Thus, while unskilled manual and service workers have limited educational credentials in common, they differ in many other key respects. There are more similarities between retail sales and unskilled service workers than between the latter and unskilled manual workers.

Earnings Trends of Unskilled Service Workers

How have the earnings of unskilled service workers fared compared to those of others in the labor force? Trends in median annual earnings by major occupation are presented in Table 8.3. Real incomes of American workers were sluggish during the 1970s and 1980s. Women working full time were the only group to have made real annual earnings gains during this period. Their median earnings were 3.55 times higher in 1987 than in 1969, a 14.5 percent real increase after adjusting for inflation. Men working full time experienced an 11.3 percent decline in real annual earnings adjusted for inflation.

The biggest losers during this period, however, were part-time workers, whose earnings hardly rose at all in nominal terms. Part-time men fared particularly poorly, as their wage and salary income declined even in nominal terms. Their real earnings declined 75.8 percent, compared with a 48.4 percent decline in real earnings for part-time women. The plummeting wages of part-time workers deserve further scrutiny.

The declining position of part-time workers hit unskilled service and sales occupations especially hard as a result of the concentration of part-time workers in these occupations. Thus, the median earnings in these categories fell relative to other workers over this

Table 8.3   *Median earnings (dollars) by occupation, sex and full-time status, USA, 1969–87*

	Total labor force	Unskilled service workers	Sales workers	Unskilled manual workers
Total				
1987	14,500	6,690	11,875	12,440
1969	6,000	4,000	6,000	5,000
Ratio 1987/1969	2.42	1.67	1.98	2.49
Men				
1987	20,000	10,000	22,000	14,500
1969	8,000	6,000	8,000	6,000
Ratio 1987/1969	2.50	1.67	2.75	2.42
Women				
1987	10,000	5,000	6,125	8,690
1969	4,000	2,000	3,000	3,000
Ratio 1987/1969	2.50	2.50	2.04	2.90
Part-time men				
1987	3,000	2,000	3,160	2,500
1969	4,000	2,000	3,000	4,000
Ratio 1987/1969	0.75	1.00	1.05	0.63
Part-time women				
1987	3,190	2,500	3,000	3,000
1969	2,000	1,000	2,000	3,000
Ratio 1987/1969	1.60	2.50	1.50	1.00
Full-time men				
1987	22,000	15,000	25,000	16,000
1969	8,000	6,000	9,000	6,000
Ratio 1987/1969	2.75	2.50	2.78	2.67
Full-time women				
1987	14,190	8,500	11,970	10,000
1969	4,000	3,000	3,000	3,000
Ratio 1987/1969	3.55	2.83	4.00	3.33

Part-time: less than 35 hours

period. The decline in real annual earnings was 46.1 percent for unskilled service workers and 36.1 percent for sales workers. However, when earnings are divided into part-time and full-time workers, the trends for unskilled service workers and sales workers do not look especially unfavorable. Part-time men lagged behind inflation about as badly in all of the occupations examined. Part-time women appear to have fared somewhat better in unskilled service work than in the labor market as a whole. The earnings trends of full-time men and women were slightly behind the labor market average in unskilled service work, while full-time men and women did slightly better than average in retail sales. (The Canadian, Norwegian and Swedish data also indicate that consumer service workers are paid less than otherwise similarly situated workers, although we do not know whether the trend is the same in Sweden as in the United States.)

Unskilled manual workers fared somewhat better than unskilled service workers; indeed, their earnings growth exceeded that for the labor force as a whole. This is due to the more limited reliance on part-time workers in unskilled manual employment. Once employees are divided according to sex and full-time versus part-time work, the earnings trends for unskilled manual work resemble those found for unskilled service work.

A broader picture of the rewards of work indicates further problems with low-end service jobs (see Jacobs, 1991, for details). Their unemployment rates exceed the economy-wide average (although they were lower than manufacturing in 1987), and they are more likely than other workers to report they are under-employed. Such jobs have low levels of health and pension cover-age, especially among part-time employees. This sector of the economy is characterized by high rates of employer turnover, and occupational and industrial mobility. Thus, there can be little doubt that unskilled service jobs offer unattractive wage and fringe benefit packages when compared with other occupational groups.

Table 8.4 presents the results of a series of regression equations which predict the earnings of labor force incumbents for a combined 1969–87 sample. The strategy of these equations is to compare gross and net occupational differentials, and to examine whether the relative earnings position of different occupations remained con-stant over time. In our initial equation, the gross earnings differen-tials between unskilled service workers and other occupations are documented, along with a time-trend interaction. This term indi-cates the extent of positive or negative earnings change in unskilled service work relative to the rest of the labor force. Basic demo-graphic characteristics – sex and race – are included in this baseline model. In subsequent equations, I explore the extent to which these differentials can be attributed to various factors which differ across occupations. Model 2 indicates the extent to which earnings differ-ences between unskilled service work and other occupations are due to differences in industry distribution. Model 3 adds education and experience, and finally Model 4 adds hours and weeks worked.

The results in Model 1 document the earnings disadvantage of unskilled service workers relative to workers in the rest of the economy, and the declining trend for service workers relative to the rest of the labor force between 1969 and 1987. Thus, not only are these workers poorly paid, but they fell behind in terms of earnings compared to the rest of the labor force.

In Model 2 industry characteristics are added. The reference category here is the manufacturing sector (mining and agriculture are excluded from the earnings analysis). The addition of industry characteristics does not significantly change the time trend for unskilled service workers. Thus, the unfavorable earnings trend for unskilled service work is not due to the changing industrial composition of this group of occupations. Nonetheless, it should be noted that the earnings of workers in the consumer service and retail sales industries are substantially below those garnered by workers in other industries, even after membership in major occupational groups is controlled.

In Model 3, the addition of education and experience substantially reduces both the cross-sectional and longitudinal effects associated with unskilled service occupations. In other words, the economic 'cost' associated with being employed in unskilled service work is partly due to the relatively low education and limited labor market experience of workers in this group of occupations. Further, much of the downward time trend is due to the decline in education and experience of these workers, relative to the labor force as a whole. During the 1970s and 1980s, the earnings of those with limited educational credentials fell behind those of college graduates, and the earnings of recent entrants into the labor market have fallen behind those of experienced workers (Blackburn et al., 1990). The results in Model 3 indicate that these trends are responsible for about half of the decline in earnings of unskilled service workers relative to the rest of the labor force.

In Model 4, the addition of hours worked and weeks worked explains virtually all of the remaining decline in earnings of unskilled service workers. In other words, the earnings trends of unskilled workers would not have changed had they worked the same number of hours per week and weeks per year as other occupations. As noted above, the presence of large numbers of part-time workers depresses the position of unskilled service work relative to other occupations, and explains the lower earnings growth in this group of occupations.

It should be noted that there is still a significant negative cross-sectional effect of employment in unskilled service work. In other words, even after controlling for formal education, labor market experience and hours and weeks worked, workers employed in unskilled service occupations continue to be paid less than comparable individuals in other occupations. Further, wage 'penalties' associated with the consumer services, retail sales and social service industries persist after these controls are introduced.

The problem with low-end service employment, then, is not only

Table 8.4   *Determinants of wages by occupation, USA,*
1969–87 (dependent variable: log of annual earnings)

	Model 1	Model 2	Model 3	Model 4
	Beta (SE)	Beta (SE)	Beta (SE)	Beta (SE)
Intercept	1.986* (.005)	1.979* (.006)	0.412* (.018)	−1.824* (.019)
Year	0.766* (.007)	0.776* (.007)	0.707* (.007)	0.814* (.006)
Female	−0.714* (.007)	−0.703* (.008)	−0.641* (.007)	−0.443* (.006)
Black	−0.374* (.017)	−0.385* (.016)	−0.219* (.016)	−0.168* (.012)
Black female	0.399* (.024)	0.399* (.024)	0.311* (.023)	0.190* (.018)
Unskilled service	−0.436* (.015)	−0.348* (.015)	−0.199* (.014)	−0.182* (.012)
Trend in unskilled service	−0.329* (.022)	−0.309* (.021)	−0.272* (.020)	−0.030* (.016)
Industries				
Consumer services		−0.458* (.015)	−0.516* (.014)	−0.356* (.011)
Retail sales		−0.397* (.010)	−0.421* (.010)	−0.273* (.008)
Social services		0.160* (.010)	−0.159* (.010)	−0.054* (.008)
Public administration		0.276* (.017)	0.086* (.017)	0.038* (.014)
Business services		0.174* (.012)	−0.013* (.012)	0.007 (.010)
Wholesale		0.095* (.017)	−0.020 (.016)	−0.035* (.013)
Utilities/transport		0.234* (.013)	0.158 (.013)	0.104* (.010)
Education			0.112* (.001)	0.085* (.001)
Experience			0.014* (.001)	0.008* (.001)
Hours worked				
0–29				−
30–4				0.395* (.013)
35–9				0.613* (.012)
40				0.697* (.008)
41–8				0.765* (.010)

Table 8.4 *continued*

	Model 1	Model 2	Model 3	Model 4
	Beta (SE)	Beta (SE)	Beta (SE)	Beta (SE)
Hours worked *continued*				
49–59				0.838* (.012)
60+				0.723* (.013)
Weeks worked				
0–25				–
26–38				1.097* (.016)
39–46				1.586* (.016)
47–8				1.883* (.016)
49–51				2.018* (.018)
52				2.133* (.014)
Adjusted R^2	0.190	0.228	0.292	0.545

* $p < 0.05$ SE standard error   N = 95,530

that these jobs pay less than other jobs, but that their earnings position relative to employment in other occupations has deteriorated. We have seen that this change is due to the concentration of individuals with limited education and experience who work less than a standard full-time, full-year schedule. While the unfavorable earnings trends have been evident for these groups throughout the economy, the concentration of workers with these characteristics in unskilled service jobs has meant a deterioration in the relative position of unskilled service work.

Table 8.5 presents age–earnings profiles for unskilled service workers. The age–earnings profile of unskilled service workers became somewhat steeper between 1969 and 1987, and the peak in earnings moves to a later age group. In 1969, the peak earnings period for this group was age 25–34, after which earnings remained flat over the balance of the life-course. In 1987, earnings of unskilled service workers climbed faster than in 1969 and peaked in the 35–44 age bracket.

Full-time men make the most of any group considered, and have the steepest age–earnings trajectory. The earnings curve for this group is steeper and peaks later in 1987 than in 1969. In contrast, full-time women's earnings curve remains much flatter than men's in

Table 8.5   *Age–earnings profiles of unskilled service workers,*
USA, 1969 and 1987 (median annual earnings, dollars)

	Total	Age groups					
		16–24	25–34	35–44	45–54	55–64	65+
Total							
1987	6,888	2,250	9,375	10,563	10,438	9,500	3,688
1969	4,000	2,000	5,000	4,000	4,000	4,000	2,000
Part-time men							
1987	2,000	1,188	3,938	5,000	4,188	4,000	3,500
1969	2,000	1,000	6,000	5,000	5,000	3,000	1,000
Part-time women							
1987	2,500	1,688	3,500	3,400	4,000	3,500	2,250
1969	1,000	1,000	2,000	2,000	2,000	1,000	1,000
Full-time men							
1987	15,000	6,000	15,000	20,000	19,000	15,656	10,000
1969	6,000	4,000	7,000	7,000	7,000	6,000	4,000
Full-time women							
1987	8,500	5,000	9,000	9,688	10,000	10,750	6,280
1969	3,000	2,000	3,000	3,000	3,000	3,050	2,000

Part-time: less than 35 hours

1987, and is not markedly steeper than it was in 1969. On a more
positive note, it should be remembered that women working full
time garnered the largest wage increases of any group between 1969
and 1987.

A flat earnings profile continues to characterize part-time
unskilled service workers. From age 25 on, there is no clear trend in
the earnings of unskilled part-time workers in either 1969 or 1987
for either men or women. As I noted in discussing Table 8.3, the
decline in real earnings of part-time workers throughout the US
economy is a troubling development.

In analyses not shown, I found that these age–earnings profiles
are steeper in unskilled manual jobs than they are in unskilled
service occupations, but that this difference is principally due to a
greater concentration of part-time jobs in unskilled service occupations. Among full-time workers, the manual workers had only
slightly higher pay and a slightly steeper age–earnings profile
than the service workers. Sales occupations also paid better and
had a steeper earnings trajectory than the unskilled service occupations. In this case, the difference remained even among full-time
workers.

The trend toward a sharper age–earnings profile among unskilled
service workers partly reflects a steeper age–earnings profile in the
US labor force as a whole. In related analyses not included in this
chapter, I have found a similar increase in the slope of the age–

earnings profile for all full-time workers, both male and female. Not surprisingly, part-time workers do not earn substantially more as they get older.

Two important caveats about these age–earnings profiles are in order. These data are cross-sectional, and consequently do not necessarily reflect the experience of individuals over the course of their careers, for two separate reasons. First, this analysis implies that the earnings of young workers are likely to rise as they get older because older workers earn more than younger workers. This inference would be incorrect if the future earnings growth were stymied for any reason. In this case, the earnings of today's younger cohorts would not climb in the same way as has been the case for earlier groups. Secondly, the substantial career.mobility of individuals means that the occupational age–earnings profile does not apply to the same people at different ages. This caveat is especially pertinent in the case of unskilled service workers, who enter and leave these jobs with great frequency during the early stages of their labor force experience. Thus, even with data comparing cohorts, occupational mobility during the career would make inferences about the earnings experiences of individuals a hazardous endeavor.

The pessimistic view of these data is that the earnings position of young workers has seriously eroded over the last two decades. Proponents of this view might well worry that the future prospects of this cohort might also be dim. On the other hand, a more optimistic inference that might be drawn from these analyses is that employers see an increase in work performance from more experienced workers. That might account for the willingness of employers to pay older workers so much more than younger ones. Economists would no doubt maintain that in the absence of such a relationship employers would substitute cheap young workers for older expensive workers. If a growing age–performance relationship accounts for the heightened age–earnings profiles we see in Table 8.5, then we may be entitled to expect continued earnings growth for those entering service occupations.

These data clearly indicate a decline in the real earnings of young unskilled service workers between 1969 and 1987, as well as a sharp decline in the real earnings of part-time workers during this period. Whether there will be steep earnings gains for the full-time unskilled service workers who remain in these jobs remains to be seen.

The last question we must examine, however, is whether individuals tend to remain in these jobs for their entire careers, or whether they tend to occupy them only briefly.

Career Mobility of Unskilled Service Workers

For the mobility analysis, I employ Current Population Survey data for both time points because these data include a comparable one-year retrospective occupation and industry question. The mobility analyses compare movement during the 1971–2 period to that observed during the 1987–8 period.[4]

Table 8.6 reports exit rates from unskilled service occupations for four types of moves. Overall, the rate of exit from unskilled service jobs increased slightly between 1971–2 and 1987–8, to 11.91 from 10.75 percent in a one-year period. Most of this change was probably associated with movements into sales and clerical occupations, and one may question whether these moves truly represent upward mobility. The rate of mobility into white-collar employment increased to 7.81 from 6.29 percent, but the rate of movement into managerial, professional and technical jobs declined slightly. The balance represents moves into skilled service, sales and clerical occupations. Finally, the rate of movement into both skilled and unskilled manual occupations declined slightly during this period.

The demographic breakdown of movers presented in Table 8.6 is revealing. The annual exit rate from unskilled service work is remarkably high for young workers. For both years considered, the annual rate of exit from unskilled service jobs exceeded 20 percent for 16- to 24-year-olds, and exceeded 10 percent for 25- to 34-year-olds. Thus, there is a great deal of flux in the membership of unskilled service work, especially during the early stages of workers' careers. The high rate of mobility in the United States is lower than indicated by the Canadian data: some of this excess may be due to methodological differences.[5] Nonetheless, the qualitative result is the same: young individuals move in large numbers into and out of unskilled service work. The Scandinavian countries also exhibit substantial mobility: the exceptions in this regard are Britain and, even more strikingly, Germany.

Between 1971–2 and 1987–8, all exit rates increased for workers aged 16–24. For those aged 25–54, almost all exit rates increased except moves into professional and managerial occupations. Among older workers, the pattern of change was more mixed. These data suggest that unskilled service work represents a temporary status for many young American workers, and that incumbency in such jobs is slightly more temporary today than during the 1970s.

Women's exit rates increased for all types of moves except moves into professional, managerial and technical occupations, and women's exit rates exceeded men's for all except moves into manual occupations. Blacks, in contrast, had lower rates of mobility than Whites, and all their exit rates from unskilled service jobs increased except for moves into manual occupations.

Table 8.6   *Exit rates of unskilled service workers, by worker attributes, USA, 1971–2 and 1987–8*

	Left	Non-manual[a]	Moved into Professional/ managerial[b]	Manual
Total				
1987–8	11.91	7.81	2.49	4.10
1971–2	10.75	6.29	2.52	4.46
Female				
1987–8	12.05	9.91	2.67	2.15
1971–2	10.40	8.66	3.46	1.74
Male				
1987–8	11.77	5.72	2.32	6.05
1971–2	11.08	3.96	1.59	7.12
Black				
1987–8	8.74	5.51	1.78	3.24
1971–2	6.08	2.73	0.77	3.36
White				
1987–8	12.45	8.20	2.61	4.25
1971–2	12.04	7.28	3.00	4.76
Full-time				
1987–8	9.15	5.29	1.57	3.86
1971–2	10.54	6.11	2.62	4.43
Part-time				
1987–8	16.89	12.34	4.15	4.54
1971–2	11.06	6.56	2.36	4.50
Full year worked				
1987–8	6.56	4.53	1.34	2.04
1971–2	6.14	3.67	1.60	2.46
Part year worked				
1987–8	21.47	13.67	4.56	7.80
1971–2	18.10	10.47	3.97	7.63
Age 16–24				
1987–8	22.25	15.86	5.42	6.40
1971–2	21.21	12.78	3.96	8.43
Age 25–34				
1987–8	12.97	7.35	2.01	5.62
1971–2	11.93	6.50	3.20	5.43
Age 35–44				
1987–8	7.66	5.12	1.87	2.53
1971–2	8.37	4.47	2.38	3.90
Age 45–54				
1987–8	6.08	3.83	1.17	2.25
1971–2	4.82	3.14	1.61	1.68
Age 55–64				
1987–8	3.75	2.50	0.52	1.25
1971–2	4.71	2.79	1.25	1.92
Age 65+				
1987–8	3.82	2.50	0.52	1.25
1971–2	2.75	1.25	1.00	1.50

[a] Includes managerial, professional, technical, clerical and sales occupations.
[b] Includes professional, managerial and technical occupations.

Surprisingly, exit rates from unskilled service jobs were higher for part-time and part-year workers than for full-time and full-year workers. This pattern may indicate that employment in unskilled service jobs is used as a temporary holding measure for many workers who are subsequently mobile. In contrast, full-time and full-year workers in unskilled service jobs may be more likely to represent a post-industrial proletariat with much more limited prospects for career mobility. All exit rates increased for part-time and part-year workers, while many of the exit rates declined for full-time and full-year workers.

Table 8.7 displays each type of exit rate by industry. The rate of mobility out of unskilled service occupations was highest for retail sales workers (other than the exceedingly small case of agriculture). Consumer and business services follow, with social services and public administration exhibiting substantially lower exit rates. Of the industries with substantial numbers of unskilled service workers, only public administration lagged behind manufacturing in the rate of exit from unskilled service jobs. Retail sales and consumer services saw increases in the rate of exit from unskilled service jobs between 1971 and 1987, while social services and public administration saw declines. The same industry differentials hold for mobility into white-collar jobs. However, for movement into managerial, professional and technical occupations, the inter-industry differentials are much narrower.

Two findings should be noted about mobility into these relatively elite occupations. First, retail sales continues to exceed other industries in the rate of upward mobility. This may reflect the widespread availability of relatively low-level managerial positions in the retail sales industry. Secondly, all service industries exceed manufacturing in the rate of upward mobility.

Occupational mobility tables were constructed for 1971–2 and 1987–8 for all workers, and for full-time and part-time workers separately (these results are presented in Jacobs, 1991). As far as the destinations of unskilled service workers are concerned, between 1987 and 1988 one-third of leavers went to sales and clerical occupations, one-third to manual jobs, one-sixth to skilled service jobs, and one-sixth to managerial, professional and technical jobs. Between 1971 and 1972, almost 40 percent of leavers went to manual occupations, almost one-quarter to managerial, professional and technical jobs, with the remaining third entering sales, clerical and skilled service occupations. The biggest change in the interim, then, was the decline in exits to manual jobs and elite jobs, with a corresponding rise in entry into sales, clerical and skilled service jobs.

Table 8.8 presents the results of a pooled mobility analysis of each

Table 8.7 Exits from unskilled service occupations, by industry and type of move, USA, 1971–2 and 1987–8

	Consumer service	Retail sales	Social service	Public admin.	Business service	Manufac-turing	Whole-sale	Utility/ Transport	Agri-culture/ other	Mining	Total
Leavers											
1987–8	12.00	17.58	8.82	5.39	12.25	7.96	7.59	4.91	22.52	0.00	11.91
1971–2	9.62	15.25	9.45	5.88	12.18	6.72	4.05	7.46	25.78	0.00	10.75
Non-manual occupations											
1987–8	7.87	13.23	6.40	3.59	7.17	2.80	3.45	2.00	8.40	0.00	7.81
1971–2	6.00	9.83	6.36	2.52	5.18	2.34	1.35	3.51	7.03	0.00	6.29
Managerial, professional and technical occupations											
1987–8	2.10	3.97	2.32	1.80	2.31	1.47	1.38	0.91	2.29	0.00	2.49
1971–2	2.31	3.48	3.21	0.84	2.07	0.94	1.35	0.66	2.34	0.00	2.52
Manual occupations											
1987–8	4.13	4.35	2.41	1.80	5.09	5.16	4.14	2.91	14.12	0.00	4.10
1971–2	3.63	5.42	3.10	3.36	6.99	4.38	2.70	3.95	18.75	0.00	4.46

Table 8.8 *Determinants of exit from unskilled service occupations, USA, pooled analysis, 1987–8 and 1971–2*

	All leavers	To non-manual occupations	To professional, managerial, and technical occupations	To manual occupations
	Beta (SE)	Beta (SE)	Beta (SE)	Beta (SE)
Intercept	−2.873* (.277)	−6.427* (.411)	−9.355* (.657)	−0.961* (.344)
Industries				
Consumer services	0.347* (.164)	0.671* (.237)	1.132* (.413)	0.012 (.219)
Retail sales	0.357* (.156)	0.566* (.229)	0.984* (.403)	0.128 (.204)
Social services	0.084 (.159)	0.332 (.232)	1.127* (.400)	−0.191 (.216)
Business services	0.393 (.208)	0.515 (.314)	0.920 (.519)	0.167 (.259)
Manufacturing	−0.199 (.205)	−0.115 (.330)	0.284 (.549)	−0.246 (.250)
Reference[a]	0.432 (.366)	1.667* (.523)	2.112* (.857)	−0.398 (.465)
Year interaction terms				
Consumer services	−0.108 (.214)	−0.045 (.303)	−0.722 (.521)	0.154 (.291)
Retail sales	−0.109 (.203)	0.132 (.291)	−0.388 (.500)	0.460 (.276)
Social services	−0.118 (.210)	0.019 (.297)	−0.587 (.502)	0.215 (.296)
Business services	−0.053 (.258)	0.102 (.378)	−0.308 (.624)	0.084 (.334)
Manufacturing	0.259 (.273)	0.132 (.436)	0.239 (.688)	−0.293 (.336)
Female	−0.095 (.093)	0.916* (.126)	0.781* (.191)	−1.581* (.163)
Black	−0.474* (.126)	−0.763* (.181)	−1.115* (.324)	−0.029 (.171)
Education	0.131* (.019)	0.307* (.027)	0.400* (.039)	−0.068* (.025)
Full time	0.522* (.094)	0.518* (.117)	0.474* (.178)	0.371* (.143)
Full year worked	−0.981* (.094)	−0.699* (.119)	−0.649* (.180)	−1.230* (.145)

Table 8.8 *continued*

	All leavers	To non-manual occupations	To professional, managerial, and technical occupations	To manual occupations
	Beta (SE)	Beta (SE)	Beta (SE)	Beta (SE)
Year interaction terms				
Female	−0.018	−0.504*	−0.868*	0.487*
	(.120)	(.156)	(.245)	(.211)
Black	0.305	0.612*	1.110*	−0.104
	(.170)	(.228)	(.401)	(.247)
Education	0.001	−0.078*	−0.038	0.045
	(.025)	(.035)	(.053)	(.033)
Full time	−0.770*	−0.863*	−1.045*	−0.386*
	(.123)	(.150)	(.240)	(.195)
Full year worked	−0.117	−0.150	−0.291	−0.181
	(.121)	(.150)	(.239)	(.193)
Age groups				
16–24	–	–	–	–
25–34	−0.544*	−0.681*	−0.099	−0.195
	(.121)	(.156)	(.229)	(.180)
35–44	−0.701*	−0.805*	0.001	−0.353
	(.135)	(.176)	(.251)	(.204)
45–54	−1.218*	−1.064*	−0.342	−1.311*
	(.151)	(.187)	(.269)	(.250)
55–64	−1.126*	−0.992*	−0.396	−1.154*
	(.169)	(.217)	(.325)	(.265)
65+	−1.602*	−1.631*	−0.450	−1.717*
	(.319)	(.467)	(.535)	(.437)
Year interaction terms				
16–24	–	–	–	–
25–34	0.219	0.111	−0.689*	0.360
	(.150)	(.190)	(.299)	(.229)
35–44	−0.089	0.006	−0.680*	−0.227
	(.177)	(.222)	(.335)	(.281)
45–54	0.267	0.064	−0.615	0.666*
	(.206)	(.253)	(.402)	(.338)
55–64	−0.224	−0.298	−1.228*	−0.084
	(.250)	(.311)	(.570)	(.411)
65+	−0.067	−0.323	−2.217*	0.653
	(.433)	(.630)	(1.147)	(.593)
Percentage reduction in χ^2	0.116	0.145	0.144	0.121

* $p < 0.05$ SE standard error   N = 6,598
[a] Industry reference group includes wholesale, utilities/transportation, public administration, mining, agriculture and other.

of the four types of exits from unskilled service occupations for the 1971–2 period and the 1987–8 period. The design of this analysis tests whether the overall rate of exit changed during this period, and examines whether the impact of industrial and individual variables changed over time.

The 'year' term is significantly positive for mobility into white-collar jobs and for mobility into managerial, professional and technical jobs. This finding indicates that these rates of mobility increased, net of changes in the attributes of workers in these jobs and net of changes in the effect of independent variables on the process of mobility.

None of the industry interaction terms is significant for any of the four types of exits. Consequently, we can conclude that any industry-specific changes in rates were due to changes in the attributes of incumbents in these industries.

The changes in the impact of two demographic factors was somewhat surprising. While the increase in the exit rates of Blacks seems plausible, the declining rate of exit of women, particularly into managerial, professional and technical occupations, was unexpected, given the general improvement in managerial employment opportunities for women in the United States (Jacobs, 1992). Also intriguing is the decline in mobility rates for full-time workers. By 1987–8, part-time and part-year workers had higher exit rates than full-time and full-year workers with similar attributes. As I suggested above, this pattern may reflect differences in attributes and strategies between those who rely on employment in unskilled service jobs versus those who use such jobs in more of a 'stop-gap' manner.

The age group interaction terms which are significant are generally negative. This indicates an increase in the mobility rate of the reference group, 16- to 24-year-olds, relative to those at older ages. These changes are most evident in overall exits and in mobility into managerial, professional and technical jobs.

The results in Table 8.8 on trends in exit rates are difficult to reconcile with an image of an increasingly trapped group of unskilled service workers. To be sure, most of the 'upward' mobility is into sales and clerical occupations. While one may question the extent to which these moves truly represent upward mobility, it is nonetheless hard to maintain that unskilled service workers represent a fixed strata with extremely circumscribed mobility prospects.

The analysis of mobility into unskilled service occupations for the 1971–2 and 1987–8 periods (data not shown) indicates that entry into unskilled service occupations declines sharply with age, education and employment in professional, technical, sales and clerical jobs. Employment in consumer services and retail sales increased one's chances of moving into unskilled service occupations between 1987 and 1988, while manufacturing employment reduced one's chances. Women, Blacks and part-year workers were more likely to move into unskilled service occupations between 1987 and 1988. The patterns are similar during the 1971–2 period, except that industry differentials grew and the chances of managers and sales workers moving into unskilled service occupations declined.

Conclusions

In the United States employment in unskilled service occupations edged up only slightly between 1969 and 1987. These jobs were disproportionately filled by young employees with limited educational credentials. Blacks and women were over-represented in unskilled service jobs, but their concentration in these jobs declined during this period.

Unskilled service jobs paid far less than the economy-wide average. This earnings deficit persisted after basic productivity-related attributes (education, experience, hours and weeks worked) were controlled. Further, the earnings gap between low-end service industries and the rest of the economy grew substantially between 1969 and 1987. This lag was due to the concentration of part-time workers in unskilled service jobs, whose earnings fell dramatically behind the rest of the labor force. Exit rates were very high for young employees in unskilled service jobs, and relatively few individuals entered such jobs from other types of employment after age 25.

Our analysis of the employment prospects of unskilled service workers indicates that this group is not growing rapidly nor is it becoming increasingly disconnected from other career opportunities. Our results suggest that sales and clerical occupations might be combined with unskilled service occupations in a broader analysis of the emerging post-industrial disadvantaged. Yet sales and clerical workers appear increasingly reluctant to switch into unskilled service jobs, which suggests that these occupations continue to be perceived as more desirable than unskilled service jobs. The data indicate much higher levels of early career mobility for unskilled service workers in the United States than is evident in Germany. In this respect there is greater similarity with the Scandinavian countries and Canada.

In the introduction I outlined several distinctive features of the US labor market that might be responsible for these patterns. The

United States has a lower level of unionization, has a weaker connection between formal education and the labor market, and relies more heavily on part-time employment than many other countries. Each of these factors contributes to the high rate of mobility in unskilled service. Explicitly comparative research will be needed to assess the role these arrangements play in accounting for the distinctive outcomes in the United States. In particular, more detailed comparisons of the distribution of part-time workers within the economies of different industrial countries would be highly desirable.

A vigorous debate over the causes of growing inequality has been underway in the United States since the early 1980s. The optimists point to the notion that the emerging service economy is likely to produce a continuing bevy of opportunities at the top of the occupational structure in the United States, albeit at a slower rate than in the past (Hout, 1988; Diprete and Grusky, 1990), while the pessimists fear that the US economy is becoming increasingly dominated by low-wage, low-skill positions (Harrison and Bluestone, 1988). Service employment is heterogeneous, including highly skilled social service and business service professions as well as low-level consumer service jobs. Since employment has been growing at both the top and the bottom end of the service economy, each group can marshall evidence in support of its position.

The decline in the earnings of unskilled service work reflects in part the political economy of the labor market. More research on the political economy of growing inequality is needed, as Harrison and Bluestone have called for. Political decisions affect many aspects of the service economy: the size and make-up of social service employment; minimum wage levels, which in turn affect the size of the unskilled service labor force; and finally union regulations, which by affecting unionization levels indirectly affect wages, working conditions and employment stability and security. The political system is perhaps more important in shaping the contours of the post-industrial class structure than that of the traditional industrial economy. Since industrial countries continue to differ in their political configurations, and since politics will be crucial in shaping the post-industrial future, there is every reason to expect each country to display unique features in the shape of its post-industrial class structure.

This chapter has principally focused on one aspect of the emerging post-industrial economy and social inequality in the United States: whether this process is generating a new, closed social class, namely a post-industrial proletariat. Our answer has primarily been a negative one. The principal changes in class structure conditioned by the emergence of a post-industrial economy in the United States remain uncertain at this time.

Nonetheless, we can speculate about emerging trends. The good news is that the bottom of the post-industrial society is far from closed, and shows little sign of becoming more closed over the last two decades. The bad news is that the economic distance from the bottom to the top is growing. Social class analysis should be as concerned about the marginals as it is about mobility. In other words, growing levels of inequality in a context of slow growth in real incomes may result in an increasing polarization of the class structure and potentially the political system as well. The deteriorating prospects for the young workers with limited educational credentials is disturbing, yet thus far they have continued to make gains as they enter their thirties. In the last twenty years the young have become increasingly conservative when they have not been apathetic (perhaps disaffected would be more accurate).

A key question this chapter leaves unanswered is whether the earnings and career profiles implied by cross-sectional age comparisons will be borne out in the lived experience of today's youngest cohorts. While the immiserization of this group has not ignited social unrest thus far, we will have to wait to see what happens if this group's expectations of improving lifestyles over the course of their lives are not realized. The career trajectories of younger cohorts will play an important role in shaping the political economy of post-industrialism.

Notes

1 In 1988, 2.6 percent of managers earned the top amount allowed in the coding scheme ($99,999). The overwhelming majority of these were men. These individuals probably earned more than $99,999, and consequently this figure was adjusted upward to correct for the bias imposed by this 'top-coding' procedure.

2 While the *level* of sex segregation varies with the precision of measurement, the direction of change is typically the same regardless of the aggregation of the data. See Jacobs and Lim (1992) for evidence of this empirical generalization. See Jacobs (1989) for evidence regarding the decline in sex segregation during the 1970s and 1980s.

3 Racial segregation as measured across major industrial categories fell for the labor force as a whole from 13.37 to 10.11 between 1969 and 1987, and fell even faster for part-time workers (it fell from 25.37 to 6.98 in this time period).

4 Using these data required translating the occupational and industry coding scheme into the 1970 codes. I estimate over 95 percent accuracy in this matching process (based on an analysis of the 1970 Census data, for which both sets of codes were available).

5 The United States results are based on a retrospective question, while the Canadian results are based on the comparison of individuals at two points in time in a large data base. It may be that the retrospective question employed in the

United States reduces the documented rate of mobility compared with the Canadian data because of under-reporting of change, while comparing panels across time tends to increase reports of mobility due to incomplete matching. Further, the Canadian analysis indicates the extent of occupational change, including changes within unskilled service work, while the US analysis counts as change only movements between major occupational groups.

9

Mobility Regimes and Class Formation

Gøsta Esping-Andersen

Should the concept of social classes still be regarded as an indispensable tool for understanding our society? In a sense, the answer to this question depends on how we interpret historical evolution. One view holds that the class-divided society was but a historical aberration, a pathology peculiar to the early stages of capitalist industrialization. Its salience diminished with the advent of welfare capitalism and the rise of the new middle classes; and, as we march towards the post-industrial society, we shall be leaving the world of classes behind us entirely. Post-industrial theorists, like Daniel Bell, prefer to speak of situs groups.

There is little doubt that the kind of polarization depicted by traditional class theory has lost much of its face validity. But in its place novel social cleavages are being identified. The neo-Marxists insist that the long-run trend towards proletarianization now also encompasses the broad white-collar strata; others note the emergence of new sources of division, such as the crystallization of a new scientific ruling class, the institutionalization of labor market and other dualisms, insider and outsider classes, or the consolidation of a new underclass. Still, are these phenomena real, and, if so, do they legitimately warrant the concept of class?

The empirical case against the neo-Marxist degradation cum white-collar proletarianization thesis is overwhelmingly strong (Erikson and Goldthorpe, 1992). Sørensen (1991) has a point when he maintains that the relevant social inequalities that sociologists seek to explain with the new theories of dualism and segmentation are, in reality, reducible to neoclassical economic theory. In this view, too, class can make no legitimate claim to theoretical primacy.

Sørensen's dismissal is, however, grounded in an essentially *static* analysis of the relations of exploitation and inequality. It ignores the case for a class theory based on a dynamic class-formative approach. Thus, following Goldthorpe (1987) and Erikson and Goldthorpe (1992), the question of class depends on whether, and to what degree, there exist forces which systematically structure collective life-chances, and thus create class closure.

An alternative interpretation of historical evolution springs from the recognition that the social basis for a class theory is being revolutionized, that we need to rethink the meaning of class to take into account the simultaneous decay of the traditional industrial order and rise of the new service society. The most recent class theories of Wright and Goldthorpe belong to this kind of interpretation, but do not, in our view, go far enough in breaking with theoretical orthodoxy.

Central to the efforts of both Wright and Goldthorpe is their attempt to reconstruct class theory to take into account the rise of new 'post-industrial' strata. As we discussed in Chapter 1, Wright (1985, 1989) follows the Marxist legacy of defining a priori the structural bases of class in terms of empty slots. He expands the concept of exploitation to include human capital assets, and is thus able to insert the new 'post-industrial' positions in a general class matrix. The ensuing empirical task is to validate the pre-defined classes.

The approach chosen by Goldthorpe (1982, 1987) and Erikson and Goldthorpe (1992), in contrast, sees classes as being formed through processes that mold distinctive, collectively shared life-chance scenarios. It is thus people's mobility experiences rather than their occupancy in 'empty slots' that elucidate their class membership. Goldthorpe's class scheme is defined with reference to hypothesized uniformities in life-chances. Of major importance is the recognition that class formation may have multiple roots.

The criterion of life-chances and the identification of multiple sources of class formation are, in our view, crucial to the study of stratification patterns in an evolving post-industrial society. If our social order is in great flux, undergoing a fundamental restructuration, and if new criteria govern people's life-choices, fluidity is likely to increase and traditional patterns of social closure may no longer prevail. It follows that the correlation between current position and final destination may be quite low: a static picture of the occupational structure may therefore be deceptive. The key issue, then, is whether the flux that exists confirms the 'end-of-classes' view of history, or whether it harbors the mainsprings of new regimes of class formation.

The great weakness of the static approach to classes is that it assumes one of the following: either that the degree of mobility across classes is so marginal as not to matter, or that the occupancy of any given 'empty slot' overwhelms an individual's identity formation to such a degree that prospects of mobility do not matter.

The static approach, as found in the research of Wright and associates, may be informative in an era of great stability. The 'fordist' industrial order conformed in many respects to this kind of scenario in that the life-cycle of the working-class masses was predictable and, mobility-wise, generally flat. Hence, if we knew where in the system a person had entered, we would be fairly sure to know that person's final destination.

The traditional view of classes assumes, in a sense, a 'fordist' type of mobility regime. This, however, is everywhere coming apart: its working-class incumbents are declining dramatically in absolute and relative terms, and are often being replaced either by upgraded functionally flexible core workers, or by a new army of 'disponible', peripheralized workers (Michon, 1981; Goldthorpe, 1990). It is safe to assume a concomitant change in authority hierarchies, promotional ladders and reward systems. Moreover, with the decline of fordism has come a rapid expansion of both professional and semi-professional cadres, and of lower-end service occupations. In neither case can we assume that life-chances and mobility behavior will follow the stable, predictable patterns of the conventional fordist life-cycle. Novel selection criteria are emerging. First, job and career opportunities depend increasingly on the self-servicing nexus, on welfare state policies, and on people's leisure preferences. Secondly, new kinds of labor supply characteristics are gaining in influence, including education, scientific expertise and immeasurable qualities such as social graces, inter-personal skills and adaptability. The kind of human capital needed in service production differs in qualitative ways, and social skills will almost certainly gain in value. Additionally, social skills are acquired mainly in the family or in expensive elite schools, not in the classrooms of mass education systems. Inherited privilege may therefore reappear as a decisive class-filter within post-industrial economics.

Our study began with the observation that the structure of jobs has changed dramatically in what, for want of better, we have termed a post-industrial direction. Its core attribute is a recast nexus between working life, the family and the state. The fordist nexus was built around the now standard model of a full-time male breadwinner, the full-time dedication of women to family self-servicing, both coupled to the welfare state's life-cycle guarantees. The post-industrial nexus, in turn, de-familializes social reproduction, frees women for labor supply, and creates a new and potentially huge demand for services in both production, reproduction and leisure. The life-cycle of all concerned is therefore open to more variety and less predictability. And, most important of all, life-chances are guided and structured by institutions, such as the welfare state, that have no analytical role within conventional class theory.

The erosion of fordism means that class formation as a dynamic phenomenon cannot be deduced from current class occupancy. This is principally why we chose to identify the coming class structure on the basis of a heuristic approach. As such, several options were available. We could have followed Breiger's (1981) approach, refraining from any kind of a priori class specification. Instead, classes would be deduced from the dividers that appear in the scrutiny of mobility tables. If, however, our intent is to establish the class-formative propensities of occupational groupings already identified by ourselves as theoretically important (such as our unskilled service class), it would be more apropos to subject a set of pre-defined job classes to empirical verification. In other words, our approach follows in the tradition of Goldthorpe (1987), Mayer and Carroll (1987) and Carroll and Mayer (1986). But, in contrast to Goldthorpe, our method of empirical specification is limited to intra-generational class formation. We cannot examine the influence of social inheritance on class destinies, that is, inter-generational mobility.[1]

Patterns of Post-industrial Class Formation

The class scheme used in this book differs from existing models in two important respects. First, it is based on the idea that the fordist and post-industrial hierarchies are fundamentally different. They should be distinguished for reasons of both employment relations and mobility patterns. Thus, the nature of hierarchy, authority and rewards, on the one side, and the patterns of career mobility, on the other side, should be qualitatively different. The validity of our class scheme depends, therefore, on whether 'post-industrial' jobs and mobility patterns are distinct: does a post-industrial stratification regime exist?

To support this claim, we should be able to detect very different *patterns* of employment relations and career behavior in the two hierarchies. We should also anticipate a certain degree of closure between the two hierarchies. This implies that we should find patterns of job moves that are hierarchically distinct. If the intra-hierarchy flows and the inter-hierarchy flows in *both directions* are of roughly similar magnitude, the case for our post-industrial distinction would be severely weakened.[2]

Our post-industrial mobility regime also incorporates the possibility of an 'outsider class'. Outsiders are most likely to be formed into a class where barriers to labor market entry are huge, where their life-chances converge around similar dependencies (on welfare state transfers, for example), and where outsider 'careers' emerge (such as when laid-off workers slide into long-term unemployment and subsequently take early retirement).

Secondly, our class scheme differs from the 'conventional view', held by Goldthorpe (1983), that (married) women should be assigned to the class position of their male partners. Indeed, there are numerous reasons why our 'post-industrial' perspective compels us to treat women as independent agents. For one, huge sections of the service economy constitute, almost by definition, a female labor market. This is pre-eminently the case in the social services. These services are likely to be gendered labor markets in the sense that women and men hardly engage in direct competition and, more importantly, in the sense that they offer a gender-distinctive mobility and career trajectory. If the post-industrial labor market is also a women's labor market and if, additionally, it is welfare state dominated, chances are that gender-specific processes of class formation will emerge. A second major reason for examining women as separate agents follows from the post-industrialization of the family self-servicing nexus. While social services create a female occupational hierarchy, they also loosen women's identification with their familial role; they allow women to design career scenarios and life-cycle destinies independently of any male partner. Indeed, women increasingly delay, and even refrain from, marriage, let alone child-bearing, for career-specific reasons (Blossfeld and Huinink, 1991). Vice versa, the integration of women in working life may simultaneously compel males to re-design *their* life-cycles. As we know, the life-cycle profile of men and women is converging (Oppenheimer, 1988).

The Case for a Post-industrial Proletariat

The unskilled service workers are, in our study, the analytical prism through which we have sought to establish the contours of an emerging class structure. If, as was generally the case for the traditional manual worker, the unskilled service jobs are emerging as a relatively closed, dead-end career road, from which improvement is unlikely and in which life-chances are strongly pre-ordained to be poor, there would be a case in favor of the pessimistic theory of post-industrial society: we would be able to speak of a post-industrial proletariat.

The overall trends in industrial and occupational change that we examined in Chapter 2 indicated an essentially positive development. Everywhere, the occupational structure is being upgraded in that the qualified professional, technical and semi-professional jobs have grown considerably faster than bottom-end servicing jobs (or, for that matter, traditional clerical and sales jobs). Industry shifts (towards services) have been more powerful than the occupational shifts. Yet, as previous research shows, occupational upgrading also occurs independently of industrial transformation (Singelmann and Browning, 1980; Singelmann and Tienda, 1985). The structural trends appear positive, but this does not rule out the possibility of polarization and proletarianization.

In the late 1980s and early 1990s unskilled service jobs constituted anywhere from five percent (in Germany) to 15 percent (in Sweden) of the active labor force. Both their size and composition depend on how social institutions have helped resolve the Baumol 'cost-disease' problem; they will grow where industrial relations and welfare states allow a low-wage market, or where social services are expanded.

In contrast to most unskilled manual work, the prospects for labor substitution or productivity growth with technology are slim in the low end of the services. Hence, further growth will depend on the magnitude of the low-wage labor markets or on the threshold of popular tax tolerance. In neither case do we have reason to believe that the relative size of unskilled service jobs will increase much in the future. Therefore, if unskilled service workers are emerging as a distinct class, such a proletarian class is likely to remain numerically less influential than was its fordist manual parallel. And if, again, it were to constitute a class, its internal composition would doubtlessly be considerably more heterogeneous than is the manual proletariat. The latter are heavily male, while unskilled services have a large female bias; manual workers find themselves in a relatively homogeneous world of factories, while service workers are scattered across an exceedingly heterogeneous and often highly individualized work environment: from day-care centers and hospitals to restaurants and taxis.

Our data have shown that there are distinctive traits associated with the unskilled service jobs. There are no marked material disadvantages in the welfare state sector where pay, fringe benefits, job security and related conditions equal those of the mainstream manual or clerical worker. Unskilled service jobs in the private sector tend, however, to be characterized by sometimes severe disadvantages: very low pay, no fringe benefits, precarious job rights and weak trade union representation. These fit the description of the 'disponible' labor force: 'stand-by' workers, available when needed and discarded when not. For most of our countries, (lower-end) sales workers exhibit similar characteristics. There is, accordingly, the potential for a particular kind of class closure, one defined in terms of a relatively closed mobility circuit between unskilled service jobs, sales jobs, and including probably also unemployment and household work.

The central question, nonetheless, remains whether indeed we see the emergence of a new service proletariat, meaning a class imprisoned in a collectively shared, underprivileged dead-end career. Given the typical profile of working conditions, pay and security, the existence of such a proletariat would also indicate the emergence of substantial class polarization, at least for private sector workers.

Patterns of Social Recruitment

There is no clear, uniform profile of unskilled service worker recruitment, valid across all nations. Instead, our analyses suggest three main types. There is, first, a distinct Scandinavian model in which inflows are dominated by women with little education. They are likely to be part-time workers, seeking to harmonize family and work obligations within a welfare state setting. North America (and, perhaps, the United Kingdom) constitutes a second model. Here, the unskilled service jobs are more likely to be in private consumer (and also private social) services, and the typical recruit is very young (often minority) and uneducated; the degree of female over-representation is much less accentuated. Germany appears as a third model. Women are very over-represented, but unskilled service jobs also function as an important reservoir for redundant (even skilled) industrial labor, perhaps of immigrant status, and not old enough to qualify for early retirement. In Norway, too, unskilled service jobs absorb large numbers of 'de-industrialized' manual workers.

Patterns of Class Mobility

Class formation has mainly to do with life-cycle closure, and in this respect there are no indications of proletarianization. In all countries, except Germany, there is a high degree of social fluidity among the unskilled service workers; the majority remain for brief periods and move onwards – and upwards.

The mobility periods that we have monitored differ between the countries. For most countries we have roughly ten-year interludes, but for Canada and the United States the periods are of only one to two years. All things considered, we would expect much higher rates of mobility over a ten-year span than over a one- to two-year span. We must also note differences in timing. For most countries, we are observing mobility behavior during the 1980s; for Norway, however, the period in question is the 1970s. Mobility differences may be a function of a period effect.

Except for Germany, unskilled service jobs (together with sales) show dramatically lower stability than all other occupational categories. For example, in the United States, the annual rate of outflow was 12 percent in the 1980s, up from ten years earlier. The retention rates in Canada are even lower. In Norway, almost 65 percent of the 1970 unskilled service workers had moved within ten years. A ten-year cumulation would, of course, not produce a 120 percent outflow in the United States, but as Jacobs' analyses suggest, most of the unskilled service workers of the 1970s would be unlikely to have remained as such in the 1980s. Similar levels of fluidity obtain for Sweden and the United Kingdom. Germany is the dramatic exception. Here, as Blossfeld shows, the majority (almost 60 percent) of unskilled service workers remain immobile.

Everywhere but in Germany, the unskilled service jobs look like transitional stop-gap jobs, especially for the young. In the United States, as in Sweden, the probability of outward mobility was twice as high for the youngest cohorts. Yet it would be completely false to view the unskilled service jobs as a catalyst for rags-to-riches mobility. The dominant pattern everywhere is one of mainly short-range, or at the most medium-range, mobility. But the patterns differ substantially between the countries. In the *Scandinavian* countries, the main pattern of mobility is, predictably, concentrated within the welfare state hierarchies: from, say, nursing aides or homehelper to skilled nurse or social worker. In Norway, upward mobility in the welfare state hierarchy is especially pronounced. This is almost certainly a function of the later, but very rapid, growth of social services in Norway: a catch-up effect. As the social services reach saturation point, which is now more or less the case in Sweden, the capacity to count on the welfare state hierarchy for an escape from unskilled service work may diminish.

In the *United States* and *Canada*, unskilled service jobs are heavily concentrated in the consumer service industries, and the data suggest quite different mobility trajectories. Here there is, of course, no equivalent to the Nordic welfare state hierarchy. These jobs are evidently very much bridging jobs for youth, but the bridging is usually to modest careers in alternative, slightly more skilled and qualified private sector services, administrative-clerical jobs or sales jobs. In the United States in the 1980s, about 17 percent of workers experienced long-range moves into managerial, professional and technical jobs, compared to 30 percent who moved to clerical and sales. The similarity between unskilled service jobs and sales occupations seems especially pronounced in the American study.

The *British* unskilled service workers are, as in North America, a sizable stratum and mainly concentrated in private sector services. They are, however, clearly less mobile and when they do move it is much less likely to be in an upward direction. Indeed, for males the most likely move is to manual work. For a full sixteen-year period, Gershuny shows that 54 percent of males and 70 percent of women were non-mobile, unskilled service workers. Hence, unskilled service workers in Britain seem to combine the worst features of the American and German model: large but relatively immobile – a potential proletariat.

The feminization of the unskilled service jobs is, in comparison to Scandinavia, much less pronounced in North America. The gender bias in terms of mobility seems, however, quite high among the short-range movers, but much less so among the long-range career movers. Thus, in the United States, short-range female movers will tend to favor clerical and sales jobs, while males have a higher chance of moving to manual jobs. In terms of highly upward career mobility, the American data suggest a phenomenal gender equalization. By the 1980s, males' and females' chances of moving from unskilled service to professional-managerial jobs were almost identical.[3]

Germany, like Britain, exhibits low rates of mobility out of the unskilled service occupations. And, like Britain, where mobility occurs, it tends to be either horizontal (to unskilled clerical and sales for example) or short-range. The probability of moving into professional-managerial jobs was, indeed, zero; into technical semi-professional jobs about 5 percent. Upward moves are thus essentially into skilled administrative, sales or manual jobs. Instead, the most likely moves for German unskilled service workers are *outward*: 10 percent ended up as unemployed, almost 50 percent as housewives.

Our focus on the mobile workers obscures the fact that, in all countries, there remains a core of workers destined to remain in unskilled service jobs through most of their employment career. This proportion is especially high in Germany and Britain. This may seem less troubling in Germany, where unskilled service work accounts for such a small share of total employment (its share is only half as large as in the United States and a full three times as small as in Sweden). Still, be it proportionately large or small, the question is whether the residual core that remains constitutes a peculiar 'class', a proto-proletarian margin. Our data are considerably less well equipped to answer this question.

There are some common characteristics among the stayers that may add up to a basic profile. First (and primarily), education emerges as the *alpha and omega* of escape; this is perfectly consistent with mainstream post-industrial theory, namely that human capital will evolve as the hegemonic determinant of life-chances. Education is everywhere the single most salient precondition for mobility out of unskilled service work. In Sweden, for example, you are four times as likely to move with a university education, and twice as likely with a secondary education.

Secondly, women are more likely to remain imprisoned in a proto-proletarian core. This may partially be a function of their lower educational attainment, but may also reflect their rotation between family and unskilled service jobs. This 'family effect' should be prevalent especially outside Scandinavia where women cannot easily count on a service apparatus (and lenient absenteeism policies) to permit them to harmonize work with child care. There is some evidence in favor of this argument. In Germany, 45 percent of unskilled service workers moved to housewife status, compared to 18 percent in Norway. Unfortunately, the data for many of our countries do not permit us to identify the 'family effect'.

The core that remains in unskilled service jobs may, therefore, be a permanent or a fluid one. The United States chapter (like the German) identifies a permanent core of older, uneducated, steadily employed unskilled service proletarians, working on a full-time basis, and with little possibility of escape. This full-time core co-exists with possibly two kinds of fluid groups: women rotating between unskilled service work and the family, and another group (probably more likely male) rotating between unskilled work and unemployment. Here then, are, the makings of a new post-industrial 'stand-by' class, a class that seems functionally equivalent to the migrant rural workers and peasant-workers of early industrialism.

In the United States, there exists also the possibility of an alternative kind of 'underclass core'. As the recent Jencks and Peterson (1991) study indicates, the large concentration of urban poverty can be attributed to principally two causes: the increased number of single mothers, and extremely low youth wages. The low-wage phenomenon in North America is, on one hand, what accounts for the dynamic growth of low-end service jobs; on the other hand, it generates poverty. For many, if not most, this kind of poverty may be transitional, but there is almost certainly a large core of uneducated persons for whom it will remain chronic within their own life-cycle as well as being passed on to their offspring.[4]

Post-industrial Mobility Regimes and Class Structuration

It seems safe to conclude that the specter of a massive post-industrial service proletariat seems unwarranted. From the point of view of class formation, fluidity and mobility patterns are simply too strong for any significant social closure to occur. Where, as in Germany, social closure is pronounced, the numerical importance of this kind of proletariat is quite insignificant. There may very well be a marginal core of non-mobiles in every country, but (except for Britain) its size is nowhere huge, and we must assume that it is socially quite heterogeneous and variegated.

If we take into account prevalent mobility patterns, however, there emerges the possibility of a more broadly-based class formation. For *women* lacking in skills, there is clearly a closed mobility circuit between unskilled services, (low-end) sales and (low-end) clerical work. This circuit could easily come to constitute a common underprivileged female 'class'. For *men*, a similar kind of inter-occupational closure is less evident. For one, males are typically a numerically marginal group among the unskilled service workers and, in some cases (like Germany and Norway), they are there because of industrial redundancies. When they move, they are either young and educated, and thus likely to engage in either long-range upward mobility, or they move into manual jobs (at least in Britain and the United States).

If, then, we can identify a broader-based class closure within which the (uneducated) unskilled service workers find themselves, it clearly is sexually differentiated. It is tempting to conclude that the unskilled service jobs function as two distinct links in an increasingly gender-divided process of class formation.

There is certainly a bottom end in the new service society, but its degree of class closure is highly uncertain. It is a stop-gap for those with education or for those who return to the family. Only a minority will usually remain unskilled service workers for long, but if they do not possess higher qualifications, their (high) rates of mobility imply basically a mobility within a circuit of essentially similarly unattractive jobs. If this circuit turns out to be a form of class closure, then it will be a very different kind of proletariat than is the traditional fordist industrial working class.

Our study has disclosed a seeming paradox: the basically high levels of mobility from the post-industrial bottom go hand-in-hand with a noticeable degree of closure within the post-industrial elite jobs. Everywhere, recruitment to the professional (and now even managerial) posts is closing up to all but those with post-secondary, and mainly university-level, educational credentials. The role of education in the post-industrial order may, accordingly, be to assure openness at the lower rungs of the stratification system, but solidification and class closure at the top. The distribution of access to higher education, and the degree of inter-generational transmission of human (and social) capital advantages, may be decisive for the extent to which class closure will evolve within the post-industrial elite. Access to educational credentials (and social skills) is clearly a potential catalyst of a new class axis.

The trends in occupational structure that we presented in Chapter 2 suggested substantial international divergence: a distinct North American, Scandinavian and German model. By and large, these nation differences remain salient in terms of the dynamics of life-cycle mobility. We should, nonetheless, not ignore the presence of a number of cross-national similarities. First, the service economy is everywhere associated with the evolution of two gendered labor markets. Except for routine administrative and sales jobs, the traditional fordist economy remains predominantly male. The evolving services are becoming a women's labor market. It is hardly an exaggeration to say that the post-industrial economy, as we have defined it, is a female economy; in the United States, the female bias is modest (and in decline), but in Scandinavia it is extreme. Accordingly, hidden behind the common general trend we find sharp differences, and these have to do with nation-specific institutional arrangements.

The degree of sectorial sex-segregation may be a function of the institutional embeddedness of labor markets, but we should also note the effect of timing. Women were once an important source of manual labor in industries such as textiles, clothing and many food industries. These were also the first to rationalize or 'de-industrialize', shedding huge numbers of women workers. Therefore, as the new services began to expand after the 1960s, there was a ready-made supply of women to fill them. Male-dominated industries, in contrast, were later to de-industrialize, and when this began to occur in a massive way, early retirement existed as a major option to unemployment. The sex-based differential in labor supply certainly helped mold the post-industrial jobs into a female labor market, whether they were welfare state jobs, as in Scandinavia, or private sector service jobs, as in North America.

A second commonality is that the unskilled service workers are almost everywhere a mobile stratum. They tend to be young, and enter these jobs for 'stop-gap' reasons: as a bridge between education and careers, as a temporary source of earnings between (or before) family obligations, or as a labor market entry point for immigrants or returning wives. That unskilled service jobs can also perform the function of a dumping ground for redundant industrial manpower is evident in Germany and Norway. But, once again, the common trend is composed of great national variety. In Germany, the lion's share of mobility is accounted for by the pendulum movement of women between work and family. This is clearly not the case in Scandinavia and North America where full-time female family activity has ceased to be a norm, and where mobility is therefore between jobs.

A third common trend is that the unskilled service jobs are less distinct than we initially assumed. Our countries seem to converge in the sense that these jobs form part of a larger, essentially unskilled, labor market that includes sales jobs and probably also the lower end of clerical occupations. For men, there is also a certain overlap between unskilled service and unskilled manual jobs.

The fourth, and most visible, convergence has to do with the role of education. It is clear that life-chances and class formation are everywhere increasingly a function of education: the spread of mass education at higher than primary school levels means also that the bottom end of the job structure will be more mobile; limited access to professional degrees tends to close the top.

What our study shows, however, is that convergent trends find very different national expression. The nations exhibit distinct mobility regimes and, as such, convergent macro-trends camouflage different outcomes. This is most clearly seen in the mobility behavior. Given the gendered specificity of the labor market, there are also indications of emerging mobility hierarchies. This is most pronounced in the Scandinavian welfare state model, where the social service job hierarchies function as a relatively closed female career system. Compared to elsewhere, Scandinavian women have good opportunities for longer-range upward mobility, especially into the semi-professional occupations. This is no doubt an attribute of (expanding) welfare state hierarchies and these countries' accent on continued adult training. In contrast, women in North America follow mobility trajectories that favor movement between unskilled service jobs, sales and clerical occupations. There is less sectoral closure in the United States and also a high probability of long-range career moves for women. In Scandinavia, it seems, women pay the price for good mobility opportunities by suffering greater sectoral segregation; this is less the case in the United States.

The German service economy is substantially less developed than in either of the two other models. It is, nonetheless, also quite female dominated. However, in Germany the possibility of an emerging divide between the fordist and post-industrial labor market is overwhelmed by the much more powerful skill barrier. Germany exhibits a dual labor market structure with two distinct mobility regimes. At the bottom we find a closed system occupied by the unskilled, unable to move out. Above the skill barrier, we find a labor market characterized by high levels of mobility; indeed, a skilled worker has surprisingly good chances of upward mobility into technical and semi-professional/managerial positions.

These regime differences must certainly be attributed to institutional factors, the welfare state and education being of primary importance. As others have previously argued (Haller et al., 1985; König and Müller, 1986; Allmendinger, 1989a,b), the rigidity of the German labor market has to do with its educational and vocational training system: job entry is defined by credentials and certifications. Hence, those lacking in skills will automatically find themselves exiled into the secondary, unskilled labor market. In contrast, the schooling–job nexus is much looser in all our other countries. In the American system, on-the-job training within an 'organizational mobility space' plays a very large part in promotional trajectories; in the Swedish system, active adult training and retraining schemes permit greater mobility chances across the life-cycle.

Besides education, the welfare state is obviously decisive; indeed, in two ways. First, if it is service oriented, it creates a labor market *and* an internal mobility hierarchy that maximizes women's participation within an essentially female career structure. Secondly, it allows women to become class structural agents in their own right because it grants them the opportunities to design career paths regardless of child and family obligations.[5] A service-heavy welfare state, as in Scandinavia, will therefore create an interaction effect: men's and women's career profiles will tend to converge, but in an extremely segregated setting. A welfare state-led post-industrialization may be both egalitarian and at the same time segmentary in terms of life-chances.

The absence of social services, on the other hand, inhibits female participation. From a life-cycle perspective, young women may enter employment, but will be much less capable of choosing careers. Germany is the archetypical case of this. The propensity of women to opt for an unskilled entry job may be related to their anticipation of soon thereafter withdrawing into housewife status. But even among skilled and professional women, the probability of leaving employment within ten years is comparatively very high.

Conclusion

A distinct post-industrial class structure may be emerging. If it does, national differences will be substantial and probably nowhere will it conform to the image of either the gloomy pessimists or the starry-eyed optimists. Clearly, we shall not be able to dispense with the unattractive jobs. The servant classes of the past were largely composed of *personal* servants, of nannies, butlers and coachmen tending to the needs of one household; the servant workers of post-industrial society service perform very similar tasks, but on behalf of anonymous masses; their character is more collective. Most of our new collective servants are not, as in the past, condemned to life-time servitude. Hence, the pessimists are wrong when they see a future of mass proletarianization.

They are also wrong if they draw parallels between the new unskilled service masses and the industrial unskilled proletariat. The industrial worker was by and large condemned to a pre-determined class destiny, a destiny that was gradually made toler-able by the life-cycle guarantees and job rights that the welfare state and the industrial relations apparatus introduced. The fordist proletarian was decidedly a class animal, even when affluence delivered the two-car garage, a decent pension and a Visa Card. The unskilled service workers, in contrast, are not condemned to know their future. They are structurally quite undetermined, fluid particles on the way to something else, be it careers, unemployment or mothering. They are not a class, but people temporarily willing or forced to take unpleasant jobs. In the Scandinavian welfare state setting, they are granted the trappings of the fordist worker; but in the private sector, these are jobs that deliver neither life-cycle safety and 'affluence', nor a two-car garage and a decent pension.

The post-industrial labor market may be more or less closed. Where it is heavily social service-biased, as in the Nordic countries, it seems also a very closed internal hierarchy; where not, as in the United States, career prospects will be less sectorally constrained. In any case, education has become the determinant of life-chances, and this is where the post-industrial optimists are mistaken. Instead of being the great leveller of classes, education may very well create a deep post-industrial class divide. We have seen this tendency emerging in different ways. The German system creates a barrier between skilled and unskilled; the system is open for the former, but closed for the latter. The other countries exhibit a much looser and less formal connection between schooling and careers, and the net result is almost the exact opposite: the system is generally quite open to upward mobility at the bottom, but closing at the top.[6] Post-industrial class formation will therefore depend on patterns of educational access and attainment. It is not inconceivable that future reforms will greatly democratize access to prized educational credentials and thereby diminish the threat of class closure at the top. But if social skills emerge as an additional vital asset, socially inherited privilege will probably still manage to assert its influence on life-chances and class closure.

Our post-industrial job hierarchy turns out to be heavily female. This may very well be due to a period effect. Our study happens to bridge a historical watershed: service jobs expanded in the, relatively brief, era during which women (or, to a much lesser degree, immigrants) happened to be the main labor force reservoir. This kind of period effect is almost certainly combined with a gender effect: post-industrial jobs are often natural female jobs (requiring, indeed, many traditional female social skills) that once were performed exclusively within the family. Where they require few skills, housewives can enter employment with no further ado; and where skills are required, they are the kind that trained women are very likely to possess.

The post-industrial labor market is feminine for another reason. Historically, when women left industrial jobs their destiny was typically that of the housewife. The fordist system, indeed, was built on the logic of a full-time housewife and mother. But when men left industrial jobs during the past decades, the welfare system assured that employment exit became entry into retirement. Hence, during the expansionary period of service jobs, there existed no male labor supply pressure of a scope similar to women's.

The larger implications of this period effect can be quite dramatic, and this means that the generalizations we have reached may very well be invalid for even the next decade. This can be illustrated by a simple, and also probable, example. Let us assume that Sweden will be incapable of any further expansion of its social service apparatus. This means that the female labor market *and* career hierarchy will freeze up. The new cohorts entering the labor force, male and female, will accordingly find themselves competing within the same, essentially private service sector. It is possible that women will be crowded out, and perhaps return to their traditional self-servicing role. It is also possible that over-supply within the private sector will create severe downward pressures on wages, and that a low-wage-based, American-style 'McJobs scenario' will evolve. In brief, the uniquely Scandinavian post-industrial mobility regime that we have identified may easily transform itself into a German or an American look-alike; the institutions that gave rise to a given mobility regime are permeable and therefore so is class formation.

It follows that we have identified three *possible* post-industrial stratificational scenarios. They may, perhaps, not produce a new class *polarization*, but new cleavages seem unavoidable. We can escape a mass of bad jobs, but will instead have to accept a mass of outsiders. We can accept a mass of bad jobs and endow them with acceptable conditions, as in the welfare state model, or base their growth on low pay and minimal security, as in the American model.

If we can assure universal access to skills, those who find themselves in bad jobs will hardly evolve into a proletarian class. We may even wish to encourage their growth as a means of facilitating youth, female and immigrant labor market entry. Regardless of which road we choose, inegalitarian results are unavoidable. If opportunities for training and education become part and parcel of the citizen's guarantees, we should be able to avoid the kind of polarized inequality associated with a class of chronic post-industrial proletarians. For policy-makers, the implications are clear: we should reconsider the welfare state's commitment to educational citizenship.

Notes

1 Our lack of information on inter-generational class-transmission is especially lamentable if it is true that social skills are emerging as privileged human capital assets.

2 Note that the distinct 'post-industrial' hierarchy remains valid if we observe only one-way flows from the 'fordist' to the post-industrial hierarchy. Just as labor surpluses from agrarian economies were absorbed in the rising industrial labor markets, it is also possible that redundant industrial labor will be absorbed in service jobs.

3 Note that this conclusion is based on highly aggregated occupational strata. Disaggregation might very well show that females move into low-grade management (managing restaurants for example) while males have a greater likelihood of attaining top-level managerial jobs.

4 Recent data and analyses of this phenomenon in the United States are also presented in Burtless, ed. (1990). It emerges that the low-wage experience is especially associated with an interaction effect between low skills and youth.

5 We may add to this the more marginal effect on men's life-cycle. Parental leave programs and the like will, when utilized, bend the male life-cycle in the direction of women's, thus narrowing the traditional sex-specific life-cycle differential.

6 However, here we should not forget the probability of uneducated youths (inner-city, minority in particular) becoming trapped in a underclass poverty status. As both Wilson (1991) and Kasarda (1989) indicate, there is also a spatial cause behind the solidification of an urban underclass (truly disadvantaged to Wilson): the attractive jobs are located far away from where the disadvantaged are physically located. Unfortunately, our study has not considered the issue of geographical mobility.

Bibliography

Aaron, Henry and Burtless, Gary (eds) (1984) *Retirement and Economic Behavior*. Washington, DC: Brookings Institution.

Åberg, Rune (1984) 'Market-independent income distribution: Efficiency and legitimacy', in J.H. Goldthorpe (ed.), *Order and Conflict in Contemporary Capitalism*. Oxford: Clarendon Press. pp. 209–30.

Adler, Max (1933) 'Wandlung der Arbeiterklasse?', *Der Kampf*, 26: 367–414.

Ahrne, Goran and Wright, Erik (1983) 'Classes in the United States and Sweden: A comparison', *Acta Sociologica*, 26 (3/4): 211–35.

Alber, Jens (1982) *Vom Armenhaus zum Wohlfahrtsstaat: Analysen zur Entwicklung der Sozialversicherung in Westeuropa*. Frankfurt a.M.: Campus.

Aldrich, John H. and Nelson, Forrest D. (1984) *Linear Probability, Logit, and Probit Models*. Beverly Hills, CA, and London: Sage.

Allison, Paul D. (1984) *Event History Analysis: Regression for Longitudinal Event Data*. Beverly Hills, CA, and London: Sage.

Allmendinger, Jutta (1989a) *Career Mobility Dynamics*. Berlin: Max-Planck-Institut für Bildungsforschung.

Allmendinger, Jutta (1989b) 'Educational systems and labor market outcomes', *European Sociological Review*, 5: 231–50.

Applebaum, E. and Albin, P.S. (1988) 'Differential characteristics of employment growth in tertiary service and information and knowledge service industries'. Paper presented at symposium on 'The Impacts of Structural and Technological Change on the Labor Market'. Wissenschaftszentrum, Berlin (March).

Assimakopoulou, Zina, Esping-Andersen, Gøsta and van Kersbergen, Kees (1992) 'Post-industrial class structures'. Working Papers, SPS 92/18, European University Institute, Florence.

Auletta, Ken (1982) *The Underclass*. New York: Random House.

Baldwin, John R. and Gorecki, P.K. (1990) 'Structural change and the adjustment process'. Statistics Canada and the Economic Council of Canada, Ministry of Supply and Services, Ottawa, Canada.

Baumol, William (1967) 'Macroeconomics of unbalanced growth', *American Economic Review*, 57 (3): 415–26.

Beck-Gernsheim, Elisabeth (1976) *Der geschlechtsspezifische Arbeitsmarkt*. Frankfurt a.M.: Campus.

Beck-Gernsheim, Elisabeth and Ostner, I. (1978) 'Frauen verändern – Berufe nicht?', *Soziale Welt*, 29: 257–87.

Bell, Daniel (1960) *The End of Ideology*. New York: Free Press.

Bell, Daniel (1976) *The Coming of Post-Industrial Society*. 2nd edn. New York: Basic Books.

Betts, Julian (1990) 'Technological change and the labour market: Explorations in the theory of human capital'. Unpublished PhD dissertation, Department of Economics, Queen's University, Kingston, Ontario.

Blackburn, McKinley L. and Bloom, David E. (1990) 'Changes in the distribution of family income in Canada and the United States'. Paper presented at the annual meeting of the Canadian Economics Association (May).

Blackburn, McKinley L., Bloom, David E. and Freeman, Richard B. (1990) 'The declining economic position of less skilled American men', in Gary Burtless (ed.), *A Future of Lousy Jobs? The Changing Structure of US Wages*. Washington, DC: Brookings Institution. pp. 31–76.

Blau, Peter and Duncan, Otis Dudley (1967) *The American Occupational Structure*. New York: Wiley.

Block, Fred (1990) *Postindustrial Possibilities*. Berkeley: University of California Press.

Blossfeld, Hans-Peter (1987a) 'Labor market entry and the sexual segregation of careers in the FRG', *American Journal of Sociology*, 93: 89–118.

Blossfeld, Hans-Peter (1987b) 'Entry into the labor market and occupational careers in the FRG', *International Journal of Sociology*, 17: 86–115.

Blossfeld, Hans-Peter (1989) *Kohortendifferenzierung und Karriereprozess: Eine Längsschnittstudie über die Veränderung der Bildungs – und Berufschancen im Lebenslauf*. Frankfurt a. M.: Campus.

Blossfeld, Hans-Peter (1990) 'Changes in educational careers in the Federal Republic of Germany', *Sociology of Education*, 63: 165–77.

Blossfeld, Hans-Peter (1991) 'Is the German dual system a model for a modern vocational training system? A cross-national comparison of how different systems of vocational training deal with the changing occupational structure'. EUI Working Paper SPS no. 91/7, European University Institute, Florence.

Blossfeld, Hans-Peter and Becker, Rolf (1989) 'Arbeitsmarktprozesse zwischen öffentlichem und privatwirtschaftlichem Sektor', *Mitteilungen aus der Arbeitsmarkt- und Berufsforschung*, 22: 233–47.

Blossfeld, H.P., Giannelli, G. and Mayer, K.O. (1991) 'Expansion of the tertiary sector in the Federal Republic of Germany'. Working Papers, SPS 91/8, European University Institute, Florence.

Blossfeld, Hans-Peter, Hamerle, Alfred and Mayer, Karl Ulrich (1989) *Event History Analysis: Statistical Theory and Application in the Social Sciences*. Hillsdale, NJ: Lawrence Erlbaum Associates.

Blossfeld, Hans-Peter and Huinink, Johannes (1991) 'Human capital investments or norms of role transition? How women's schooling and career affect the process of family formation', *American Journal of Sociology*, 97: 143–68.

Blossfeld, Hans-Peter and Mayer, Karl Ulrich (1988) Arbeitsmarktsegmentation in der Bundesrepublik Deutschland, *Kölner Zeitschrift für Soziologie und Sozialpsychologie*, 40: 262–83.

Bluestone, Barry and Harrison, Bennett (1982) *The Deindustrialization of America*. New York: Basic Books.

Bluestone, Barry and Harrison, Bennett (1986) *The Great American Job Machine: The Proliferation of Low-Wage Employment in the US Economy*. Washington, DC: Joint Economic Committee of the United States Congress.

Bluestone, Barry and Harrison, Bennett (1989) 'Increasing inequality and the proliferation of low-wage employment in the US: A review of the debate and some new evidence'. Mimeo.

Boyd, Monica (1990) 'Sex differences in occupational skill: Canada, 1961–86', *Canadian Review of Sociology and Anthropology*, 27 (3): 285–315.

Boyd, Monica and Pryor, Edward (1989) 'The cluttered nest: The living arrangements of young Canadian adults', *Canadian Journal of Sociology and Anthropology*, 14 (4): 461–77.

Boyer, Robert (1988) *The Search for Labour Market Flexibility*. Oxford: Clarendon Press.

Braverman, Harry (1974) *Labor and Monopoly Capital: The Degradation of Work in the Twentieth Century*. New York: Monthly Review Press.

Braverman, Harry (1977) *Die Arbeit im Modernen Produktionsprozess*. Frankfurt a.M. and New York: Monthly Review Press.

Breiger, Ronald (1981) 'The social class structure of occupational mobility', *American Journal of Sociology*, 87 (3): 578–611.

Browning, Harley and Singelman, Joachim (1978) 'The transformation of the US labor force: The interaction of industry and occupation', *Politics and Society*, 8 (3–4): 481–509.

Brynjolfsson, Erik, Malone, Thomas, Gurbaxani, Vijay and Kambil, Ajit (1989) 'Does information technology lead to smaller firms?' Center for Coordination Science, MIT and UC Irvine.

Burtless, Gary (ed.) (1990) *A Future of Lousy Jobs? The Changing Structure of US Wages*. Washington, DC: Brookings Institution.

Carroll, Glenn R. and Mayer, Karl Ulrich (1986) 'Job-shift patterns in the Federal Republic of Germany: The effects of class, industrial sector and organizational size', *American Sociological Review*, 51: 323–41.

Clark, Colin (1940) *The Conditions of Economic Progress*. London: Macmillan.

Clement, W. and Myles, John (1994) *Relations of Ruling: Class, Gender and Postindustrialism in Comparative Perspective*. Montreal: McGill-Queen's University Press.

Cohen, Stephen and Zysman, John (1987) *Manufacturing Matters: The Myth of the Post-industrial Economy*. New York: Basic Books.

Colbjornson, Tom (1986) *Dividers in the Labor Market*. Oslo: Norwegian University Press.

Collins, R. (1979) *The Credential Society*. New York: Academic Press.

Connor, Steven (1989) *Postmodernist Culture: An Introduction to Theories of the Contemporary*. Oxford: Basil Blackwell.

Crompton, Rosemary and Jones, Gareth (1984) *White-Collar Proletariat: Deskilling and Gender in Clerical Work*. London: Macmillan.

Dahrendorf, Ralph (1959) *Class and Class Conflict in Industrial Society*. Stanford, CA: Stanford University Press.

Davis, S.J. and Haltiwanger, J. (1990) 'Gross job creation, gross job destruction and employment reallocation'. Discussion paper 90–4, Center for Economic Studies, US Bureau of the Census, Washington, DC.

Dex, Shirley (1984a) 'Women's occupational profiles'. *Department of Employment Gazette*, December.

Dex, Shirley (1984b) 'Women's work histories: an analysis of the Women and Employment Survey'. Department of Employment Working Paper no. 46.

Diprete, Thomas A. and Grusky, David B. (1990) 'Structure and trend in the process of stratification for American men and women', *American Journal of Sociology*, 91 (1): 107–43.

Doeringer, Peter B. and Piore, Michael J. (1971) *Internal Labor Markets and Manpower Analysis*. Lexington, MA: Heath.

Economic Council of Canada (1989) *Good Jobs, Bad Jobs*. Ottawa: Economic Council of Canada.

Economic Council of Canada (1991) *Employment in the Service Economy*. Ottawa: Economic Council of Canada.

Ehrenreich, B. and Ehrenreich, J. (1979) 'The professional-managerial class', in P. Walker (ed.), *Between Labor and Capital*. Boston, MA: South End Press. pp. 5–45.

Erikson, Robert (1990) 'Politics and class mobility: Does politics influence rates of social mobility?', in I. Persson (ed.), *Generating Equality in the Welfare State: The Swedish Experience*. Oslo: Norwegian University Press. pp. 247–66.

Erikson, Robert and Goldthorpe, John H. (1985) 'Are American rates of social mobility exceptionally high? New evidence on an old issue', *European Sociological Review*, 1: 1–22.

Erikson, Robert and Goldthorpe, John H. (1992) *The Constant Flux. A Study of Class Mobility in Industrial Societies*. Oxford: Clarendon Press.

Esping-Andersen, Gøsta (1990) *The Three Worlds of Welfare Capitalism*. Cambridge: Polity Press, and Princeton, NJ: Princeton University Press.

Esping-Andersen, Gøsta (1991) 'Post-industrial class structures: An analytic framework'. Unpublished manuscript, European University Institute, Florence.

Featherman, David, Selbee, Kevin L. and Mayer, Karl Ulrich (1989) 'Social class and the structuring of the life course in Norway and West Germany', in David I. Kertzer and Warner K. Schaie (eds), *Age Structuring in Comparative Perspective*. Hillsdale, NJ: Lawrence Erlbaum Associates. pp. 55–93.

Flora, Peter (1976) 'Modernisierung und die Entwicklung der westeuropäischen Wohlfahrtsstaaten.' Habilitationsschrift, University of Mannheim.

Foot, D.K. and Li, J.C. (1988) 'Youth unemployment: A reply', *Canadian Public Policy*, XIV (1): 109–11.

Freeman, Richard B. and Holzer, Harry J. (1986) *The Black Youth Employment Crisis*. Chicago, IL: University of Chicago Press.

Freeman, Richard B. and Medoff, James L. (1984) *What Do Unions Do?* New York: Basic Books.

Fuchs, Victor R. and Leveson, Irving F. (1968) *The Service Economy*. New York: National Bureau of Economic Research.

Gershuny, Jonathan (1978) *After Industrial Society: The Emerging Self-servicing Economy*. London: Macmillan.

Gershuny, Jonathan (1983) *Social Innovation and the Division of Labour*. Oxford: Oxford University Press.

Gershuny, Jonathan (1988) 'Changing times: A report to the Joseph Rowntree Memorial Trust'. University of Bath.

Gershuny, Jonathan and Marsh, Katherine (1993) 'Unemployment in work histories', in K. Marsh and D. Gallie (eds), *Unemployment*. Cambridge: Cambridge University Press.

Giannelli, Gianna and Esping-Andersen, Gøsta (1991) 'Labour costs and employment in the service economy', *Labour*, 4 (3): 107–31.

Giddens, Anthony (1973) *The Class Structure of Advanced Societies*. London: Hutchinson.

Goldthorpe, John H. (1982) 'On the service class, its formation and future', in A. Giddens and G. Mackenzie (eds), *Social Class and the Division of Labour*. Cambridge: Cambridge University Press. pp. 162–87.

Goldthorpe, John H. (1983) 'Women and class analysis: in defence of the conventional view', *Sociology*, 17 (4): 465–88.

Goldthorpe, John H. (1985) 'Soziale Mobilität und Klassenbildung: Zur Erneuerung einer Tradition soziologischer Forschung', in H. Strasser and J.H. Goldthorpe (eds), *Die Analyse sozialer Ungleichheit.* Opladen: Westdeutscher Verlag. pp. 155–73.

Goldthorpe, John H. (1987) *Social Mobility and Class Structure in Modern Britain.* 2nd edn. Oxford: Clarendon Press.

Goldthorpe, John H. (1990) 'Employment, class and mobility: A critique of liberal and Marxist theories of long-term change'. Paper presented at the first National Norwegian Conference on Sociology, Geiranger (May).

Goldthorpe, John and Marshall, Gordon (1991) 'The promising future of class analysis: A response to recent critiques'. Unpublished paper, Nuffield College, Oxford.

Goldthorpe, John H. and Payne, Clive (1986) 'Trends in intergenerational class mobility in England and Wales, 1971–1983', *Sociology*, 20 (1): 1–24.

Gouldner, A. (1979) *The Future of Intellectuals and the Rise of the New Class.* London: Macmillan.

Grubb, Norton W. and Wilson, Robert H. (1989) 'Sources of increasing inequality in wages and salaries, 1960–1980', *Monthly Labor Review*, 112 (4): 3–13.

Gustafsson, Björn and Uusitalo, Hannu (1990) 'Income distribution and redistribution during two decades: Experiences from Finland and Sweden', in I. Persson (ed.), *Generating Equality in the Welfare State: The Swedish Experience.* Oslo: Norwegian University Press. pp. 73–96.

Hagen, Kåre (1991) 'Where did the employees of the welfare state come from?', in J.E. Kolberg (ed.), *The Welfare State as Employer.* New York: M.E. Sharpe. pp. 59–90.

Haller, Max (1989) *Klassenstrukturen und Mobilität in fortgeschrittenen Gesellschaften.* Frankfurt a.M.: Campus.

Haller, Max, König, Wolfgang, Krause, Peter and Kurz, Karin (1985) 'Patterns of career mobility and structural positions in advanced capitalist societies', *American Sociological Review*, 50: 579–603.

Hamilton, Stephen F. (1990) *Apprenticeship for Adulthood.* New York: Free Press.

Hanefeld, Ute (1987) *Das Sozio-ökonomische Panel: Grundlagen und Konzeption.* Frankfurt a.M.: Campus.

Hannan, Michael T., Schömann, Klaus and Blossfeld, Hans-Peter (1990) 'Sex and sector differences in the dynamics of wage growth in the FRG', *American Sociological Review*, 55: 694–713.

Hanratty, Maria and Blank, Rebecca (1990) 'Down and out in North America: Recent trends in poverty in Canada and the United States'. Paper presented at the annual meeting of the Canadian Economics Association (May).

Harrison, Bennett and Bluestone, Barry (1988) *The Great U-Turn.* 2nd edn. New York: Basic Books.

Hartman, H. (ed.) (1986) *Computer Chips and Paper Clips.* Vols 1 and 2. Washington, DC: National Research Council.

Håvorsen, P. (1987) *Arbeidstidsundersøkelsen 1985: Dokumentasjon og frekvensfordelinger.* Bergen: Norsk Samfunnsvitenskapelig Datatjeneste, NSD Rapporter nr 68.

Hedström, Peter (1987) 'Disability pension: Welfare or misfortune?', in R. Erikson,

E. J. Hansen, S. Ringen and H. Uusitalo (eds), *The Scandinavian Model: Welfare States and Welfare Research*. New York: M.E. Sharpe.

Hibbs Jr, Douglas A. (1990) 'Wage dispersion and trade union action in Sweden', in I. Persson (ed.), *Generating Equality in the Welfare State: The Swedish Experience*. Oslo: Norwegian University Press. pp. 181–200.

Hofbauer, Hans (1983) 'Berufsverlauf nach Abschluss der betrieblichen Berufsausbildung', *MittAB*, 16: 211–31.

Holm, L. (1988) 'The Norwegian census data bank and the Norwegian Social Science Data Service', in L.J. McCrank (ed.), *Databases in the Humanities and Social Sciences*. Medford, NJ: Learned Information Inc.

Hout, Michael (1988) 'More universalism, less structural mobility: The American occupational structure in the 1980s', *American Journal of Sociology*, 93 (6): 1358–400.

Howell, David and Wolff, Edward (1988) 'Changes in the skill requirements of the US labour force'. Research Report 88–26, C.V. Starr Center for Applied Economics, New York University.

Hunt, Allan H. and Hunt, Timothy L. (1985) *Clerical Employment and Technological Change*. Kalamazoo, MI: Upjohn Institute.

Jacobs, Jerry A. (1989) *Revolving Doors: Sex Segregation and Women's Careers*. Stanford, CA: Stanford University Press.

Jacobs, Jerry A. (1991) 'Consumer, social and business service industries in the United States, 1969–1987'. EUI Working Paper SPS no. 92/15, European University Institute, Florence.

Jacobs, Jerry A. (1992) 'Women's entry into management: Trends in earnings, authority, values and attitudes among salaried managers', *Administrative Science Quarterly*, 37: 282–301.

Jacobs, Jerry A. and Lim, Suet T. (1992) 'Trends in occupational and industrial sex segregation in 56 countries 1960–1980', *Work and Occupation*, 19 (4): 450–86.

Janossy, Franz (1966) *Das Ende der Wirtschaftswunder*. Frankfurt a.M.: Campus Verlag.

Jencks, Charles (1987) *The Language of Post-modern Architecture*. New York: Rizzoli.

Jencks, Christopher and Peterson, Paul E. (eds) (1991) *The Urban Underclass*. Washington, DC: Brookings Institution.

Kalleberg, Arne (1988) 'Comparative perspectives on work structures and inequality', *Annual Review of Sociology*, 14: 203–25.

Kalleberg, Arne and Berg, Ivar (1987) *Work and Industry: Structures, Markets, and Processes*. New York: Plenum Press.

Kasarda, John (1989) 'Urban industrial transition and the underclass', *Annals of the American Academy of Political and Social Sciences*, 501: 26–47.

Kaufmann, Robert L. and Spilerman, Seymour (1982) 'The age structure of occupations and jobs', *American Journal of Sociology*, 87: 827–51.

Kern, Horst and Schumann, Michael (1984) *Das Ende der Arbeitsteilung?* Munich: C.H. Beck.

Kerr, C., Dunlop, J.T., Harbison, F.H. and Myers, C.A. (1973) *Industrialism and Industrial Man*. 2nd edn. Cambridge, MA: Harvard University Press.

Kiberg, D. (1989) *Levekårsundersøkelsen 1987: Kodebok og frekevnsfordelinger*. Bergen: Norsk Samfunnsvitenskapelig Datatjeneste, NSD Rapporter nr 77.

Kocka, Jürgen and Prinz, Michael (1983) 'Vom "neuen Mittelstand" zum angestellten Arbeitnehmer: Kontinuität und Wandel der deutschen Angestellten seit der

Weimarer Republik', in W. Conze and M.R. Lepsius (eds), *Sozialgeschichte der Bundesrepublik Deutschland*. Stuttgart: Klett-Cotta. pp. 210–55.

Kolberg, Jon Eivind and Kolstad, Arne (1991) Table Annex, 'The post-industrial stratification order: The Norwegian experience'. Mimeo, Department of Sociology, University of Bergen.

König, Wolfgang and Müller, Walter (1986) 'Educational systems and labor markets as determinants of worklife mobility in France and West Germany', *European Sociological Review*, 2: 73–96.

Krueger, Alan B. and Summers, Lawrence H. (1988) 'Effiency wages and the inter-industry wage structure', *Econometrica*, 56 (2): 259–93.

Krupp, Hans-Jürgen (1985) *Das Sozio-ökonomische Panel*. Frankfurt a.M./Berlin: Campus.

Kumar, Krishan (1978) *Prophecy and Progress: The Sociology of Industrial and Post-industrial Society*. Harmondsworth: Penguin.

Kurz, Karin and Müller, Walter (1987) 'Class mobility in the industrial world', *Annual Review of Sociology*, 13: 417–42.

Kutscher, R. (1988) 'Structural change in the United States, past and prospective: Its implication for skill and educational requirements'. Paper presented at symposium on 'The Impacts of Structural and Technological Change on the Labor Market', Wissenschaftszentrum, Berlin (March).

Kuttner, Robert (1983) 'The declining middle', *The Atlantic Monthly*, July: 60–72.

Lawrence, R.Z. (1984) 'Sectoral shifts and the size of the middle class', *The Brookings Review*, Fall: pp. 3–11.

Le Grand, Carl (1989) *Interna Arbetsmarknader, ekonomisk segmentering och social skiktning* [Internal Labour Markets, Economic Segmentation, and Social Stratification]. Stockholm: Almqvist & Wiksell International.

Le Grand, Carl (1991) 'Explaining the male–female wage gap: Job segregation and solidarity wage bargaining in Sweden', *Acta Sociologica*, 34: 261–78.

Levy, Frank (1988) *Dollars and Dreams: The Changing American Income Distribution*. New York: W.W. Norton.

Levy, Frank and Murnane, Richard (1992) 'US earnings levels and earnings inequality: A review of recent trends and proposed explanations', *Journal of Economic Literature*, 30: 1333–81.

Lillard, Lee and Macunovich, Diane (1988) 'Why the baby bust cohorts haven't boomed yet: A reconsideration of cohort variables in labor market analyses'. Paper presented at the annual meeting of the Population Society of America, Baltimore.

Lindbeck, Assar and Snower, Dennis (1984) 'Involuntary unemployment as an insider–outsider dilemma'. Seminar paper 282, Institute for International Economic Studies, Stockholm.

Loveman, Gary W. and Tilly, Chris (1988) 'Good jobs and bad jobs: What does the evidence say?', *New England Economic Review*, January/February: 47–65.

Lundgreen, Peter (1980–1) *Sozialgeschichte der deutschen Schule im Überblick. Teil I: 1770–1918; Teil II: 1919–1980*. Göttingen: Vandenhoeck und Ruprecht.

McMahon, John and Tschetter, John (1986) 'The declining middle class: A further analysis', *Monthly Labor Review*, September: 22–8.

Mahon, Rianne (1991) 'Post-fordism: Some issues for labour', in D. Drache and M. Gertler (eds), *The New Era of Global Competition*. Montreal and Kingston: McGill-Queen's University Press. pp. 316–34.

Maurice, Marc, Sorge, Arndt and Warner, Malcolm (1980) 'Societal differences in organizing manufacturing units', *Organizational Studies*, 1: 63–91.

Mayer, Karl Ulrich and Brückner, Erika (1988) *Lebensverläufe und Wohlfahrtsentwicklung.* Materialien aus der Bildungsforschung n. 35, Max-Planck-Institut für Bildungsforschung, Berlin.

Mayer, Karl Ulrich and Carroll, Glenn R. (1987) 'Jobs and classes: Structural constraints on career mobility', *European Sociological Review*, 3 (1): 14–38.

Mayer, Karl Ulrich, Featherman, David, Selbee, Kevin L. and Colbjornson, Tom (1989) 'Class mobility during the working life: A comparison of Germany and Norway', in M.L. Kohn (ed.), *Cross-National Research in Sociology*. London: Sage. pp. 218–39.

Mayer, Karl Ulrich and Müller, Walter (1986) 'The state and the structure of the life course', in A.B. Sörensen, F.E. Weinert and L. Sherrod (eds), *Human Development and the Life Course: Multidisciplinary Perspectives*. Hillsdale, N.J.: Lawrence Erlbaum Associates. pp. 217–45.

Melucci, Alberto (1989) *Nomads of the Present: Social Movements and Individual Needs in Contemporary Society*. Philadelphia, PA: Temple University Press.

Melz, Noah M. (1969) 'Manpower in Canada 1931–1961: Historical statistics of the Canadian labour force'. Department of Manpower and Immigration. Ottawa: Queen's Printer.

Michon, F. (1981) 'Dualism and the French labor market', in F. Wilkinson (ed), *The Dynamics of Labor Market Segmentation*. London: Academic Press. pp. 81–97.

Mishel, Lawrence and Teixeira, Ruy (1990) 'The myth of the coming labour shortage: Job skills and incomes of the America's workforce 2000'. Economic Policy Institute, Washington, DC.

Morisette, René (1991) 'Are jobs in large firms better jobs?', *Perspectives on Labour and Income*. Ottawa: Statistics Canada. pp. 40–50.

Morisette, René, Picot, Garnett and Pyper, Wendy (1992) 'Patterns of quits in the Canadian economy: Perspectives on labour and income'. Statistics Canada, Ottawa (May).

Müller, Walter (1985) 'Mobilitätsforschung und Arbeitsmarkttheorie', in H. Knepel and R. Hujer (eds), *Mobilitätsprozesse auf dem Arbeitsmarkt*. Frankfurt a.M. and New York: Campus Verlag. pp. 17–40.

Myles, John (1988), 'The expanding middle: Some Canadian evidence on the deskilling debate', *Canadian Review of Sociology and Anthropology*, 25 (3): 335–64.

Myles, John (1990) 'States, labour markets and life cycles', in R. Friedland and S. Robertson (eds), *Beyond the Marketplace: Rethinking Economy and Society*. New York: Aldine de Gruyter. pp. 271–98.

Myles, John and Fawcett, Gail (1990) *Job Skills and the Service Economy*. Ottawa: Economic Council of Canada.

Myles, John, Picot, Garnett and Wannell, Ted (1988) 'Wages and jobs in the 1980s: Changing youth wages and the declining middle'. Research Paper no. 17, Analytical Studies Branch, Statistics Canada, Ottawa.

OECD (1984, 1985, 1987, 1990a, 1991) *Employment Outlook*. Paris: OECD.

OECD (1990b) *Labour Force Statistics, 1968–1988*. Paris: OECD.

Offe, Claus (1985) *Disorganized Capitalism: Contemporary Transformation of Work and Politics*. Cambridge, MA: MIT Press.

Olsson, Sven E. (1990) *Social Policy and Welfare State in Sweden*. Lund: Arkiv.

Oppenheimer, Valerie (1988) 'A theory of marriage timing', *American Journal of Sociology*, 94: 563–91.

Oppenheimer, Valerie (1990) 'Life-cycle jobs and the transition to adulthood'. Unpublished paper, Department of Sociology, UCLA, Los Angeles.

Osterman, Paul (1980) *Getting Started: The Youth Labor Market*. Cambridge, MA: MIT Press.

Parkin, Frank (1968) *Middle Class Radicalism*. Manchester: University of Manchester Press.

Parkin, Frank (1979) *Marxism and Class Theory: A Bourgeois Critique*. New York: Columbia University Press.

Parsons, Talcott (1960) *Structure and Process in Modern Societies*. Glencoe, IL: Free Press.

Petersen, Trond (1989) 'The earnings function in sociological studies of earnings inequality: Functional form and hours worked', *Research in Social Stratification and Mobility*, 8: 221–50.

Picot, W. Garnett (1986) *Canada's Industries: Growth in Jobs over Three Decades*. Ottawa: Statistics Canada.

Picot, Garnett and Baldwin, John (1990) 'Patterns and layoffs in the Canadian economy', *Canadian Economic Observer*, October. pp. 5.9–5.11.

Picot, W. Garnett, Myles, John and Wannell, Ted (1990) 'Good jobs/bad jobs and the declining middle: 1967–86'. Research Paper Series 28, Analytical Studies Branch, Statistics Canada, Ottawa.

Piore, Michael J. (1969) 'On-the-job training in the dual labor market: Public and private responsibilities in on-the-job training of disadvantaged workers', in A.R. Weber, F.H. Cassel and E.L. Ginsburg (eds), *Public–Private Manpower Politics*. Industrial Relations Research Association Series. Madison, WI. pp. 101–32.

Piore, Michael and Sabel, Charles (1984) *The Second Industrial Divide*. New York: Basic Books.

Priebe, John A. (1985) '1970 Census sample with industry and occupation descriptions'. Unpublished manuscript, US Bureau of the Census, Washington, DC.

Reich, Robert (1989) 'As the world turns', *The New Republic*, May, 1: 23–8.

Renner, K. (1953) *Wandlungen der Modernen Gesellschaft*. Vienna: Wiener Volksbuchhandlung.

Rosenbaum, James E. and Kariya, Takehiko (1989) 'From high school to work: Market and institutional mechanisms in Japan', *American Journal of Sociology*, 94 (6): 1334–65.

Rosenbaum, James E. and Kariya, Takehiko (1991) 'Do school achievements affect the early jobs of high school graduates in the United States and Japan?', *Sociology of Education*, 65 (2): 78–95.

Rosenthal, Neal (1985) 'The shrinking middle class: Myth or reality', *Monthly Labor Review*, March: 3–10.

Runciman, W.G. (1990) 'How many classes are there in contemporary British society?', *Sociology*, 24 (3): 377–96.

Ryder, Norman B. (1965) 'The cohort as a concept in the study of social change', *American Sociological Review*, 30: 843–61.

Singelmann, Joachim (1974) 'The sectoral transformation of the labor force in seven industrialized countries, 1920–1960'. PhD dissertation, Department of Sociology, University of Texas, Austin.

Singelmann, Joachim (1978) 'The sectoral transformation of the labor force in seven industrialized countries, 1920–1970', *American Journal of Sociology*, 83 (5): 1224–34.

Singelmann, Joachim and Browning, H. (1980) 'Industrial transformation and occupational change in the United States, 1960–1980', *Social Forces*, 59: pp. 246–64.

Singelmann, Joachim and Tienda, M. (1985) 'The process of change in a service society: The case of the United States, 1960–1980', in B. Roberts, R. Finnegan and D. Gallie (eds), *New Approaches to Economic Life*. Manchester: Manchester University Press. pp. 48–67.

Smeeding, Timothy, O'Higgins, Michael and Rainwater, Lee (1990) *Poverty, Inequality and Income Distribution in Comparative Perspective*. New York: Harvester/Wheatsheaf.

Sobel, R. (1989) *The White Collar Working Class: From Structure to Politics*. New York: Praeger.

Solow, Robert M. (1990) *The Labor Market as a Social Institution*. Oxford: Basil Blackwell.

Sørensen, Aage B. (1977) 'The structure of inequality and the process of attainment', *American Sociological Review*, 42: 965–78.

Sørensen, Aage B. (1983) 'The structure of allocation to open and closed positions in social structure', *Zeitschrift für Soziologie*, 12: 203–24.

Sørensen, Aage B. (1991) 'On the usefulness of class analysis in research on social mobility and socioeconomic inequality', *Acta Sociologica*, 34: 71–87.

Sørensen, Aage, B. and Blossfeld, Hans-Peter (1989) 'Socioeconomic opportunities in Germany in the post-war period', *Research in Social Stratification and Mobility*, 8: 85–106.

Sørensen, Aage B. and Tuma, Nancy Brandon (1981) 'Labor market structures and job mobility', *Research in Social Stratification and Mobility*, 1: 67–94.

Streeck, Wolfgang (1984) *Industrial Relations in West Germany: A Case Study of the Car Industry*. London: Heinemann.

Streeck, Wolfgang (1987) 'The uncertainties of management in the management of uncertainty', *International Journal of Political Economy*, 17 (3): 57–87.

Tåhlin, Michael (1992) 'Class mobility in a Swedish city', in R. Erikson, E.J. Jansen, S. Ringen and H. Uusitalo (eds), *Scandinavian Trends in Welfare and Living Conditions*. New York: M.E. Sharpe.

Thurman, Joseph E. and Trah, Gabriele (1990) 'Part-time work in international perspective', *International Labor Review*, 129 (1): 23–42.

Tilly, Chris, Bluestone, Barry and Harrison, Bennett (1987) 'What is making American wages unequal?', in *Proceedings of the 39th Annual Meeting of the Industrial Relations Research Association*. Madison, WI: Industrial Relations Research Association. pp. 338–48.

Touraine, Alain (1971) *The Post-industrial Society*. New York: Random House.

Treiman, Donald J. (1970) 'Industrialization and social stratification', in E.O. Laumann (ed.), *Social Stratification: Research and Theory for the 1970s*. Indianapolis: Bobbs Merrill. pp. 207–34.

Treiman, Donald J., Bielby, William T. and Cheng, Man-Tsun (1988) 'Evaluating a multiple-imputation method for recalibrating 1970 US Census detailed industry codes to the 1980 standard', *Sociological Methodology*, 18: 309–45.

Tuma, Nancy Brandon (1976) 'Rewards, resources and the rate of mobility', *American Sociological Review*, 41: 338–60.

Tuma, Nancy Brandon (1985) 'Effects of labor market structure on job-shift patterns', in J.J. Heckman and B. Singer (eds), *Longitudinal Analysis of Labor Market Data*. Cambridge: Cambridge University Press. pp. 327–65.

Tuma, Nancy Brandon and Hannan, Michael T. (1984) *Social Dynamics: Models and Methods*. New York: Academic Press.

US Bureau of Labor Statistics (1988) *Employment and Earnings*, January.

US Congress (1978) *Historical Statistics of the United States, 1776–1976*, Series D 233–682. Washington, DC: US Government Printing Office.

Van Parijs, Philippe (1987) 'A revolution in class theory', *Politics and Society*, 15 (4): 453–82.

Vogel, J., Andersson, L.-G., Davidsson, U. and Häll, L. (1988) *Inequality in Sweden: Trends and Current Situation*. Living Conditions Report no. 58. Stockholm: Statistics Sweden.

Wannell, Ted (1991) 'Trends in the distribution of employment by employer size: Recent Canadian evidence'. Analytical Studies Branch, Statistics Canada, Ottawa.

Weber, Max (1978) *Economy and Society*. Volume 2. Berkeley: University of California Press.

Welch, Finis (1979) 'Effects of cohort size on earnings: The baby boom babies', *Journal of Political Economy*, 87 (5): S65–S98.

Western, Mark (1991) 'Class structure and demographic class formation in Australia'. PhD dissertation, University of Queensland, Brisbane.

Willms-Herget, Angelika (1985) *Frauenarbeit: Zur Integration der Frauen in den Arbeitsmarkt*. Frankfurt a.M.: Campus.

Wilson, William Julius (1991) 'Public policy research and the truly disadvantaged', in Christopher Jencks and Paul E. Peterson (eds), *The Urban Underclass*. Washington, DC: Brookings Institution. pp. 460–82.

Wolfson, Michael (1989) 'Inequality and polarization: Is there a disappearing middle class in Canada?'. Paper presented at the proceedings of the Statistics Canada symposium of 'Analysis of Data in Time', Ottawa (October).

Wright, Eric O. (1978) *Class, Crisis and the State*. London: New Left Books.

Wright, Eric O. (1979) *Class Structure and Income Determination*. New York: Academic Press.

Wright, Eric O. (1980) 'Class and occupation', *Theory and Society*, 9: 177–214.

Wright, Eric O. (1985) *Classes*. London: Verso.

Wright, Eric O. (1989) *The Debate on Classes*. London: Verso.

Wright, Eric O. and Martin, B. (1987) 'The transformation of the American class structure, 1960–1980', *American Journal of Sociology*, 93 (1): 1–29.

Wright, Eric O. and Singelmann, Joachim (1982) 'Proletarianization in the changing American class structure', *American Journal of Sociology*, 88: 176–209 (supplement).

Yamaguchi, Kazuo (1991) *Event History Analysis*. London: Sage.

Zeitlin, Maurice (1989) *The Large Corporation and Contemporary Classes*. Cambridge: Polity Press.

Index